Advance praise for *Analysis of Customer Satisfaction Data*

"I found this to be a very thorough and comprehensive study of advanced customer satisfaction and loyalty analysis. In particular, the chapters on Dependence Models: Towards Relative Importance (Chapter 5) and Casual Modeling (Chapter 7) offer a great deal of helpful insight to Motorola as we drive our entire corporation toward total customer satisfaction. I've already used the 'glossary of terms' numerous times as a great reference source."

—*Bob Bovee*
Director of Quality
Motorola

"Here is a book that clearly provides a broad overview of all the tools relevant to the measurement and analysis of customer satisfaction issues. Within its nine chapters, it moves the reader through the total landscape of customer satisfaction and loyalty measurement and analysis. The authors' in-depth coverage of all the relevant statistical tools, from the simplest univariate statistics to advanced multivariate analysis, makes this a very useful reference book. This book is a 'must have' in all research managers' libraries."

—*Manuel Gutierrez*
Director, Market Research, K & B Group
Kohler Company

"Anyone looking for a comprehensive overview of advanced analytical techniques in the area of customer satisfaction research that is rigorous, without being overwhelming, will find a rich resource in this very readable book. The authors make extensive use of case studies from a variety of industries, using actual data to illustrate applications of advanced multivariate analytical methods. By emphasizing the fundamental assumptions that underlie these methods, they also draw attention to potential misapplications or limitations of certain analytical techniques that arise when these assumptions are violated. Throughout, the authors' focus is on illustration and interpretation of concepts, rather than on their mathematical derivation, which makes this book such a useful resource in the practitioner's tool kit—a tour guide through the 'no longer impenetrable' forest of advanced multivariate analytical methods."

—*Al Grabenstein*
Vice President, Corporate Marketing-Research & Consulting
Comerica Incorporated

"This book is a must read for anyone who is developing a customer satisfaction survey. Critical decisions in survey design such as placement of the overall satisfaction question and interval scaling are explained and evaluated."

—*Richard Yorio*
Customer Satisfaction and Loyalty Manager
Xerox Corporation

Analysis of Customer Satisfaction Data

Analysis of Customer Satisfaction Data

A comprehensive guide to multivariate statistical analysis in customer satisfaction, loyalty, and service quality research.

Derek R. Allen, Ph.D., & T.R. Rao, Ph.D.

ASQ Quality Press
Milwaukee, Wisconsin

NEW AGE

First Indian Sub-Continent Edition : 2010
by New Age International (P) Ltd., Publishers

This special low-priced edition is for sale in India, Bangladesh, Bhutan, Mayanmar (Burma), Sri Lanka, Nepal and Pakistan only.

Originally Published by *American Society for Quality, USA*

Branches:
- 36, Malikarjuna Temple Street, Opp. ICWA, Basavanagudi **Bangalore**. ✆ (080) 26677815
- 26, Damodaran Street, T. Nagar, **Chennai**. ✆ (044) 24353401
- CC-39/1016, Carrier Station Road, Ernakulam South, **Cochin.** ✆ (0484) 4051303
- Hemsen Complex, Mohd. Shah Road, Paltan Bazar, Near Starline Hotel **Guwahati**. ✆ (0361) 2543669
- No. 105, 1st Floor, Madhiray Kaveri Tower, 3-2-19, Azam Jahi Road, Nimboliadda **Hyderabad**. ✆ (040) 24652456
- RDB Chambers (Formerly Lotus Cinema) 106A,1st Floor, S.N. Banerjee Road **Kolkata**. ✆ (033) 22275247
- 16-A, Jopling Road, **Lucknow**. ✆ (0522) 2209578
- 142C, Victor House, Ground Floor, N.M. Joshi Marg, Lower Parel **Mumbai**. ✆ (022) 24927869
- 22, Golden House, Daryaganj, **New Delhi**. ✆ (011) 23262370, 23262368

Printed in India at Anand Sons, Delhi
C-09-09-4074

ISBN: 978-81-224-2800-1
Original Edition Price: $ 66.00
Indian Edition Price: Rs. 395.00

PUBLISHING FOR ONE WORLD
NEW AGE INTERNATIONAL (P) LIMITED, PUBLISHERS
4835/24, Ansari Road, Daryaganj, New Delhi - 110002
Visit us at **www.newagepublishers.com**

Contents

List of Figures .... *xi*
Preface .... *xv*
Acknowledgments .... *xvii*

Chapter 1. The Historical Roots of Customer Satisfaction Research 1

Introduction 1
The Six Sigma Approach 3
Linking Satisfaction to the Bottom Line 5
Customer Loyalty versus Customer Satisfaction 7
Case Study: Modeling Customer Retention 10
Introduction to Model Development 12
The Significant Predictor Variables 13
Model Validation 14
Model Implementation 15
Intervening to Save Profitable Customers 16
The Future of Customer Satisfaction Research 17

Chapter 2. Instrumentation and Scale Selection 19

Introduction 19
Scaling Issues 20
How Many Scale Points? 25
Case Study: Scale Equivalencies 29
Survey Instrument Design 34
Dependent Variable Placement 35
The Structured Instrument 37

Chapter 3. Preparing Customer Satisfaction Data 41
Introduction 41
Missing Data in Customer Satisfaction Research 41
Distributional Abnormalities 51
The Correlation Matrix as Data 52

Chapter 4. Analysis Framework for Customer Satisfaction Data 55
Analytical Approaches to Satisfaction Data 55
Univariate Data Analysis 56
Bivariate Data Analysis 57
Multivariate Data Analysis 58
Key Driver Analysis 61
Multivariate Interdependence Models 65
Multivariate Hybrid Models 66

Chapter 5. Dependence Models: Toward Relative Importance 69
Introduction 69
The Nature and Derivation of Importance 69
Marginal Resource Allocation Models 70
Regression Techniques and Importance 72
The Correlation Coefficient 73
Simple Linear Regression 75
Multivariate Correlation Analysis 76
Multiple Linear Regression 78
Multiple Linear Regression with Stepwise Selection 80
Kruskal's Relative Importance Approach 81
Dominance Analysis 83
Canonical Correlation Analysis 86
Multiple Logistic Regression 87
Presentation of Derived Importance Data 91
Integrating Performance and Importance Data 92

Chapter 6. Exploratory Data Analysis and Problems in Regression Analysis **97**

Introduction 97
Exploratory Data Analysis 97
Variable Profiles 104
The Diagnosis of Collinearity 116
Influential Observations in Regression Analysis 121

Chapter 7. Causal Modeling: Multiple Dependencies in Path Analysis **129**

Causal Modeling 129
The Nature of Causality 130
Path Analysis Assumptions 134
Confirmatory versus Exploratory Models 136
Model Input 137
Case Study: Discount Auto Parts 139
Case Study: OilTech 142

Chapter 8. Interdependence Models: The Dimensionality of Satisfaction **149**

Introduction 149
Principal Components and Factor Analysis 150
Exploratory versus Confirmatory Analysis 150
Data Structures for Factor Analysis and Principal Components Analysis 152
Principal Components Analysis 154
Common Factor Analysis 156
How Many Factors or Components? 159
Rotating Factors or Components 161
Case Study: Personal Computer Purchase Experience 163
Factor Analysis Variants 169
Confirmatory Factor Analysis 171

Chapter 9. Structural Equations with Latent Variables..... 177

Introduction 177
Matrix Algebra 178
The Measurement Model 186
The Structural Model 188
Assessing the Model 189
Identification 190
Case Study: Aquarian Electric Utility 192
Latent Variable Path Modeling with Partial Least Squares 198

Appendix A. Matrix Algebra in Statistics 203
Glossary 215
Bibliography 231
Index 235

List of Figures

Figure 1.1.	Principle disparities affecting service quality.
Figure 1.2.	SERVQUAL scale dimensions.
Figure 1.3.	Six sigma process variance reduction.
Figure 1.4.	Reasons for automobile repurchase.
Figure 1.5.	Affective and cognitive dimensions of loyalty.
Figure 1.6.	Relationship between loyalty and satisfaction.
Figure 1.7.	SuperBank data warehouse.
Figure 1.8.	Attrition by risk agency.
Figure 1.9.	Integrating profitability and attrition risk.
Figure 2.1.	Four levels of data measurement.
Figure 2.2.	Nominal-level (binary) predictors followed by an interval-level dependent variable.
Figure 2.3.	An ordinal-level letter grading scale.
Figure 2.4.	The typical five-point scale has anchors only on its endpoints.
Figure 2.5.	The fully anchored five-point scale may lose its interval-level properties.
Figure 2.6.	Distribution of scores using five-point, seven-point, and 10-point scales.
Figure 2.7.	Omnikote overall satisfaction tracking graph.
Figure 2.8.	Approaches to scaling changes.
Figure 2.9.	Five-point versus 10-point scales.
Figure 2.10.	Survey instrument with nested structure.
Figure 2.11.	Analysis architecture.
Figure 3.1.	Globe Bank customer satisfaction survey instrument.
Figure 3.2.	Effect of mean substitution imputation method.
Figure 3.3.	Common data transformations.
Figure 4.1.	Levels of customer satisfaction data analysis.
Figure 4.2.	Framework for customer satisfaction data analysis.
Figure 4.3.	Multiple regression analysis.
Figure 4.4.	Example of relative importance measure.
Figure 4.5.	Canonical correlation analysis.

Figure 4.6. Data reduction example.
Figure 4.7. Structural equation model with latent variables.
Figure 5.1. Sample survey instrument with 10-point scales.
Figure 5.2. Simplification of canonical correlation analysis.
Figure 5.3. Five service and product quality issues for XYZ Airlines.
Figure 5.4. Differences across binary dependent variable.
Figure 5.5. Pie graph used to depict differences across nominal variable categories.
Figure 5.6. Scaled and raw derived importance data.
Figure 5.7. Integrating performance and derived importance.
Figure 5.8. Performance and importance data.
Figure 6.1. Sources of problems in regression and other multivariate models.
Figure 6.2. Effect of influential observation.
Figure 7.1. Minimal criteria for establishing causality.
Figure 7.2. Simple causal relationship.
Figure 7.3. Multiple predictor causal model.
Figure 7.4. Path analysis model with two dependent variables.
Figure 7.5. Quasi-confirmatory model-building approach.
Figure 7.6. Saturated model for Discount Auto Parts.
Figure 7.7. Discount Auto Parts path model.
Figure 7.8. OilTech quarterly performance summary.
Figure 7.9. Hypothesized OilTech path model.
Figure 7.10. Final OilTech path analysis.
Figure 8.1. Exploratory versus confirmatory factor analysis.
Figure 8.2. Iterative nature of confirmatory factor analysis.
Figure 8.3. Principal components of bivariate data.
Figure 8.4. Common and unique variable variance.
Figure 8.5. common factor model.
Figure 8.6. Example of a scree test.
Figure 8.7. Action PC questionnaire excerpt.
Figure 8.8. *R*-factor analysis approach.
Figure 8.9. Transposing a data matrix.
Figure 8.10. Correlation matrix based on transposed data matrix.
Figure 8.11. Confirmatory factor analysis—Action PC data.
Figure 8.12. Final confirmatory factor analysis of Action PC data.
Figure 9.1. Structural equation model with latent variables.

Figure 9.2. GIFCO products CSM instruments.
Figure 9.3. Assessing model goodness-of-fit.
Figure 9.4. Aquarian Electric CSM instrument.
Figure 9.5. Hypothesized Aquarian Electric model.
Figure 9.6. Aquarian Electric model.
Figure 9.7. Direct versus indirect effects.
Figure 9.8. Reflective and formative indicators in SEM.

Preface

This book is intended for advanced service quality managers and marketing researchers with more than a modest exposure to statistical data analysis. Our objective is to provide the reader with a fundamental understanding of how service quality data may be approached with multivariate statistical techniques. Above all, this book is intended for the *practitioner* and, as such, relies upon numerous industry examples to illustrate key points. Whenever possible, we provide actual results and discuss the appropriate interpretation and presentation.

The scope of this book ranges from a treatment of scaling issues and data collection methodologies to substantive discussions concerning analytical approaches such as derived importance models, structural equations, and the empirical link between customer satisfaction and profitability. We have avoided as much as possible an overly technical treatment of these subjects. Instead, a more descriptive approach was taken in an effort to facilitate an understanding of how the most sophisticated techniques can be applied and, more importantly, what they can tell us about our data. Nonetheless, we cannot avoid some technical discussions because our objective is to demonstrate the power of a variety of advanced statistical techniques.

Wherever possible, we have attempted to include actual industry examples to illustrate how techniques were applied, how the results were interpreted, and finally, how critical strategic marketing decisions were affected. Note that although the case studies may be real, company names, variable labels, and key scores have been changed to ensure anonymity. We have also addressed some of the most problematic aspects of service quality data, including data scaling, ill-conditioned data, the impact of missing values, and the violation of key assumptions underlying various models. A glossary that includes virtually all of the technical terms referenced in the book should prove to be a useful resource to readers.

This book provides the advanced service quality manager or marketing researcher embarking on customer satisfaction research with a comprehensive overview in terms of the most sophisticated analytical techniques, interpretation and results presentation. There are, of course, much more in-depth treatments available for each of these topics. Several excellent books concerning conditioning diagnostics are available, for example. We provide references to key sources for readers interested in further exploring any of these areas.

Researchers or managers with an interest in the quantitative analysis of customer satisfaction data will find many useful examples in this book. Those practicing quality management approaches such as six sigma, which was developed at Motorola, will find a wide variety of analytical techniques that may be used to further an understanding of customer satisfaction and its antecedents.

Two families of analytical techniques define the book's overall structure. The first involves *dependence* models. These statistical techniques involve demonstrating how one or more outcome variables are affected by a set of predictor variables. These models are critical in derived importance techniques. The derivation of importance using regression-based models is well-regarded but has critical limitations. We review derived importance models and introduce a powerful means of producing importance metrics with ratio-level properties.

The second family of techniques involves *independence* among sets of variables. The application of this type of model to service quality data involves the underlying dimensionality of satisfaction perceptions or whether customers may be *grouped* based upon similar satisfaction profiles. Techniques such as factor analysis, principal components analysis, and cluster analysis are reviewed and discussed with respect to customer satisfaction data.

Within this broad structure, we have attempted to include discussions concerning many new analytical techniques that may not be familiar to all researchers. Included are discussions of *partial least squares* and an algorithm developed to provide a powerful metric relating to the derivation of importance. In this vein, we have endeavored to document the leading edge of customer satisfaction data analysis.

Acknowledgments

This book would not have been possible without the theoretical and technical foundations laid by many applied and academic researchers over the past 25 years. The completion of this work was greatly facilitated by the administrative skills of Sandy Cummings, who produced most of the graphics and spent many hours ensuring that editorial changes were implemented. Karen Garvin, Al Fraser, and Jennifer Helt provided proofreading services that were invaluable. Bonnie Lockwood also helped keep this project on track. Jill Crawford was also instrumental in the production of various figures throughout the book. Barbara Carpenter was also extremely helpful in her role as research analyst. Thanks also go to the anonymous ASQ reviewers whose insights and valuable comments enhanced this volume's contribution to the customer satisfaction research literature.

Chapter 1

THE HISTORICAL ROOTS OF CUSTOMER SATISFACTION RESEARCH

INTRODUCTION

That customer satisfaction is intractably related to the quality revolution in the United States is practically incontrovertible. The formalization of customer satisfaction as a quality component in national competitions such as the Malcolm Baldrige National Quality Award further validated the customer satisfaction research agenda. This chapter provides a succinct history of customer satisfaction research and reviews more contemporary attempts to link satisfaction to retention and, ultimately, corporate profitability.

The first forays into the measurement of customer satisfaction occurred in the early 1980s. These typically involved assessing the drivers of satisfaction. Early works by Oliver (1980), Churchill and Surprenant (1982), and Bearden and Teel (1983) tended to focus on the operationalization of customer satisfaction and its antecedents. By the mid-1980s, the focus of both applied and academic research had shifted to construct refinement and the implementation of strategies designed to optimize customer satisfaction according to Zeithaml, Berry, and Parasuraman (1996, 31).

Rigorous scientific inquiry and the development of a general service quality theory can be attributed to Parasuraman, Berry, and Zeithaml (1985). Their discussion of customer satisfaction, service quality, and customer expectations represents one of the first attempts to operationalize satisfaction in a theoretical context. Parasuraman, Berry, and Zeithaml proposed that the ratio of perceived performance

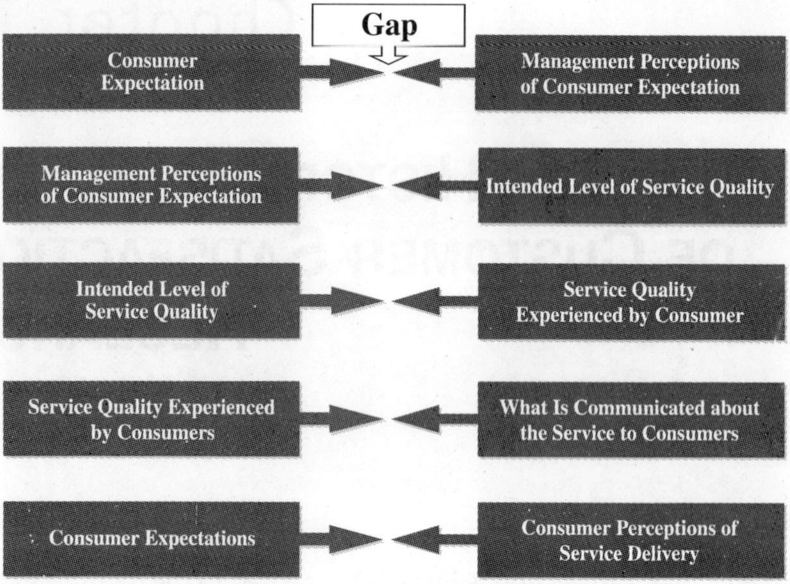

FIGURE 1.1 Principle disparities affecting service quality.

to customer expectations was key to maintaining satisfied customers. The disparity between performance and expectations was presumed to take five forms as shown in Figure 1.1.

Several years later, Parasuraman, Berry, and Zeithaml (1988) published a second, related discussion that focused more specifically on the psychometric aspects of service quality. Their multi-item SERVQUAL scale is considered to be one of the first attempts to operationalize the customer satisfaction construct. The SERVQUAL scale focused on the performance component of the service quality model in which quality was defined as the disparity between expectations and performance. The battery of items used in the SERVQUAL multi-item scale is still used today as a foundation on which instrument development is often based. The primary areas considered in the scale are depicted in Figure 1.2.

Throughout the 1980s, both applied and academic researchers focused on these (and other) issues and their effects on overall customer satisfaction according to Zeithaml, Berry, and Parasuraman (1996, 31). That is, the primary research question involved which of the five areas was most important vis à vis customer expectations. Much of the earliest applied work involving the derivation of attrib-

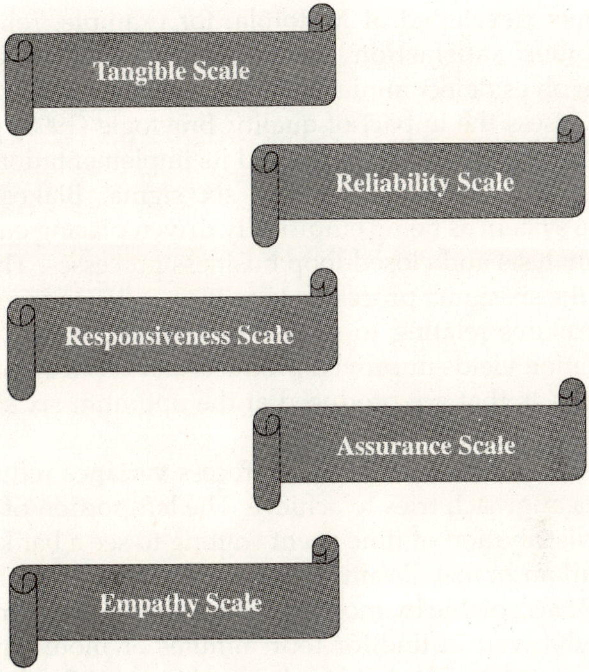

FIGURE 1.2 SERVQUAL scale dimensions.

ute importance involved stated measures. It was not uncommon to encounter surveys in which for every item both importance and performance measures were sought. The gap between these two measures was considered instrumental in resource allocation. Large gaps demanded the most attention. It is important to note, however, that Parasuraman, Berry, and Zeithaml (1988) employed regression analysis to assess the effect of each dimension relative to a dependent measure in their introduction of the SERVQUAL model. The use of regression analysis and other dependency models to derive the importance of attributes relative to an outcome measure is now considered *de rigueur.* The development of dependency models to ascertain attribute importance is discussed in greater detail in chapter 5.

THE SIX SIGMA APPROACH

Although customer satisfaction measurement enjoys a substantial position as a criterion in the Malcolm Baldrige National Quality Award, it is even more integral in other quality programs. The "six sigma" system developed at Motorola, for example, relies heavily upon customer satisfaction measurement and tracking. This approach involves defect minimization and employs the normal distribution to assess the impact of quality. Breyfogle (1999) provides a comprehensive review of six sigma and its implementation.

In an excellent article outlining six sigma, Blakeslee (1999) describes the system as being empirically driven placing emphasis on root cause analysis and closed-loop business processes. The primary objective of the six sigma process is to reduce variance around critical business measures relating to service or product quality. Reducing process variation yields improved products and services. Indeed, services or products that are produced at the optimum six sigma level yield a mere four defects per million.

Figure 1.3 illustrates the type of process variance reduction that the six sigma approach tries to achieve. The left portion of the figure depicts the distribution of time spent waiting to see a bank teller at a typical suburban branch. Waiting in line more than four minutes is considered unacceptable by most customers. In the six sigma context, customers who wait in line for four minutes or more have experienced a service defect. The left-hand side of Figure 1.3 presents a distribution in which a significant proportion of bank customers experience defective service levels.

One of six sigma's *operational* objectives is to reduce process variance and provide zero defect services and products. Perhaps more

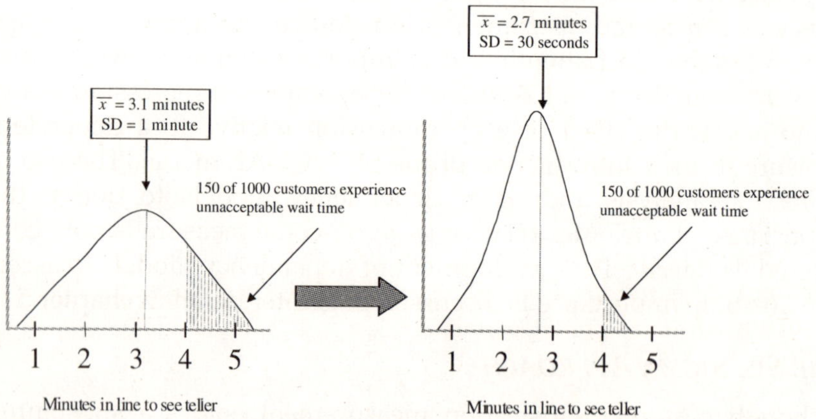

FIGURE 1.3 Six sigma process variance reduction.

important is that at the *strategic* level six sigma is intended to keep the organization focused on and aligned with customer needs. The right-hand side of Figure 1.3 presents an improved process. The distribution of waiting time is now markedly more peaked. This is reflected in the smaller standard distribution around the mean waiting time. Clearly, fewer customers experience defective service levels in this distribution as well.

A focus on customer needs and expectations at the strategic level means gathering marketplace information. Competitive intelligence plays a key role at the strategic level. Knowing how satisfied competitors' customers are and what drives their satisfaction is crucial in the six sigma framework. This type of information can help identify trends, opportunities, and service or product quality gaps.

One of the most appealing aspects of the six sigma approach involves the closed-loop relationship between business process improvements and financial accountability. That process improvements should be linked to financial outcomes is a basic requirement of the six sigma approach. It is likely, in fact, that this aspect of six sigma precipitated additional academic and applied research into linking customer satisfaction and corporate profitability.

Linking Satisfaction to the Bottom Line

That some businesses are interested in maximizing customer satisfaction does not necessarily reflect their corporate altruism. Indeed, an interest in customer satisfaction is almost always self-centered. After all, why should businesses measure, track, and attempt to improve customer satisfaction if there is no tangible benefit? Until the early 1990s, it was assumed that satisfied customers yielded greater profits; companies with more satisfied customers would be more successful, more profitable. And yet, there was only limited empirical evidence to support this notion. Buzzel and Gale (1987), for example, produced evidence to link market-share growth and service quality; however, the lack of more substantive evidence supporting the contention that customer satisfaction was instrumental in ensuring corporate profitability led the Council on Financial Competition to the following indictment in 1989: "Service quality as an issue is seriously overrated; service certainly is not as important as the mythic proportions it has taken on in industry trade publications and conferences."

This type of skepticism may have precipitated a flurry of academic and industry research aimed at linking customer satisfaction to corporate profitability and market share. Rust and Zahorik (1993), for example, focused on the retail banking industry. Their research related customer satisfaction, retention, and profitability. The authors concluded that retention rates drive market share and that customer satisfaction was a primary determinant of retention. Their model permitted Rust and Zahorik " . . . to determine the spending levels of each satisfaction element which will maximize profitability, subject to the assumptions of the model and accuracy of parameter estimation" (1993, 212).

More recent efforts by authors like Zeithaml, Berry, and Parasuraman (1996) have attempted to refine the link between customer satisfaction and profitability by focusing on an intervening variable: retention. The link between customer retention and profitability appears unequivocal to some authors. Reichheld and Sasser (1990, 105), for example, concluded that retention was a stronger predictor of corporate success than " . . . scale, market share, unit costs, and many other factors usually associated with competitive advantage." By focusing on the link between customer satisfaction and an intervening variable (retention) known to affect profitability, Zeithaml, Berry, and Parasuraman were able to build a strong case for the importance of service quality.

Danaher and Rust (1996) also focused on the financial benefits of service quality. Their study took a slightly different tack. Rather than focus on increased profitability as a result of lower attrition rates, Danaher and Rust emphasized the utility of service quality in *attracting* new customers and increasing the usage rates of existing customers. Of particular importance was the benefit of word-of-mouth advertising attributable to high service quality levels.

The effect of customer satisfaction on profitability is clearly exerted through an intervening variable such as retention. Rust, Zahorik, and Keiningham's (1994) effort to establish a return on quality (ROQ) measure, for example, linked customer satisfaction to customer retention, which, in turn, was used as a predictor of market share. Based upon a set of assumptions that included the possibility that a company could spend too much on customer satisfaction, the authors developed a computer application that would permit users to forecast the profit implications of service quality improvement efforts.

CUSTOMER LOYALTY VERSUS CUSTOMER SATISFACTION

As the customer satisfaction research environment has matured, a variety of rival and complementary constructs have emerged. Among these is customer **loyalty.** There appears to be no consensus among researchers concerning the operationalization of loyalty. A large part of loyalty may involve an attitudinal state. It is not, for example, exclusively a *behavior.* Dick and Basu (1994) suggested that customer loyalty was a combination of both behaviors and attitudes. In short, the authors maintained that loyal customers were those who had both a favorable attitude and repeated purchases. Such an approach allows for "spurious loyalty" that arises when purchases are made repeatedly by a customer who does not have a particularly favorable attitude toward the brand.

When considered exclusively as an attitudinal state, loyalty certainly has many desirable behavioral outcomes such as repurchase and lower attrition rates. Repurchase activities or switching behaviors may be *manifestations* of loyalty. The behaviors are not loyalty, they may be an outcome of loyalty. An aversion to switching and high repurchase rates do not necessarily mean that a customer base is *loyal,* per se. Clearly, many other factors can cause these desirable behaviors, including proximity and price, as shown in Figure 1.4.

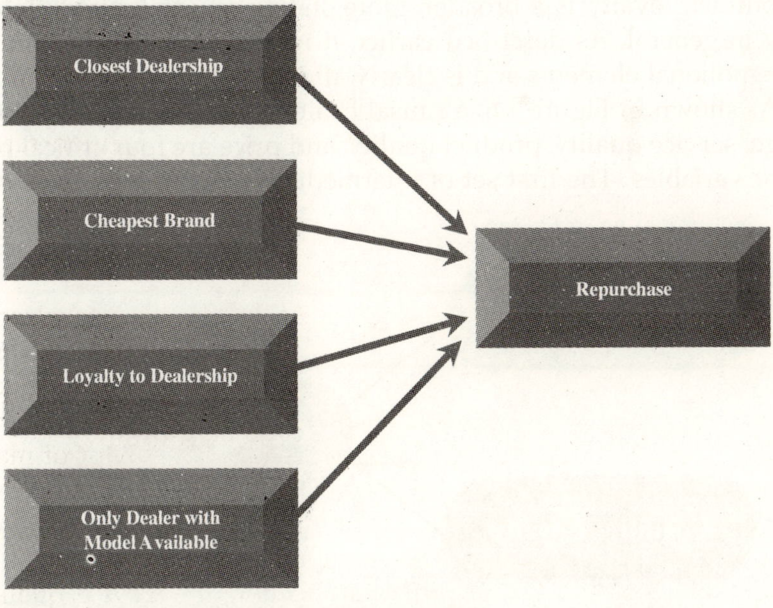

FIGURE 1.4 Reasons for automobile repurchase.

If loyalty is not a behavior or satisfaction, what is it? Recent developments in the operationalization of loyalty have yielded attitude scales designed specifically for the industrial buyer and consumer markets. Loyalty may have two primary dimensions: affective and rational as shown in Figure 1.5. The *affective* dimension of loyalty has emotional underpinnings and involves human interaction. In contrast, the *cognitive* dimension of loyalty includes evaluations of the business relationship that involve price, proximity, timeliness, and so on.

Very few applied customer satisfaction programs currently accommodate a full-developed operationalization of loyalty. Fewer still attempt to differentiate between the affective and cognitive components of loyalty. Table 1.1 presents a summary of several questionnaire items we have used in an effort to capture both dimensions of loyalty. These were developed based upon qualitative and quantitative experiences across a diverse range of industries in both consumer and business-to-business settings.

In most cases, customer satisfaction is a necessary but not sufficient condition for loyalty. We believe that satisfaction and loyalty are two different constructs. Satisfaction is directed specifically at product or service attributes and may be a relatively more dynamic measure. In contrast, loyalty is a broader, more static attitude toward a company in general. As described earlier, it may subsume both rational and emotional elements and is clearly affected by satisfaction.

As shown in Figure 1.6, a causal chain is suggested. First, brand image, service quality, product quality, and price are four critical predictor variables. The first set of intermediate variables involves cus-

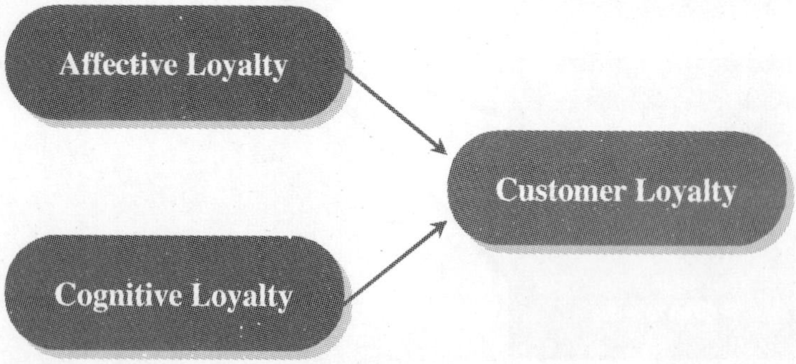

FIGURE 1.5 Affective and cognitive dimensions of loyalty.

TABLE 1.1 Questionnaire items relating to loyalty.

Cognitive Component Items

- "For our firm, staying in the relationship with XYZ Co. is a matter of necessity."
- "Discontinuing our relationship with XYZ Co. would result in a loss of business for our company."
- "Our company stays in its relationship with XYZ Co. because of the rewards and benefits it brings us."

Affective Component Items

- "The people at XYZ Co. are just like us."
- "XYZ Co. staff have our best interests at heart."
- "A lot of the employees at XYZ Co. are my friends."

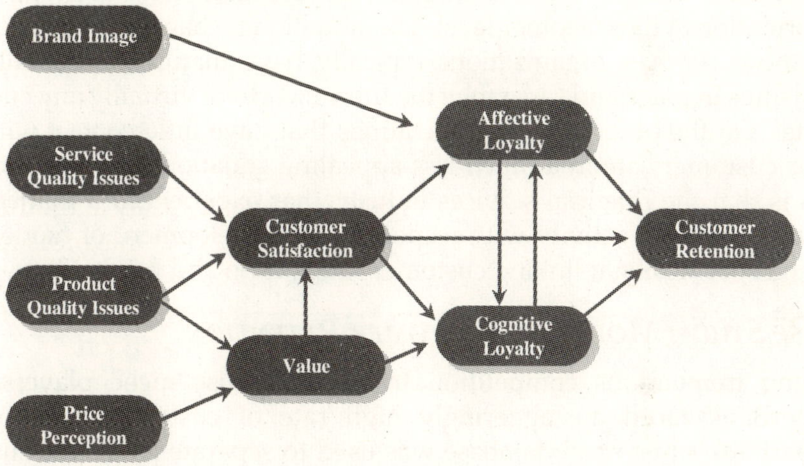

FIGURE 1.6 Relationship between loyalty and satisfaction.

tomer satisfaction and value. The former is shown to be a function of both product quality and price perceptions and directly affects customer satisfaction. The second set of intermediate variables involves the two dimensions of loyalty described earlier. Note that brand image perceptions directly affect the emotional component of loyalty whereas value perceptions and customer satisfaction have an impact on the more rational aspects of loyalty. Finally, customer satisfaction and the two loyalty measures directly affect customer retention.

Customer retention is typically measured as an attitudinal item. That is, one or more questionnaire items relating to the respondent's probable future behavior frequently serve as a measure for customer retention. In some industries, it is becoming increasingly common to encounter actual measures of retention in models similar to that depicted in Figure 1.6. Clearly, behavioral measures of retention and its tangents (that is, share of wallet) requires a mature customer database that captures actual customer loss. The implication of Figure 1.6 is that customer retention is dependent upon a complex intermingling of effects. It is likely, for example, that some level of reciprocal causation exists between the affective and cognitive components of loyalty. In effect, they cause one another. The final outcome of the hypothetical causal chain shown in the figure is customer retention. Customer retention has been used as a surrogate for profitability in some instances. Whenever possible, it is preferable to use individual-level profitability metrics. Unfortunately, companies rarely have this type of information at the customer level. This situation is changing, however. Financial services organizations typically have mature profitability measures in place and can gauge the future worth of virtually any customer. On the other hand, organizations that have little contact with their customers are in a much less appealing situation. One result of this is that the financial services industry has experienced a tremendous increase in activity with respect to the development of models aimed specifically at linking customer satisfaction and profitability.

Case Study: Modeling Customer Retention

Facing tremendous competition from numerous "niche players," SuperBank faced a staggeringly high rate of customer attrition. SuperBank's historical database was used to separate long-time customers from those who defected. Unfortunately, although a customer's departure from SuperBank was unequivocal, it was not at all clear whether the customer left to a competing bank or moved for other reasons. The key, however, was that the company's huge data warehouse held many answers concerning customer attrition. Perhaps more importantly, the data warehouse was a repository for many different types of customer data, as shown in Figure 1.7, relating to product usage, channel preference, demographics and, most importantly, customer satisfaction.

The rationale underlying this effort was grounded in the strategic and operational uses of the resulting model. In short, if a small set of accessible variables could be used to predict customer attrition, a variety of uses for the model could be considered. There are a wide

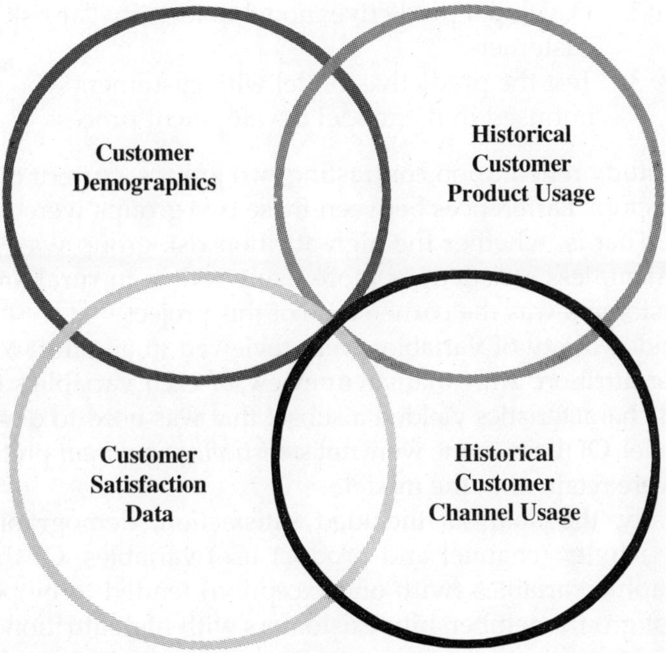

FIGURE 1.7 SuperBank data warehouse.

variety of applications for an accurate attrition forecasting model. Of paramount interest is the ability to identify customers who are at risk of leaving and empirically link this risk to customer satisfaction and its drivers. If "at risk" customers can be identified, then steps may be taken to ensure that they remain long-term customers. The bottom line is that it is significantly less expensive to retain existing customers than to attract new ones.

The system presented in this case study was directly implemented at the mainframe database level. In short, the predictive model was set up to run monthly using the entire customer database, which contained customer satisfaction data, product usage, and channel preferences. Customers identified as being at a high risk for leaving were subjected to a number of intervention measures. The primary objective of the intervention measures was to retain existing customers. The following steps were taken to achieve this goal:

Stage 1: Quantify the differences between lost customers and current customers

Stage 2: Develop a predictive model to identify "at risk" customers

Stage 3: Test the predictive model with customers who were not used in the model development process

The study relied upon contrasting two groups: current customers and defectors. Differences between these two groups were of special interest. That is, whether the high-attrition risk group was younger, less affluent, less satisfied, or more likely to live in rural areas than loyal customers was the cornerstone of this project.

A wide variety of variables were reviewed in an effort to predict customer attrition. An exhaustive review of each variable's distribution and characteristics yielded a subset that was used to develop the final model. Of these, some were not *statistically significant* predictors—others were retained in the model.

Initially, the analysis included satisfaction, demographic, and account activity (channel and product use) variables. Of these, the demographic variables (with one exception) tended to be poor predictors of group membership. Customers with high attrition risk did not differ significantly from long-term customers in terms of most of the demographic variables. For example, the group of customers who defected tended to be of the same age and gender as those who remained with SuperBank. Account history data and past customer satisfaction scores, on the other hand, emerged as strongly predictive of whether a customer would remain with SuperBank or defect.

Introduction to Model Development

For each customer in the sample ($n = 100{,}000$) both *static* and *dynamic* data were provided. Static data are those that remain relatively constant like income and household composition. Customer satisfaction data are considered static primarily because they were collected on a periodic basis. In contrast, dynamic data include loan openings or closings, payment history, and account inquiries. Both static and dynamic variables were used to develop a model capable of accurately predicting customer attrition.

Multiple logistic regression was used in this case study. The technique is discussed in chapter 5 and is used when the outcome variable in a regression model framework is binary. That is, it takes only two values. In the present case, the historical analysis of SuperBank's database involved defining the outcome variable—either the customer left the bank or did not. The logistic regression model was developed to predict whether a customer would stay or leave.

The final statistical model was composed of six variables. Of these, only one (combined monthly income) was a demographic variable. The remaining variables represented characteristics of the account relationship or customer satisfaction. Table 1.2 summarizes the model's significant variables in order of predictive impact.

THE SIGNIFICANT PREDICTOR VARIABLES

As shown in Table 1.2, the strongest predictors involved the customers' average loan and savings balances across all past and present accounts. The higher the balance of either account, the lower the customer's attrition risk. The third predictor suggests that customers who were satisfied over the past 2 years would also have a low probability of leaving the bank. The fourth predictor variable shown in Table 1.2 involved customer tenure. This *momentum effect* is not unusual and is encountered across a wide variety of industries. Quite simply, it suggests that as relationship length increases, customers are more likely to stay. This may be attributed to their comfort and familiarity or simply an inability to find suitable (for example, proximate) alternatives.

The remaining two variables, although significant predictors of customer mortality, are not as strong as the variables just discussed. Combined income, for example, exerts moderate strength in the model. A parallel empirical investigation of this phenomenon confirmed that

TABLE 1.2 Summary of the SuperBank attrition risk model.

Variable Description	Relation to Groups	Predictive Strength
Average loan balance	Higher balances suggest lower mortality risk.	Very strong
Average savings balance	Higher balances suggest lower mortality risk.	Very strong
Customer satisfaction	High satisfaction suggests lower mortality risk.	Very strong
Length of relationship	Tenure and mortality risk were inversely related.	Strong
Combined income	Customers with higher incomes had a higher mortality risk.	Moderate
Account closure	Customers who closed any account in the preceding three months had a higher mortality risk.	Strong

as customers' incomes increased, they were more likely to become targets of competitors. Finally, Table 1.2 suggests that a customer who closed any type of account with the bank within the past three months is at considerable mortality risk.

Model Validation

The model was highly successful in terms of its ability to predict attrition among the customer base used to construct the model. A more rigorous validation procedure was used to test the SuperBank model, however. This involved assigning a risk level to each of 100,000 customers who were *not* used in the model development process. These 100,000 customers were prospectively tracked over the course of nearly one year. The results were very encouraging to SuperBank management.

For simplicity's sake, the customers were assigned to one of 10 *deciles* based upon the model's assessment of their attrition risk. As shown in Figure 1.8, at the end of 10 months, fully 98.6 percent of those in the lowest risk decile were still customers. However, customers in the highest risk decile experienced a much higher dropout rate. In fact, customers in the high-risk group had an attrition rate *many times higher* than those in the low-risk group; only about 51 percent remained by the end of the tenth month.

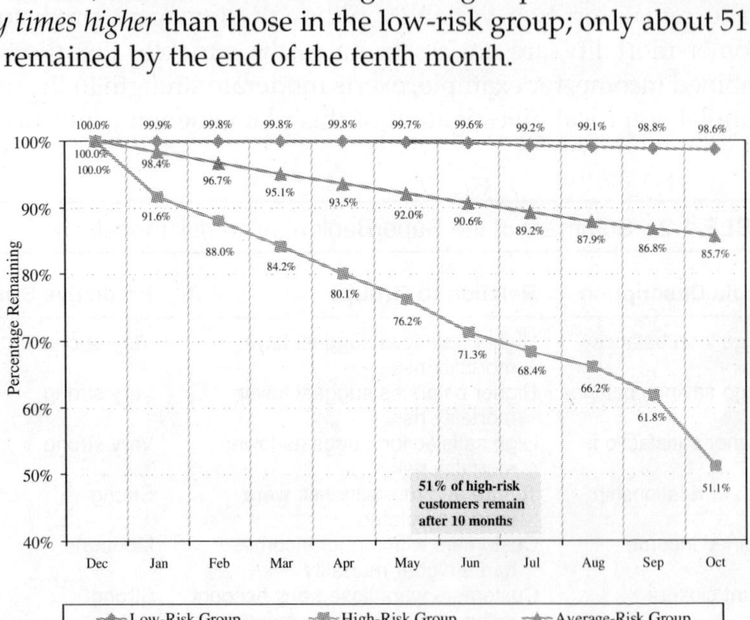

FIGURE 1.8 Attrition by risk category.

Model Implementation

The cornerstone of the model development project was the need to identify "at risk" customers before they leave. Customers vary in terms of their worth, and clearly some "at risk" customers were of greater concern than others. Specifically, *profitable* customers whom the model isolated as being at significant risk for attrition were of greatest interest. Figure 1.9 depicts the integration of individual profitability and risk data. As shown, four quadrants emerge from the integration of profitability and attrition risk data.

The horizontal axis of the quadrant diagram presented in Figure 1.9 represents attrition risk. As one moves to the right, attrition risk increases. The vertical axis of the quadrant diagram reflects customer profitability. Customers in the top-right quadrant of Figure 1.9 should be of great concern to most organizations. These customers are both very profitable and are associated with a significant dropout risk. Clearly, intervention efforts aimed at circumventing the predicted attrition would have significant utility if successful.

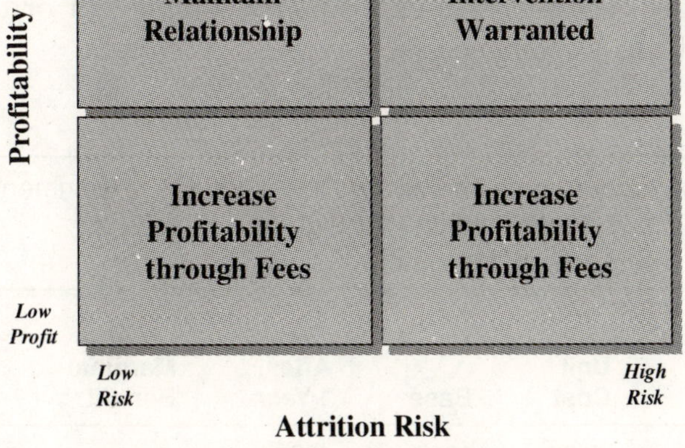

FIGURE 1.9 Integrating profitability and attrition risk.

INTERVENING TO SAVE PROFITABLE CUSTOMERS

SuperBank intervention efforts focused on the high-risk, profitable customer group. The predictive equation was migrated to a mainframe environment where it was executed monthly to identify profitable, high-risk customers. Intervening in an effort to retain the high-risk customers was the next step. Intervention took several forms and was subjected to experimental designs and cost-benefit analyses wherein the optimal communications channel was tested.

The experimental design took the form of one control group and three experimental treatment groups. In total, 1000 customers were assigned to each of the four groups. Each of the experimental groups was subjected to intervention methodologies of varying (presumed) efficacy. Although members of the control group were not contacted, two experimental groups received small gifts by mail, and the third received a personal telephone call from a SuperBank branch manager.

Table 1.3 depicts the experimental and control groups associated with SuperBank's efforts to optimize the intervention cost-benefit ratio. The table's rows relate to the four sample groups associated with the intervention analysis. The first row represents the control group of high-value, high-risk customers for whom no intervention efforts were made. These customers represent the baseline against which the various experimental interventions were contrasted. After one year, only 498 of the control group customers remained. Contrast this with the next three rows presented in Table 1.3. Each introduces an ostensibly more effective (and costly) appeal to the customer. In every case, the intent is to strengthen the relationship between the bank and the customer through either a simple gift or direct telephone call from a manager.

TABLE 1.3 Cost-benefit analysis for interventions (experimental and control groups) for high-value, high-risk SuperBank customers

Intervention Type	Unit Cost	Base	After 1 Year	Marginal Benefit	Cost per Saved Household
Control group	$0.00	1000	498		
Mail pack #1	$0.75	1000	621	123	$6.10
Mail Pack #2	$1.00	1000	686	188	$5.32
Telephone call	$1.60	1000	845	347	$4.61

Table 1.3 suggests that although most costly on a per-unit basis ($1.60), the direct telephone call to high-risk, profitable customers yielded the lowest cost per saved household. That is, it was most effective in stemming the tide of defecting customers. Although most expensive in aggregate, it produced the lowest unit cost per saved household.

A variety of cost-benefit analyses involving different intervention of strategies were tested at SuperBank. Because customer satisfaction emerged as a strong predictor of attrition, a great deal of focus has been on its antecedents. Although the financial outcome of these efforts has been highly favorable, they were based on SuperBank's very mature data warehouse. Only when financial, product usage, channel preference, demographic, and psychometric data (that is, customer satisfaction) reside in a single repository will other companies be able to enjoy the types of analysis presented in this case study.

The Future of Customer Satisfaction Research

The future of customer satisfaction research will most likely continue to establish empirical relationships with key business outcomes. The measurement of customer profitability and its surrogates will play an important role in future research. Customer retention appears to be emerging as a viable surrogate for profitability when the value of individual customer relationships cannot be quantified. Similarly, actual customer behaviors represent a reasonably good substitute for the types of profitability measures that, for example, the financial services industry enjoys. The extent to which these metrics reside in a common data warehouse will largely determine the ease with which these data can be integrated and related to both retention and profitability.

Many companies have developed robust models that permit management to test the effects of changes in customer satisfaction on customer retention and profitability. These tools may include cost-benefit analyses that match the cost of increasing customer (or employee) satisfaction to the resulting increased profits. To the extent possible, customer satisfaction researchers should have such a tool in mind when developing their survey instruments. In this framework, customer satisfaction research is part of a bigger picture in which the intent is more explicit: to increase corporate profits. After all, the corporate interest in customer satisfaction is not happenstance; there is an implicit assumption that increasing customer satisfaction will yield greater profits. And yet, without an empirical link between customer satisfaction and key business measures such as profitability, this relationship remains a mystery.

There have been numerous attempts to produce simulation applications that permit "what if?" scenarios using customer satisfaction data. One of the most comprehensive studies was conducted by Dillon, White, Rao, and Filak (1997) using American Express data. The authors' simulation model permitted managers to assess the impact of changing customer satisfaction on overt behaviors like share of spending, card retention, and spending volume. Once a structural equations model was developed and tested, it was migrated to a spreadsheet environment. Using a series of simple commands, managers could test the effects of changing satisfaction with various product and service quality issues. Share of wallet, retention, and spending volume were outcome variables that changed as the service and product quality issues were manipulated in the simulation.

Chapter 2

INSTRUMENTATION AND SCALE SELECTION

INTRODUCTION

As expected, there is a substantial body of literature relating to the optimal measurement scale. Various authors have championed a wide variety of scale types. In a somewhat controversial piece, Devlin, Dong, and Brown (1993, 12–18) compared numerous scales across six criteria: response bias, understanding, discriminating power, ease of administration, ease of use, and credibility. Using this set of criteria, the authors concluded that either a five-point expectation scale or a four-point requirements scale yielded the best results. The former is a completely anchored scale with labels as follows: much better, better, just as expected, worse, much worse. In contrast, the four-point requirements scale was labeled in the following fashion: exceeded expectations, met expectations, nearly met expectations, and missed expectations. The authors concluded that the expectations and requirements scales were most desirable given the evaluation criteria.

Grapentine (1994) was somewhat critical of Delvin, Dong, and Brown's (1993) assertion that fully anchored expectations and requirements scales were most appropriate for customer satisfaction research. Grapentine suggested that the expectation scales had questionable validity. Of particular concern was the type of inferences permissible when tracking changes over time. Grapentine wondered whether changes could be attributed to actual product or service quality differences over time or if respondent *expectations* changed over time. Assessing the source of longitudinal changes in either the expectation scale or requirements scale was seen as problematic at best.

Grapentine addressed a number of other issues surrounding the expectations and requirements scales. He argued, for example, that scale truncation was inevitable when using the requirements scale, in particular. The author found that respondents tended to use only three of the four requirements scale points when certain issues were rated. In particular, when issues such as bank statement accuracy and convenient banking hours were rated by respondents, they tended to avoid the use of the "exceeded my expectations" option. For example, respondents felt it was impossible to exceed their requirements with respect to statement accuracy. Either the statement was accurate, or it was not.

The expectations and requirements scales clearly have problems. Teas (1993) promoted a measurement framework referred to as the evaluated performance (EP) model. This type of scale typically involves soliciting agreement to a positive statement about a product or service. Teas used such a scaling approach and demonstrated higher validity coefficients than competing scales based upon expectations.

Wittink and Bayer (1994) advocated a measurement architecture characterized by a 10-point dependent variable scale and two-point experiential predictor variables. The latter are items that solicit agreement to statements concerning actual respondent experiences. Examples include whether the service person greeted the customer by name or provided an accurate and understandable invoice prior to leaving. This measurement approach is discussed in more detail later in this chapter.

It seems safe to conclude at this point that scales based upon expectations, requirements, or gaps between service experience and service expectations have only modest support in applied and academic circles. In applied settings, the multipoint scale with endpoint anchors appears to be preferred. This is not to say there are no dissenters, however. There are many instances of large corporations relying upon letter grade (that is, A through F) scales, expectation scales, and other derivatives of these. It is likely that there is more controversy surrounding the number and labeling of scale points than whether to use performance ratings, expectation, or requirements scales.

Scaling Issues

We turn now to the psychometric aspects of customer satisfaction research. In particular, the choice of measurement scales is the focus. A full understanding of measurement scales is facilitated by a review

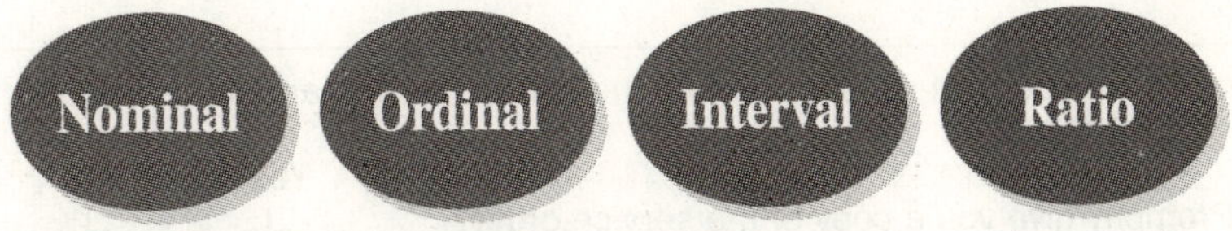

FIGURE 2.1 Four levels of data measurement.

of the four main types shown in Figure 2.1: nominal, ordinal, interval, and ratio. The scales differ tremendously in terms of what types of mathematical operations are permissible. Each scale type will be reviewed and discussed with respect to its utility in customer satisfaction research. Nunnally (1978, 12–20) provides an excellent treatment of various scale types and their psychometric properties.

Nominal Scales

Nominal scales are categorical. There is no *ordering* associated with the scale points. Examples include gender, SIC code, and job category. We typically do not employ nominal data to measure customer satisfaction, per se. The exception involves comparisons of customer satisfaction *across* nominal variable categories. For example, we might be interested in comparing the satisfaction levels of large versus small customers.

The exception to the preceding involves a *binary scale.* In a customer satisfaction context, binary scales tend to be experiential and involve actual observed behaviors. For example, one might ask respondents whether the service technician was courteous. Only two answers would be possible: yes or no. Reporting this type of customer satisfaction metric involves the proportion of answers in the affirmative. In a multivariate **dependence model,** the dependent variable is regressed on a series of binary predictor variables. The relationship is illustrated in Figure 2.2.

Advocates of binary scaling argue that these scales yield data that are characterized by relatively low levels of intercorrelation. Our research suggests binary predictor variables are just as susceptible to ill-conditioning as are either interval-level or ratio-level data. More importantly, the lack of variance invariably yields models with abysmal explanatory power! It is not uncommon for regression equations built with binary explanatory variables to account for substantially less than 50 percent of the outcome variable's variance.

Considering your last experience with the service technician, did he or she . . .

	Yes	No
1. Promptly give you a copy of the service order?	❑	❑
2. Promptly explain the problem?	❑	❑
3. Promptly give you a copy of the invoice?	❑	❑

Now considering your last service technician visit, how satisfied are you with the repair service?

Very Satisfied				Very Dissatisfied
5	4	3	2	1

FIGURE 2.2 Nominal-level (binary) predictors followed by an interval-level dependent variable.

Considering all aspects of your new digital Newtonian reflector, how satisfied are you with this product? Using the letter grade scale below, would you give the product an A, B, C, D, or F?

❑ A ❑ B ❑ C ❑ D ❑ F

FIGURE 2.3 An ordinal-level letter grading scale.

Ordinal Scales

Unlike nominal-level scales, ordinal scales are frequently used in customer satisfaction research. Ordinal scales have scale points that are ordered. Although we know one is larger than the next, we do not know *how much* larger it is. In customer satisfaction research, the ordinal-level scale typically has three to five points. The exampie presented in Figure 2.3 illustrates such an ordinal-level satisfaction scale.

The scale is clearly ordered from positive to negative, and we know that each scale point reflects an increase in the intensity of the attitude in question. Still, we do not know the magnitude of this difference. We cannot reasonably make inferences regarding the *relative* magnitude of one scale point versus another. It would be erroneous to conclude, for example, that the letter grade A implies *twice* as much satisfaction as the C grade response.

The use of ordinal-level scales in customer satisfaction measurement should be discouraged. It is meaningless to calculate any of the

Considering all aspects of your new digital Newtonian reflector, how satisfied are you with this product?

Very Satisfied				**Very Dissatisfied**
5	4	3	2	1

FIGURE 2.4 The typical five-point scale has anchors only on its endpoints.

fundamental distributional metrics so familiar to customer satisfaction researchers. The average and standard deviation, for example, are highly suspect. Similarly, most multivariate statistical methods make assumptions that preclude the use of data measured on an ordinal scale. Although there are techniques geared specifically for **ordinal data** (for example, the Spearman rank-order correlation coefficient), in general it is better to avoid these data for gauging customer satisfaction.

Interval Scales

Most, if not all, scales in customer satisfaction research yield **interval data.** Unlike ordinal scales, the interval scale permits valid inferences concerning the distances between scale points. Thus, it is reasonable to conclude that a score of 4 reflects twice the magnitude of a score of 2. Figure 2.4 illustrates the five-point **Likert scale** with endpoint anchors.

This scale is very popular with customer satisfaction researchers. Of course, the interval-level scale may have more than five points. We generally encounter interval scales in either a five-point, seven-point, or 10-point configuration. No fewer than five points are recommended, however. We will discuss later the appropriate number of scale points in more detail.

With five-point interval scales, it is important that anchors be established only for the scale endpoints. Labeling all five points implies an ordinal-level response as shown in Figure 2.5. Note that there are no absolute rules in this regard, and it is really the respondents' cognitive processes that dictate how he or she responds to a given scale. Nonetheless, by labeling each point in a scale (as in Figure 2.5), we are *implicitly* leading the subject toward an ordinal-level response. This is less of a problem with seven-point and 10-point scales because they do not lend themselves particularly well to so many labels.

The rationale underlying a fully anchored five-point scale involves the ostensible effect the labeling has on the distribution. In

Considering all aspects of your new digital Newtonian reflector, how satisfied are you with this product?				
Very Satisfied	Satisfied	Undecided	Dissatisfied	Very Dissatisfied
5	4	3	2	1

FIGURE 2.5 The fully anchored five-point scale may lose its interval-level properties.

short, it has been argued that by labeling each point and assigning the midpoint (3 on a five-point scale) a value of "Undecided," skewness will be lessened. Although there is some evidence to support this, we feel that the benefits are outweighed by the possible loss of interval-level properties.

Ratio Scales

Unlike interval-level scales, ratio-level scales explicitly accommodate a rational zero value. For example, income measured in actual dollars represents a ratio-level measurement because there is a valid zero level. Such is not the case with any of the scales presented earlier. Unfortunately, ratio scales in attitude research generally, and customer satisfaction research specifically, are rarely encountered.

The power of ratio levels of measurement lies in the types of operations that are permissible with **ratio data.** Of particular importance is the ratio scale's invariance over a wide variety of transformations. When multiplied by a constant, for example, the values of a ratio scale retain their rank ordering and ratios, and they do not affect the zero point.

It should be clear by now that researchers investigating customer satisfaction really have a limited choice with respect to measurement scales. The interval-level scale represents the best option for a variety of reasons. First, it is generally accepted that endpoint anchored measurement scales yield interval data that may be subjected to various mathematical manipulations. And, although the ratio-level scale has much to offer in terms of its invariance to mathematical transformations and the power of inferences relating data to a true zero baseline, ratio-level scales in customer satisfaction research are rarely encountered.

In reality, most scales in customer satisfaction research are of the interval variety. The *number* of scale points has been the basis for the most disagreement. Those in favor of a five-point scale typically note its simplicity and, more importantly, the presence of a natural midpoint. The latter is of little consequence for a five-point scale with endpoint anchors. Customer satisfaction data generally yield skewed distributions. It is not at all unusual to encounter **top-two box scores** greater than 90 percent reported by world-class organizations. The addition of a labeled midpoint on a five-point scale generally does not appreciably reduce the extent to which customers give ratings of 4 or 5 on such a scale.

How Many Scale Points?

Alternatives to the five-point scale include the seven-point and 10-point versions. A key remaining question involves the relative strength of each configuration. There is no unequivocal answer, unfortunately. From a purely univariate reporting perspective, the three versions are equally appealing.

The multipoint scale yields more data variability than, for example, binary scales that elicit yes or no responses (Hayes, 1998, 70–71). For organizations performing at stellar levels (for example, top-two box scores of 90 percent or greater on a five-point scale), it may be worth considering either a seven-point or 10-point scale. There are at least two reasons for this. Consider a hypothetical organization with 75 national sales districts. The company sells and services a premium product that is universally considered "best in class." Assume this company has a mature customer satisfaction measurement and tracking program that relies upon a five-point scale. Feedback is provided on a quarterly basis at the sales district level. If most sales districts receive quarterly scores of better than 90 percent, differentiating performance levels among them will be difficult at best. It is the ability to discriminate between top performers and poor performers that adds tremendous utility to CSM (Customer Satisfaction Measurement) programs that are linked to compensation and bonus plans. Clearly, if the reporting metric produces a distribution of scores so *narrow* that statistically differentiating performance levels is impossible, then the program will have only modest utility.

In reality, choice of measurement scales is frequently determined by univariate reporting requirements. A company that routinely receives 90 percent top-two box scores on a five-point scale will likely only enjoy about a 85 percent top-two box score on a seven-point scale. On a 10-point scale, the same company would expect a score of only about 75 percent. In addition, the distribution of districts around the average top-two box score will be more diffuse. The wider distribution of scores around the mean gives us more discriminating power. The enhanced discriminating power enables us more reliably to isolate poor performers, as shown in Figure 2.6.

The second reason a seven-point *or* 10-point scale is preferred involves *covariance.* In general, it is easier to establish covariance between two variables with greater dispersion (that is, variance) around their means. It is this covariance that is so critical to establishing strong multivariate dependence models used in key driver assessments. Thus, from a model development perspective, the 10-point scale is preferred. Sophisticated statistical software such as Jöreskog and Sörbom's **LISREL-8** structural equation modeling package, for example, *assume data are ordinal* if five or fewer scale levels are present.

In an empirical review of several scale types, Wittink and Bayer (1994) concluded that a 10-point dependent measure was preferred. The authors also maintained that a 2-point *experiential* predictor variable scale should be adopted. This scale type solicits a yes or no response to statements involving specific service or product experiences and was illustrated in Figure 2.2. For example, "Did the service person provide you with an accurate invoice?" can only be answered with a yes or no. Although the 10-point dependent measure is well-accepted in both academic and industry research settings, the two-point predictor variable has been met with some trepidation. One reason is that models based upon this measurement approach tend to have lower predictive (R^2) capacities.

Not surprisingly, the configuration that Wittink and Bayer advocated has not been widely adopted. Nonetheless, their comparison of the five-point and 10-point dependent variable scales is valuable. The authors relied upon a total of 13 criteria. These included issues involving the respondent (for example, simplicity and understandability) and statistical issues such as response bias, reliability, power, and sensitivity. Response bias involves the extent to which target respondents are excluded due to inability or refusal to participate. To the extent measurement error is minimal we can conclude that a metric is reliable. Reliability connotes the extent to which a measurement is repeatable with the same- or nearly same-result. Power involves the extent to which the scale can detect changes over time (or differences between groups). Finally, sensitivity was defined as having the greatest room for improving customer satisfaction. Given this set of criteria, Wittink and Bayer concluded that the 10-point endpoint anchored measurement scale was preferred to the five-point alternative.

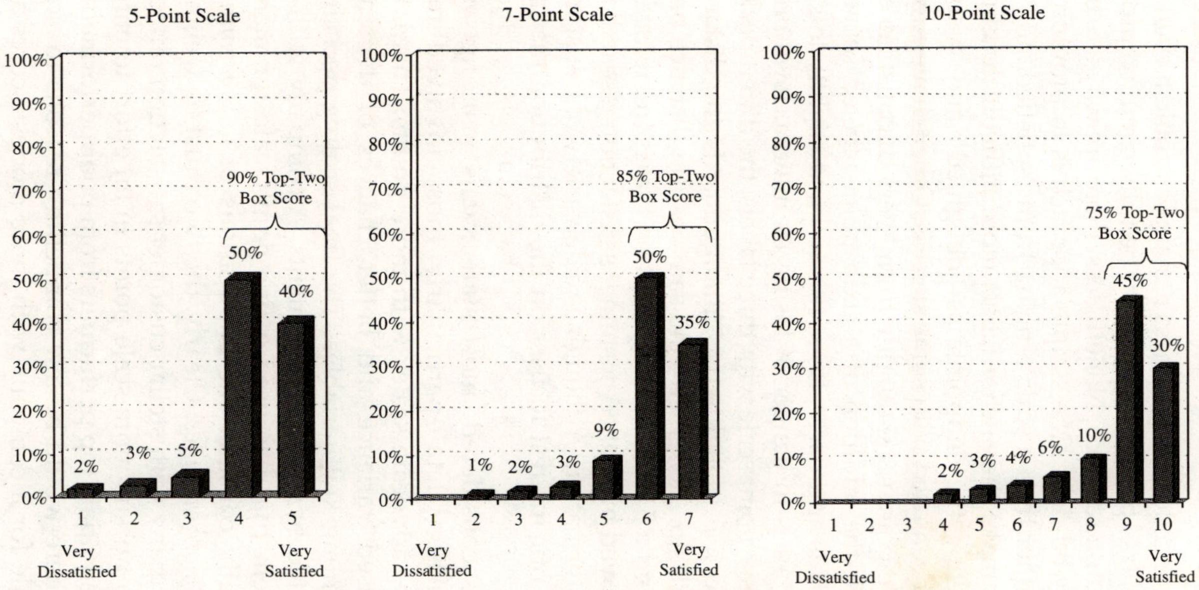

FIGURE 2.6 Distribution of scores using five-point, seven-point, and 10-pcint scales.

We must concede that skewness remains a problem even with the 10-point scale; this problem may never be fully circumvented in customer satisfaction research. Nonetheless, there are ways to lessen the impact of skewed data. One simple approach is to provide extreme endpoints. Rather than a scale ranging from "satisfied" to "dissatisfied," we can make the anchor labels more difficult to achieve. For example, labeling the endpoints as "delighted" and "very disappointed" has been used with some success. Others have suggested a traditional five-point scale ranging from "very dissatisfied" to "very satisfied" with the addition of a sixth point labeled separately as "delighted." This approach also seems to yield slightly less skewed distributions but is in danger of losing its interval-level properties. That is, it is a six-point scale with three labels; the difference between a 5 rating and a 6 (delighted) is ambiguous. Is the distance from "very satisfied" to "delighted" the same as the distance between a rating of a 4 and a 5? An additional option that is (regrettably) infrequently employed in applied customer satisfaction research involves the data transformation. Although a wide variety of transformations are available, our interest focuses on the distribution that is highly skewed.

All things considered, most statisticians working with customer satisfaction data—particularly those involved in model development—advocate scales with more points. This is because of the increased variance and better chances of demonstrating covariance among key variables. The final scaling decision is frequently dictated by past measurements. A company with a stable tracking system that has used a five-point scale for many years should carefully consider the implications of *losing continuity* in its search for *more variance.* Clearly, the two must be weighed judiciously; a company with stellar customer satisfaction ratings might be inclined to pursue more scale points in an effort to enhance its ability to differentiate top performers from poor performers. On the other hand, there would be few compelling reasons to explore an expanded scale for a company with more modest scores and very little interest in multivariate statistical models.

There are no unequivocal answers when it comes to the number of points for a scale. Each case is characterized by the current distribution of scores, need for tracking continuity, benchmarking, and, in many cases, personal preference. It should be clear that *fewer* than five points veers dangerously from the interval properties assumed by most of the multivariate statistical procedures described in this book. Similarly, more than 10 points is very uncommon and may be too unmanageable for the respondent.

Case Study: Scale Equivalencies

One persistent problem in customer satisfaction tracking studies involves situations that result in the measurement scale being changed. This often involves moving from a five-point scale to a seven-point or 10-point scale. The key question that faces researchers interested in changing scales is how to retain the value of historical data and make the transition essentially transparent.

Unfortunately, the transition from a five-point scale to, for example, a 10-point scale is not as simple as simply multiplying the former scale scores by two! We have found that the most defensible approach is built upon an empirical foundation. If at all possible, a measurement using *both* the existing and proposed scales is preferred. This approach permits the development of a predictive model that will forecast one scale based upon the other. Simple linear regression is the obvious choice for this task. It is important that the predictive capacity of the model be evaluated before embarking on a systematic conversion of previous scores, of course.

Consider the case of Omnikote Manufacturing, which faced a scale conversion problem in late 1996. Following a merger with a Japanese conglomerate, Omnikote researchers were required to migrate from a five-point scale to a 10-point scale. Even though they had tracked the five-point scale metric on a quarterly basis for the past four years, the migration to a scale with seven points was inarguable. Despite their protestations, the Omnikote researchers adopted the 10-point satisfaction scale. The main organizational benefit was consistency with their Japanese counterparts. Nonetheless, from a tracking perspective, the researchers were in a quandary. How could they possibly integrate 10-point scale data with the tracking program they had managed for four years? Unfortunately, there is no solution to this problem that does not involve some level of compromise. The most problematic aspect of the change from the perspective of Omnikote researchers was the tracking system, which clearly showed a positive trend over the past four years (Figure 2.7).

There is no shortage of options with respect to addressing the problem Omnikote faced. Figure 2.8 summarizes the four alternatives when faced with a scale conversion. The first option is clearly the

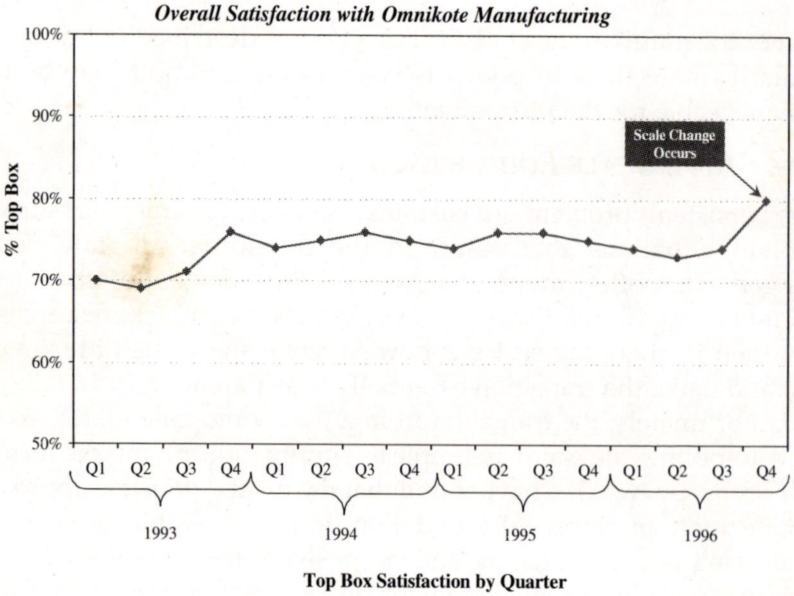

FIGURE 2.7 Omnikote overall satisfaction tracking graph.

1. Start over—shelve the existing tracking program
2. Continue to gather and track *both* types of data
3. Create a simple scale equivalency and convert historical data to new scale
4. Empirically convert historical data to new scale

FIGURE 2.8 Approaches to scaling changes.

least desirable because it requires establishing a new tracking program and dropping the old one. Nonetheless, this approach is frequently embraced—particularly when other options fail to produce appealing results.

Although often *not* an option due to political agendas, gathering overall satisfaction data using both scale types has been successfully

TABLE 2.1 Simple scale equivalencies.

5-Point Scale	10-Point Equivalent
1	1.5
2	3.5
3	5.5
4	7.5
5	9.5

implemented. We prefer that data of each type be gathered using *separate* survey instruments. That is, it would be inadvisable to place both scale types in the same survey. Two issues arise that may confound the measurement objective. First, respondents may not grasp the scaling change and provide a response based upon the first scale they encounter. Further, changing scales during an interview is at best awkward, and there is always some level of ambiguity. Second, the *position* of the overall satisfaction items must be interchanged in order to avoid bias. This requires two forms of the same questionnaire and, consequently, more administrative effort. If methodological and political hurdles can be overcome, this option provides the best of both worlds. The new scale is introduced, consistency throughout the organization is ensured, and the existing tracking system is retained.

The downside of this approach is that it yields two disparate measurements and reporting systems. Further, in the case of Omnikote, customer satisfaction data were routinely subjected to multivariate statistical analyses. These types of analysis, in general, are somewhat constrained by the lack of variation associated with five-point scales.

The third option available to the Omnikote researchers involves a simple scale equivalency. In the present case, it would be very tempting to convert the historical data to a 10-point equivalent simply by multiplying the former by two. Using this simple heuristic, the Omnikote research staff could transform the historical five-point data to the 10-point equivalent, as shown in Table 2.1.

In order to be meaningful to Omnikote researchers, the 10-point scale tracking metric had to be the top-two box score. This permits the simple linear transformation to be implemented. One trouble with this sort of approach is that it is oblivious to distributional differences. In particular, five-point scale data are frequently more skewed than 10-point scale data. The result of this difference is that the transformed tracking metric will not necessarily reflect those obtained directly using a 10-point scale. This is because data derived from a five-point scale will tend to be somewhat more heavily skewed than 10-point scale data.

Figure 2.9 illustrates how the simple numeric scale conversion approach described earlier tends to be misleading. In particular, note how the means for the five-point data and 10-point data appear to confirm the simple conversion approach. That is, the mean of the five-point scale data is almost exactly one-half of the 10-point scale data. Nonetheless, the distributions are quite clearly different. This relationship, for example, does not hold true for top-box or top-two box percentiles. Note that the original 10-point scale yielded a 60 percent top-two box score, whereas the transformed data suggest a 50 percent top-two box score.

One of the most sophisticated means of converting scales involves gathering additional data that contain *both* measures. This approach permits us to leverage the covariation that exists between the two measures. The objective here is to meaningfully convert the historical five-point scale data to a 10-point scale equivalent using simple linear regression.

This technique required Omnikote researchers to administer their survey instrument with both scales included. In half the surveys, the five-point scale was in the beginning of the survey, and the 10-point scale was placed at the end. In the other half, these positions were reversed. This approach helped avoid any positional bias associated with placing an overall satisfaction item at the beginning/end of the instrument.

With 1000 observations containing both overall satisfaction measures, it was possible to develop a simple linear regression model that predicted a five-point scale score based on a respondent's score on a 10-point scale. Using this technique, a model was developed, and historical data were successfully converted.

Scale changes in customer satisfaction research are commonplace. Not infrequently, they result in abandoning a historical tracking program because of the lack of continuity in key metrics. This need not be the case. As described earlier, there are viable solutions to the problem. Still, there is no "magic bullet," and it is the rare conversion effort that will be seamless and transparent to users.

Survey Instrument Design

Customer satisfaction surveys benefit from a highly structured approach. This structure generally should accommodate the analyti-

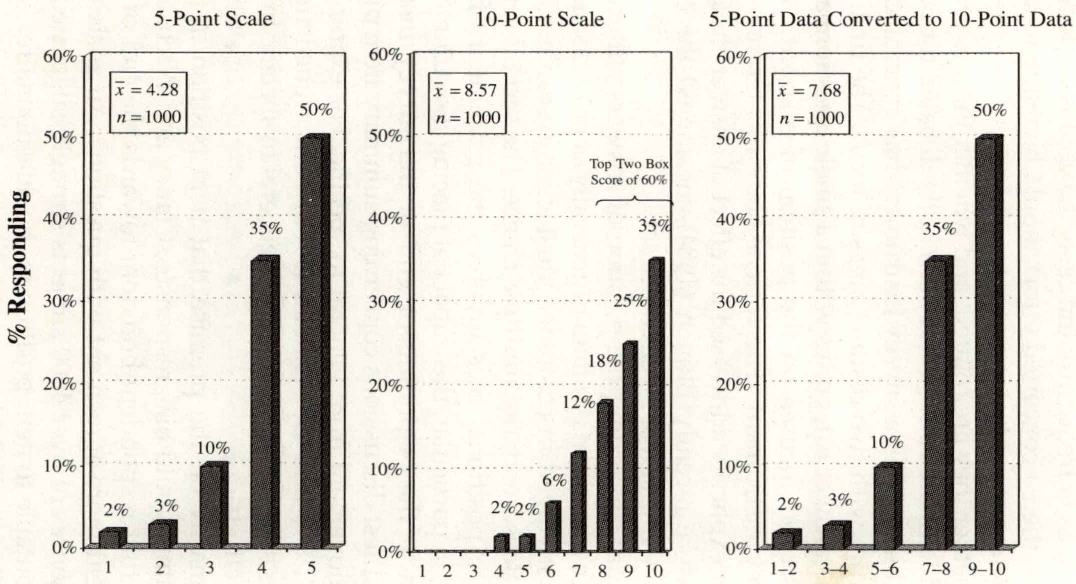

FIGURE 2.9 Five-point versus 10-point scales.

cal objectives. If, as is frequently the case, the goal is to perform key driver analyses, then a concerted effort should be made to identify *a priori* the **dependent** and **independent variables.** Where these items are placed, whether they are rotated, and whether the answer choices within a given item are rotated has been hotly debated for 50 years.

Positional bias within a survey instrument has generated its own body of literature with two distinct areas of focus. The first involves the order of the answer categories within a single questionnaire item, whereas the second focuses on the position of a specific question within a survey instrument. The former body of literature is quite mature; Becker explicitly addressed the effect of answer choice ordering in 1954. More recently Blunch (1984) considered the effects of positional bias within an answer choice set.

The literature concerning the position of answers within a single multiple-choice questionnaire item is generally of only casual interest to researchers involved in customer satisfaction research. Generally, our items are closed-end, not multiple choice. The second set of literature related to positional bias involves the placement of specific questions and, in particular, the impact of placing the summary judgment question at the beginning or end of the survey instrument. Some of the earliest discussions concerning summary item placement advocated a movement from general to specific. For example, Kahn and Cannell (1957) and Oppenheim (1966) both argued that questionnaire items should be ordered from general to specific in order to avoid biasing effects.

Based primarily on the premise that item position in omnibus studies over time would bias responses, Clancy and Wachsler (1971) hypothesized that respondent boredom towards the end of the survey would yield more agreement with questions. An analysis based upon the responses of over 4000 subjects strongly suggested that no bias was attributable to item position in the questionnaire.

Carp (1974) considered both multiple response options and item position effects. His results—based upon 899 responses—suggested that there was little difference between means when the summary judgment question was placed at the beginning and end of a two-hour survey. Carp concluded that his data " . . . cast doubt also upon the need to place general, evaluative questions first in an interview in order that responses to them not be contaminated . . . " (p. 587).

Perreault (1975) suggested that response set phenomena were highly problematic in traditional survey research platforms. As a result, he offered one of the first computer-based systems for printed questionnaire item text rotation. Clearly, the advent of personal computers at around this time revolutionized the production of questionnaires. Nearly 10 years would pass before computer-aided telephone interviews would be commonplace.

Kraut, Wolfson, and Rothenberg (1975) used a sample of over 500 to test their hypothesis that positional bias would affect survey responses. The authors were surprised to learn that items placed at the end of the survey were associated with less and less variance. Responses tended to be less discriminating and more rote toward the end of the survey. The 168-item questionnaire yielded smaller and smaller standard deviations toward the end of the survey.

The results of these and other research programs are far from unequivocal. In some instances where significant position bias has been demonstrated, the interview length was excessive. Most customer satisfaction research instruments are much shorter than those employed in some of the research cited here. With respect to very abbreviated customer satisfaction surveys involving low-involvement services or products, there may be little difference associated with placement of the dependent measure in the front or back of the survey.

Dependent Variable Placement

Despite the ambiguous results described earlier, placement of the dependent variable remains one of the most hotly debated aspects of instrument design in customer satisfaction research. One school of thought calls for placing the overall satisfaction measure at the beginning of the survey, whereas the other maintains it should appear at the end. The rationales for both approaches are intuitively appealing. Those who advocate placement of the dependent measure at the beginning of the survey argue that it evokes a "top of the mind" measure of overall satisfaction. Proponents contend this response best reflects consumers' actual cognitive processes when considering their satisfaction with a product or service. In short, this school of thought suggests that overall satisfaction reflects the consumer's highly abbreviated review of the product or service.

Placement of the dependent measure toward the end of the survey instrument has different implications. Having expressed their satisfaction with a series of specific issues relating to delivery, product quality, price, technical support, billing, sales personnel, and others, the respondent is asked to consider all of these and offer one final summarization of their satisfaction. Proponents of this approach maintain that placement of the overall satisfaction question at the end of the survey instrument is a better reflection of consumer thought processes. In a review of several competing measurement scales, Wittink and Bayer (1994, 8) argued convincingly that placement of the dependent measure at the end of the survey yields regression models with greater explanatory power. The implication is that consumers review all aspects of the product or service before settling upon a summary level of satisfaction.

Both approaches seem reasonable. Our experience suggests that placement of the dependent measure at the beginning of the instrument is most appropriate for products and services that require little introspection on the part of the consumer. Examples include low-involvement products such as cereals, soft drinks, and other consumer nondurables. Satisfaction with low-involvement products and services is more likely to be "top of mind" and require only modest introspection on the consumer's part. On the other hand, products and services that require more financial or behavioral participation such as banking relationships or complex consumer durables like automobiles tend to be evaluated differently by consumers. It seems reasonable to argue that these products and services undergo more *rational* assessments by consumers. For example, when considering his or her satisfaction with a newly acquired car, most consumers will briefly reflect on the sales process, the vehicle's aesthetics, interior, and perhaps fuel efficiency.

From a model development perspective, we prefer surveys that place the dependent measure *after* the predictor variables. Our experience confirms that more variance in the dependent measure can be accounted for with this structure. A recent test based on 3000 telephone interviews for a major utility confirmed this. Half of the respondents were asked to provide an overall satisfaction rating at the beginning of the interview, and the other half were asked the same question at the end of the survey. Parallel regression analyses were conducted, and the results confirmed that the predictor variables could account for 10 percent more variation of the dependent measure placed at the end of the survey. Of course, this is a sample of one observation, and others may have empirical evidence to contradict the example cited here. Nonetheless, it has been our experience across a variety of industries that placement of the overall satisfaction measure toward the end of the survey yields dependence models with greater explanatory power.

The Structured Instrument

In order to maximize the utility of a customer satisfaction study, it is an excellent idea to review how well it will fit your analytical objectives. We frequently encounter customer satisfaction survey instruments with no discernable dependent measure! This precludes the development of key driver analysis and other valuable treatments of customer satisfaction data.

The sample questionnaire presented in Figure 2.10 illustrates a very desirable two-stage nested structure. First, notice that there are four primary content areas: product quality, delivery and setup, warranty, and technical support. Within each content area are a number of specific issues followed by an overall assessment of satisfaction with the area. For example, the technical support section is composed of five items relating to specific issues such as ease of access. These are followed by an overall evaluation of technical support. The final item in the questionnaire elicits a satisfaction rating that reflects all four of the content areas.

This structure readily accommodates two levels of regression model development. The first involves regressing the overall content satisfaction items on the specific issues that compose each unique section. The second level of model development regresses the final overall satisfaction measure on the four summary items (product quality, delivery and setup, warranty, and technical support). Figure 2.11 illustrates the two levels of analysis permitted by the instrument structure, which is con-

Hello, this is <<*interviewer*>> calling on behalf of Newtonian Instruments. We're conducting a brief customer satisfaction interview with customers who purchased the digital Newtonian reflector. Our records show that you or someone in your household purchased one of these products in the last year. Do you have a few minutes to participate?

1. ______ Yes, purchased (***proceed***)
2. ______ Refusal (***terminate***)
3. ______ Other disposition (***terminate***)

1. Product Quality Section

First, we'd like to ask you about your satisfaction with **product quality**. For each of the items I read, please tell me how satisfied you are using a seven-point scale where one means you are very dissatisfied and seven means you are very satisfied. Of course, you can use any number in between one and seven. Using this scale, how satisfied are you with . . .

FIGURE 2.10 Survey instrument with nested structure. (*Continued*)

	Very Satisfied						Very Dissatisfied
a. The digital reflecting capacity	7❑	6❑	5❑	4❑	3❑	2❑	1❑
b. The optical resolution	7❑	6❑	5❑	4❑	3❑	2❑	1❑
c. The German equatorial mount	7❑	6❑	5❑	4❑	3❑	2❑	1❑
d. The apochromatic Barlow lens	7❑	6❑	5❑	4❑	3❑	2❑	1❑
e. Motor performance	7❑	6❑	5❑	4❑	3❑	2❑	1❑

f. Overall, considering all of these features, how satisfied are you with **product quality?** Again, please use the same seven-point scale where one means you are very dissatisfied and seven means you are very satisfied.

Very Satisfied						Very Dissatisfied
7 ❑	6 ❑	5 ❑	4 ❑	3 ❑	2 ❑	1 ❑

2. Delivery and Setup Section

Now I'd like to ask you to think about **delivery and setup.** For each of the items I read, please tell me how satisfied you are using a seven-point scale where one means you are very dissatisfied and seven means you are very satisfied. Of course, you can use any number in between one and seven. Using this scale, how satisfied are you with . . .

	Very Satisfied						Very Dissatisfied
a. The time required for delivery	7❑	6❑	5❑	4❑	3❑	2❑	1❑
b. The set-up procedures	7❑	6❑	5❑	4❑	3❑	2❑	1❑
c. Knowledge of the set-up crew	7❑	6❑	5❑	4❑	3❑	2❑	1❑
d. Resolution of set-up problems	7❑	6❑	5❑	4❑	3❑	2❑	1❑
e. Set-up crew arrival/departure times	7❑	6❑	5❑	4❑	3❑	2❑	1❑

f. Now, considering all these issues, how satisfied are you with the digital Newtonian reflector **delivery and set-up process?** Again, please use the same seven-point scale.

Very Satisfied						Very Dissatisfied
7 ❑	6 ❑	5 ❑	4 ❑	3 ❑	2 ❑	1 ❑

3. Warranty Section

Now let's turn our attention to your **warranty.** For each of the items I read, please tell me how satisfied you are using a seven-point scale where one means you are very dissatisfied and seven means you are very satisfied. Of course, you can use any number in between one and seven. Using this scale, how satisfied are you with . . .

FIGURE 2.10 *Continued*

	Very Satisfied						Very Dissatisfied
a. Detail provided in warranty	7❑	6❑	5❑	4❑	3❑	2❑	1❑
b. Length of warranty	7❑	6❑	5❑	4❑	3❑	2❑	1❑
c. Parts covered by warranty	7❑	6❑	5❑	4❑	3❑	2❑	1❑
d. Instructions in warranty manual	7❑	6❑	5❑	4❑	3❑	2❑	1❑
e. Warranty fairness	7❑	6❑	5❑	4❑	3❑	2❑	1❑

f. Now, considering all these things, how satisfied are you with the **warranty** that accompanied your digital Newtonian reflector? Again, please use the same seven-point scale.

Very Satisfied						Very Dissatisfied
7❑	6❑	5❑	4❑	3❑	2❑	1❑

4. Technical Support

Next, we'd like to ask you about your satisfaction with **technical support.** For each of the items I read, please tell me how satisfied you are using a seven-point scale where one means you are very dissatisfied and seven means you are very satisfied. Of course, you can use any number in between one and seven. Using this scale, how satisfied are you with . . .

	Very Satisfied						Very Dissatisfied
a. Ease of access	7❑	6❑	5❑	4❑	3❑	2❑	1❑
b. Courtesy of support personnel	7❑	6❑	5❑	4❑	3❑	2❑	1❑
c. Waiting time required	7❑	6❑	5❑	4❑	3❑	2❑	1❑
d. Ability to solve your problems	7❑	6❑	5❑	4❑	3❑	2❑	1❑
e. Tech support knowledge	7❑	6❑	5❑	4❑	3❑	2❑	1❑

f. Considering all of these, how satisfied are you, overall, with Newtonian Instruments' **technical support?** Once again, use the seven-point scale.

Very Satisfied						Very Dissatisfied
7❑	6❑	5❑	4❑	3❑	2❑	1❑

5. Summary

Considering the areas we've just covered—product quality, delivery, warranty, and technical support—how satisfied are you overall with your new digital Newtonian reflector? Again, use the same seven-point scale. Using this scale, **how satisfied are you overall?**

	Very Satisfied						Very Dissatisfied
Overall satisfaction rating	7❑	6❑	5❑	4❑	3❑	2❑	1❑

Thank you for your participation in this customer satisfaction research project. Your answers will help Newtonian Instruments to further enhance the services and products offered to customers. Again, thanks for participating.

FIGURE 2.10 *Continued*

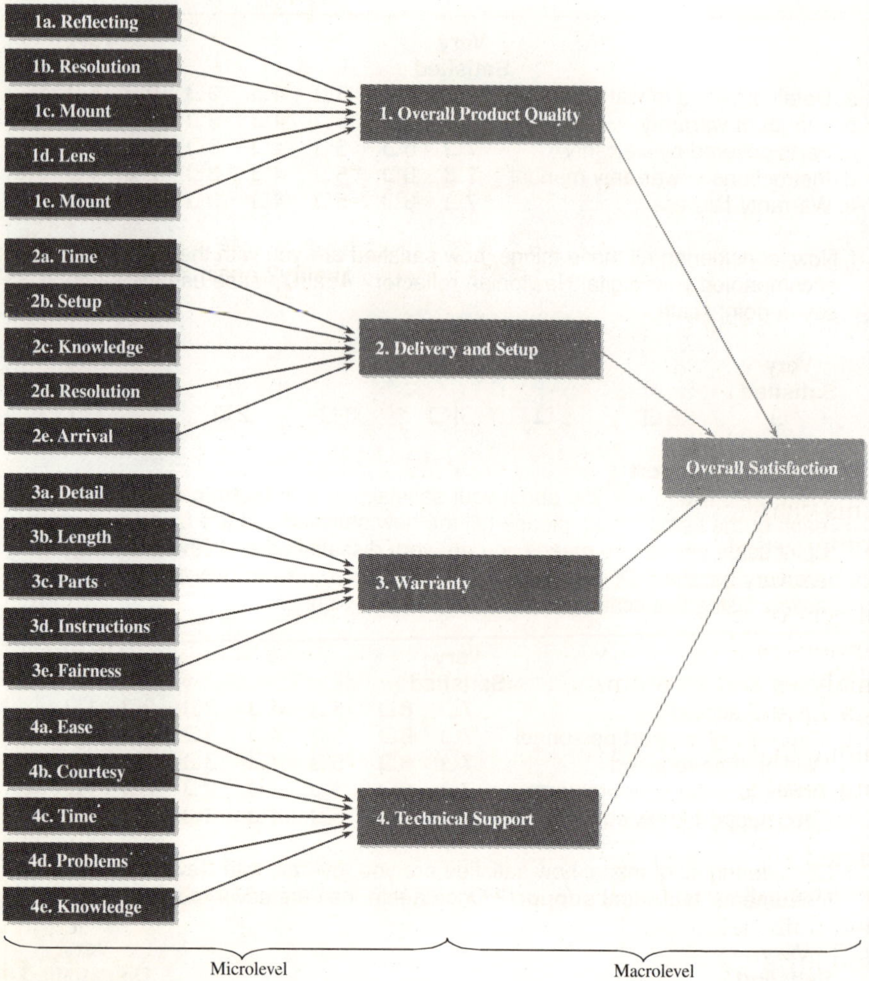

FIGURE 2.11 Analysis architecture.

ducive to a variety of multivariate techniques. At the lowest level, confirmatory factor analysis may be conducted to assess the dimensionality of each content area (that is, product quality, delivery and setup, warranty, and technical support). As just described, two levels of **regression analysis** may be conducted. Other techniques such as **path analysis** are also readily accommodated by the highly structured design presented here. These techniques are all discussed in detail later.

Chapter 3

Preparing Customer Satisfaction Data

Introduction

This chapter focuses on some of the problems associated with customer satisfaction data before they are subjected to the analytical techniques described later in this book. In an effort to demonstrate the effects of missing values, a case study is presented. This example underscores how our approach to treating missing values can affect analyses and recommendations. Missing data clearly affect the number of observations we include in our analyses. However, the technique that we choose to impute missing data can significantly affect our results.

Customer satisfaction data are subject to the same problems associated with other types of multivariate data. In particular, issues such as missing value treatment and **imputation,** data transformations, and data cleaning tend to plague the analysis of customer satisfaction and loyalty data. In most respects, how we approach these problems is not substantively different than in other fields. Still, our data tend to be characterized by more missing values and most certainly skewed distributions. In the former case, a great deal of effort has been expended developing missing value imputation techniques that preserve the characteristics of the original data.

Missing Data in Customer Satisfaction Research

Survey data—particularly data from self-administered instruments—tend to have a healthy share of **missing values.** Consider the case of Globe Bank whose customer satisfaction questionnaire is especially appropriate for this illustration due to its abbreviated length. Figure 3.1

Globe Bank Customer Satisfaction Questionnaire

Dear Customer: Thank you for your continued patronage at Globe Bank. As part of our continuous quality-improvement effort, we randomly select a sample of customers each month to participate in our customer satisfaction research program. This month, your name was drawn, and we would greatly appreciate your participation. Please use the postage-paid return envelope to return your completed survey and keep the enclosed $1.00 as a sign of our gratitude for your participation in this important program.

Please use a seven-point scale where one means you are very dissatisfied and seven means you are very satisfied. Of course, you may use any number in between these extremes.

	Very Dissatisfied						**Very Satisfied**
1. Globe Bank tellers' service level at the branch you visit most often	1	2	3	4	5	6	7
2. Globe Bank's deposit account rates	1	2	3	4	5	6	7
3. Globe Bank's rates on loans	1	2	3	4	5	6	7
4. Globe Bank's employees' willingness to help you	1	2	3	4	5	6	7

Now considering all four of these aspects of Globe Bank, *how satisfied are you overall with us?*

Very Satisfied						**Very Dissatisfied**
1	2	3	4	5	6	7

FIGURE 3.1 Globe Bank customer satisfaction survey instrument.

presents the Globe Bank survey instrument. As shown, it is composed of four specific items relating to product and service quality followed by a single, summary dependent measure. All five items employ a seven-point rating scale. Note that an eighth category to accommodate a "don't know" category was purposely excluded in an effort to minimize missing values. In the present case, bank marketing researchers were as interested in perceptions as they were in actual experiences. That a customer did not have experience with the bank's loan rates, for example, was not of great importance. The final question involved their perceptions of Globe Bank's product and service quality.

In total, 400 completed questionnaires were included in this sample analysis. Table 3.1 presents the base sample sizes, means, and correlations among the five items. As shown, the five items differ tremendously in terms of the number of valid responses. For example, while

TABLE 3.1 Profile of Globe Bank questionnaire items.

				Intercorrelations Among Questionnaire Items				
Question	***n***	**Mean**	**SD**	**Service**	**Deposit**	**Loans**	**Help**	**Overall**
1. Service	393	4.40	2.02	1.00				
2. Deposit	388	4.23	2.09	0.89	1.00			
3. Loans	330	4.61	1.87	0.61	0.58	1.00		
4. Help	382	4.21	1.94	0.58	0.59	0.51	1.00	
5. Overall	394	4.09	1.93	0.71	0.71	0.59	0.65	1.00

virtually all of the respondents answered the overall satisfaction question, only 330 provided an evaluation for the item relating to loan rates. This is unquestionably attributable to respondents' lack of experience with the bank's loan product group. Had a "don't know" option been provided, the number of usable responses would have been much lower.

The distribution and pattern of missing values were determined through additional analysis. Of the 400 responses included in the analysis, 318 had no missing values. That is, 318 respondents answered each of the five questions in the survey. Of course, this means 82 respondents failed to answer at least one of the five questions. In fact, 61 respondents failed to answer one of the five questions, 17 failed to answer two, and four respondents did not provide answers to three.

Why are we so concerned about the pattern of missing values? The answer involves nonresponse bias and the implications of data missing in some nonrandom pattern. Typically, we assume that missing values are distributed uniformly across the sample of respondents. Such is not always the case, unfortunately. In the present instance, there would be substantive grounds to believe that the data involving loan rates is missing according to some other factor such as exposure to Globe Bank loans.

Nonresponse error can also involve the sample as a whole. That certain respondents returned their questionnaires and others did not is of concern in survey research. The 400 Globe Bank responses, for example, represent a 40 percent response rate (1000 questionnaires were mailed out). Thus, our concern lies both in the differences between those who responded and those who did not *and* what factors might differentiate those who answered specific questions and those who failed to.

Nonresponse error can be expected to occur in most sample-based research methodologies and can be attributed either to noncontact or refusal to participate. In the former case, respondents may have moved or simply failed to recognize that their participation in the research was being solicited. Refusal to participate tends to be more problematic because it may not be uniformly distributed. It is often associated with socioeconomic status; the conventional wisdom suggests that more affluent consumers refuse to participate in surveys more so than others.

In applied customer satisfaction research, it is invariably easier to assess the distribution of missing values versus survey nonresponse bias. It is both time-consuming and expensive to contact consumers who failed to return their surveys. Certain types of organizations (banks, in particular) have at their disposal considerable external information that can be used to determine whether nonresponders differ from participants. For example, financial institutions have relatively detailed information concerning their customers' demographics and activity levels. If the 600 nonresponders in Globe Bank's customer satisfaction research tended to differ substantially from those who participated, there would be cause for alarm. Differences in income, account balances, account activity, and breadth should all be checked because the data are so readily available. As shown in Table 3.2, there were no noteworthy differences between the 400 survey participants and the nonresponse group. Many organizations also have access to geodemographic segmentation programs that use zip codes to assign a specific cluster affiliation to survey recipients. It is a simple matter to compare the cluster profile of responders to that of the nonresponders. Again, significant differences between the two groups should raise eyebrows.

Earlier, **univariate** and **bivariate statistics** for the Globe Bank data were presented. The correlation matrix is presented again in Table 3.3 in order to underscore how missing data affect bivariate and multivariate data. Note that under each correlation coefficient is a sample size and that under the elements are the number of valid observations for each variable. For example, 388 respondents provided a rating for the deposit item, and 330 responded to the item concerning Globe Bank loans.

When bivariate statistics like the **correlation** coefficient are calculated, there must be valid data for both variables. Thus, although

TABLE 3.2 Nonresponders versus survey participant account profiles.

Key Variable	Survey Participants	Nonresponders
Average tenure (years)	5.5	4.8
Average number accounts	2.49	2.29
Average loan balance	$852.00	$889.00
Average deposit balance	$2203.00	$2190.00

TABLE 3.3 Globe Bank survey correlations with sample sizes.

Question	Service	Deposit	Loans	Help	Overall
1. Service	1.00 *(393)*				
2. Deposit	0.89 *(381)*	1.00 *(388)*			
3. Loans	0.61 *(325)*	0.58 *(325)*	1.00 *(330)*		
4. Help	0.58 *(375)*	0.59 *(375)*	0.51 *(327)*	1.00 *(382)*	
5. Overall	0.71 *(387)*	0.71 *(384)*	0.59 *(328)*	0.65 *(380)*	1.00 *(394)*

there are 330 observations for the loan variable and 393 observations with valid data for the service variable, the correlation between the two is based upon only 325 observations. Clearly, all but five of the missing values associated with the service variable coincided with missing data on the loan variable because the number of valid observations for the correlation is 325.

The effect of missing values is more pronounced when multivariate techniques are involved. Of the 400 observations in the Globe Bank data set, only 318 observations have valid data for the first four variables. The overall satisfaction measure is associated with six missing values. Thus, we know that for any multivariate technique employing all five variables, there will be between 318 and 312 observations available. Nearly one-quarter of our sample will be excluded from multivariate techniques due to missing values.

A wide variety of approaches to imputing values for missing data have been used in applied customer satisfaction research. One of the

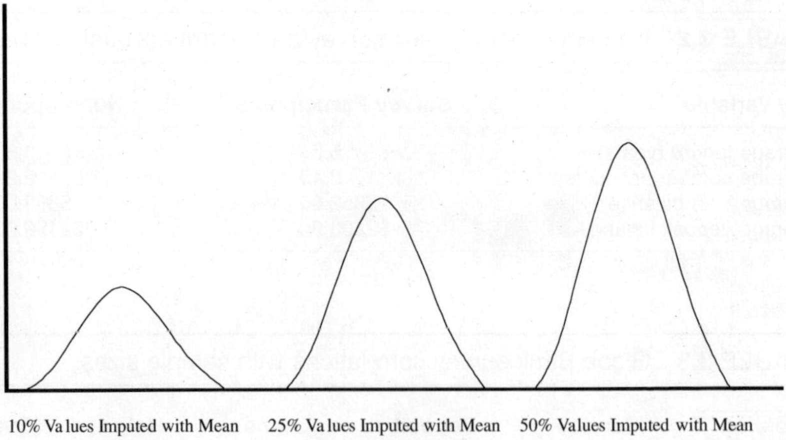

FIGURE 3.2 Effect of mean substitution imputation method.

simplest of these approaches is the mean substitution. This simply involves replacing a missing value with the mean score for the variable. Again, it is a simple solution and has some troublesome effects with respect to a given variable's distribution. As more observations are imputed with the mean, a variable's distribution becomes increasingly leptokurtic (peaked), as shown in Figure 3.2. As the proportion of mean substituted missing values increases, the variable's variance is decreased.

Table 3.4 demonstrates the effect of mean substitution on the data set. The left portion of the table presents the original relationships, whereas the right-hand side reflects the imputed data statistics. Notice that the most significant changes involve the standard deviations of the distributions. In each case, the standard deviation was reduced, reflecting reduced variation around the mean. From a univariate standpoint, this is not too concerning. But what effect does this reduction in variance have on the intercorrelations among the variables in this data set?

Table 3.5 presents the effects of mean substitution on the intercorrelations among variables in the data set. The right-hand side of the table reveals that *without exception* the magnitude of the correlations was lessened. Why is this? The most important reason is that in order for there to be covariation, there must be variation . . . that is, *variance.* The reduction in covariation should come as no surprise given

TABLE 3.4 Effect of mean substitution on variable distributions.

	Preimputation			Postimputation		
Question	***n***	**Mean**	**SD**	***n***	**Mean**	**SD**
1. Service	393	4.40	2.02	400	4.40	2.00
2. Deposit	388	4.23	2.09	400	4.23	2.06
3. Loans	330	4.61	1.87	400	4.61	1.70
4. Help	382	4.21	1.94	400	4.21	1.89
5. Overall	394	4.09	1.93	400	4.09	1.92

TABLE 3.5 Effect of mean substitution on variable correlations.

	Preimputation Correlations					Postimputation Correlations				
Question	x_1	x_2	x_3	x_4	x_5	x_1	x_2	x_3	x_4	x_5
1. Service	1.00					1.00				
2. Deposit	0.89	1.00				0.87	1.00			
3. Loans	0.61	0.58	1.00			0.55	0.52	1.00		
4. Help	0.58	0.59	0.51	1.00		0.56	0.57	0.46	1.00	
5. Overall	0.71	0.71	0.59	0.65	1.00	0.70	0.70	0.54	0.64	1.00

that the variance in each of the variables was reduced. Further, a closer examination of Table 3.5 confirms that as the number of observations subjected to the mean substitution increased, the correlation with other variables decreased. The loan satisfaction variable, for example, was associated with the greatest number of missing values. There were only 330 valid observations. Mean substitution was therefore performed on 70 cases. A review of Table 3.5 confirms that the greatest reduction in correlation magnitude involves the loan satisfaction variable. This is consistent with Table 3.4, which revealed that the largest decrease in standard deviations occurred with this variable. Clearly, the mean substitution method of missing value imputation has some undesirable effects on the data.

Another approach to imputing missing values involves multiple regression analysis (see chapter 5). This is the foundation for many more sophisticated techniques such as the MGV method (SAS Institute 1990, 1267–68) and the EM algorithm (McLachlan and Krishnan 1996). These approaches attempt to preserve the covariance structure of the data. The MGV method and EM algorithm are beyond the scope of this book; those interested in the EM algorithm should turn to McLachlan and Krishnan's (1996) book on the subject.

The multiple regression approach to missing value imputation involves regressing the variable for which missing values are to be imputed upon the remaining variables. Note that when dependency models will be based upon data with imputed values, it is critical that the dependent variable not be used to predict any of the independent variables. Such a tack will yield models that overstate the relationship between the set of predictor variables and the outcome variable. Thus, when data with imputed values will be used in regression modeling, it is critical that the dependent variable not be used in the model that imputes values for the independent variables.

In the case of Globe Bank, four multiple regression models were developed in an effort to impute missing values. These four models are summarized in Table 3.6. As shown, missing values for each variable are imputed based upon a multiple regression model that leverages the remaining three variables. The four models differ dramatically with respect to their predictive capacity. For example, the first model accounts for 81 percent of the variation in the dependent variable (service satisfaction). In contrast, the model that imputes missing values for the fourth variable (satisfaction with employees' willingness to help you) is much weaker.

Once the models depicted in Table 3.6 have been developed, they can be implemented using most statistical software packages. This involves coding the equations in the appropriate language (that is, **SAS** [Statistical Analysis System] or **SPSS** [Statistical Package for the Social Sciences]) and ensuring that the algorithms are only used when data for a given variable are missing!

TABLE 3.6 Summary of regression models used for missing value imputation.

Dependent Variable	Predictor Variables	R-Square	Model Summary
Service	x_2, x_3, x_4	81%	$x_1 = 0.23 + (0.76x_2) + (0.17x_3) + (0.04x_4)$
Deposit	x_1, x_3, x_4	79%	$x_2 = -0.03 + (0.84x_1) + (0.02x_3) + (0.11x_4)$
Loans	x_1, x_2, x_4	42%	$x_3 = 1.67 + (0.41x_1) + (0.04x_2) + (0.21x_4)$
Help	x_1, x_2, x_3	37%	$x_4 = 1.35 + (0.12x_1) + (0.30x_2) + (0.25x_3)$

It should be clear based on the sample sizes shown in Table 3.7 that the regression-based approach to missing value imputation is subject to certain constraints. In the present case, there are still observations that have been excluded from the profile presented in Table 3.7. This is because the equations shown in Table 3.6 require data to be present for each variable ($x_1 - x_4$). When data are missing, the regression-based approach will not generate a predicted score for the variable being imputed. One way to circumvent this is to permit imputed data from one variable to forecast the values of another variable. Although this approach would yield nearly 400 observations for each of the variables, it is dangerous, particularly when the number of missing values increases. Using imputed data to impute other data compounds estimation errors and is conceptually troublesome.

Despite the fact that not all observations are included in the statistics presented in Table 3.7, the regression-based imputation approach increased the base numbers. In some cases, the increase was large (that is, loan satisfaction); however, in some cases the number of new observations included was trivial. For example, before the imputation process, there were 382 observations for x_4. The imputed data include 384 observations for the same variable. The imputation did not adversely affect the variables' standard deviations although the changes that did occur appear to be strongly tied to the number of observations for which new values were imputed. For example, the loan satisfaction variable (x_4) experienced the greatest increase in observations (from 330 to 380) and the largest concomitant decrease in variance. Still, the decrease was not as great as that associated with the mean substitution approach to missing value imputation.

TABLE 3.7 Effect of regression-based imputation on variable distributions.

	Preimputation			Postimputation		
Question	***n***	**Mean**	**SD**	***n***	**Mean**	**SD**
1. Service	393	4.39	2.02	398	4.41	2.02
2. Deposit	388	4.23	2.09	392	4.24	2.09
3. Loans	330	4.61	1.87	380	4.60	1.80
4. Help	382	4.21	1.94	384	4.22	1.94
5. Overall	394	4.09	1.93	400	4.09	1.92

Note: The overall satisfaction data were imputed using the mean substitution technique.

Clearly, the ability of a missing value imputation technique to preserve means and variances is highly desirable. Perhaps even more important from a **multivariate data analysis** perspective is the ability of imputation methods to leave the correlation matrix undisturbed. Table 3.5 demonstrated that the mean substitution approach adversely affected the correlations among the variables for which imputed data were generated.

Table 3.8 contrasts the intercorrelations among the variables before and after the regression-based imputation procedure was implemented. A comparison with Table 3.5 confirms that the regression-based technique more closely preserved the correlations among the variables. Of course, we must concede that fewer values were imputed using the regression-based technique because we avoided imputing new data with imputed data as described earlier. Nevertheless, the variable associated with the largest proportion of imputed values (loan satisfaction) still closely approximated its preimputation values in terms of its relationship with the remaining variables. Such was not the case when the mean substitution approach was employed.

The imputation of missing data represents a dual-edged sword of sorts. Each time the decision is faced, one must weigh the lesser of two evils. On the one hand, we preserve the "purity" of the data set but suffer from lower sample sizes and the knowledge that data may be missing in a nonrandom fashion. On the other hand, introducing data that have, in essence, been manufactured on the basis of a heuristic approach is sometimes a bit disconcerting. As the proportion of observations that have imputed data increases, this level of discomfort increases. Each data set will be idiosyncratic with respect

TABLE 3.8 Effect of regression-based imputation on variable correlations.

	Preimputation Correlations					Postimputation Correlations				
Question	X_1	X_2	X_3	X_4	X_5	X_1	X_2	X_3	X_4	X_5
1. Service	1.00					1.00				
2. Deposit	0.89	1.00				0.89	1.00			
3. Loans	0.61	0.58	1.00			0.64	0.60	1.00		
4. Help	0.58	0.59	0.51	1.00		0.58	0.59	0.53	1.00	
5. Overall	0.71	0.71	0.59	0.65	1.00	0.71	0.71	0.60	0.66	1.00

Note: The overall satisfaction data were imputed using the mean substitution technique.

to the extent and pattern of missing values. No two will likely be the same. Among the points that should be considered when evaluating a data set for missing values are the following:

- An item-by-item analysis of the data set is the first step. Variables associated with very high proportions (that is, greater than 50 percent) of missing data should not be subjected to the imputation process.
- A separate program should be written to evaluate the distribution of missing values in the data set. In a dependence model framework, if an observation has 50 percent or more of the predictor variables missing, it should be excluded from the analysis.
- In general, mean substitution approaches to imputing missing values will decrease variance and dampen the level of intercorrelations among the variables in the data set.
- Missing value imputation approaches that leverage the covariation among variables tend to produce imputed values that more closely approximate the distribution of each variable.

Distributional Abnormalities

Fortunately, in marketing research applications in general, and customer satisfaction research in particular, variables generally are highly restricted with respect to their permissible ranges. That we employ Likert scales typically with no more points than 10 makes significant outliers indicative of, at worst, a data entry error. For example, suppose we encounter a value of 87 when we know the values must range from one to 10. In other fields, this may be a legitimate value but in attitudinal survey research applications it would be highly unusual. Thus, these extremes are uncommon and only serve to warn us that either the analysis program is not reading the data properly or that some sort of data entry problem has occurred.

Of course, outliers do occur even when the range of permissible values is highly constrained. In customer satisfaction research, a score of a 1 on a 10-point scale is not particularly unusual . . . unless 92 percent of the respondents gave ratings of 9 or 10. The most problematic aspect of customer satisfaction data is their tendency to be highly skewed. It is not uncommon for "best-in-class" companies to report top-two box satisfaction scores well above 90 percent even with a 10-point scale. Establishing univariate distributional abnormalities is not especially difficult because a simple plot reveals a great deal.

From a reporting perspective, highly skewed distributions are not that troublesome. A major food chain that experiences having 1550 of its 1600 locations with top-two box scores greater than 92 percent on a 10-point scale should not really care about the statistical problems associated with the distribution! Indeed, they are reaping the benefits of presumably superlative product and service quality. Nonetheless, from a statistical *modeling* perspective, this is not a desirable situation. Numerous multivariate statistical techniques including multiple regression models, in particular, *assume* conditional normal distributions. Egregious departures from this assumption—especially where the dependent variable is concerned—yield very poor models due to their lack of variance.

Figure 3.3 depicts three distributions that are commonly encountered in customer satisfaction research. The three distributions reflect increasing skewness. Each distribution can be normalized with a unique transformation. These are **monotonic transformations** in that they preserve the *order* of the observations in the distributions. That is, if one observation has a greater value than another *before* the transformation, it will also have a greater value *after* the transformation. Similarly, the observations with the highest and lowest values in the distribution will still represent these extremes after the transformation.

As shown, each transformation formula tends to reduce **skewness.** Even the most severe cases can be normalized, as shown. Experimentation with these techniques will yield the best results. A continuous distribution is preferred for these types of transformations; scales with fewer than seven points may not benefit. It is important to understand that these transformations cannot *create* variance. Data transformations are rarely employed in applied customer satisfaction research and yet, given the right circumstances, can have beneficial effects especially when techniques that assume normality are used.

The Correlation Matrix as Data

We typically consider customer satisfaction data in their raw form—that is, as a **matrix** with k columns corresponding to variables and n rows representing individual respondents. Many multivariate techniques will accept a correlation matrix instead of raw data. In fact, both factor analysis and principal component techniques in packages such as SAS or SPSS will convert the raw data into a correlation or **variance-covariance matrix** in order to conduct the analysis. Multiple

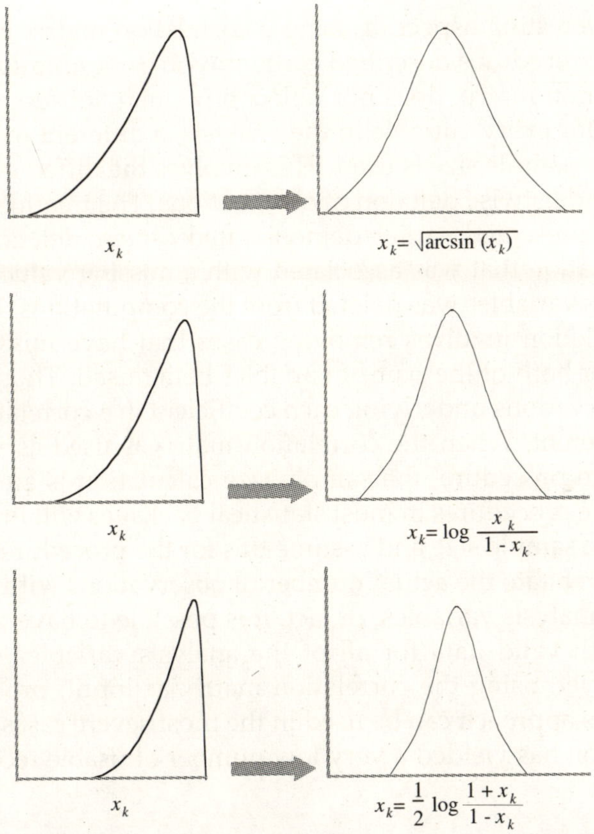

FIGURE 3.3 Common data transformations.

regression, too, can be conducted using simply a correlation matrix (and some supplemental information concerning means, standard deviations, and sample sizes). In short, most multivariate techniques will accept just a correlation matrix as input. Sometimes, we have nothing else but these matrices because it is not unusual for the original raw data to be no longer available.

There is no shortage of multivariate statistics books that provide sufficient descriptions of matrix algebra and its role in applied data analysis. With respect to the correlation and variance-covariance matrices, Searle (1982, 346–54) provides an excellent description. The variance-covariance matrix can be considered an unstandardized correlation matrix.

One interesting aspect of using a correlation matrix as input for any of the procedures described earlier involves sample size. Because the correlation matrix does not reflect how many observations have valid data for every variable in the analysis, a different means of calculating the sample size is used. This involves the difference between pairwise and listwise deletion of observations. The treatment of missing values presented earlier demonstrated *listwise* deletion. That is, any observation that was associated with a missing value for any of the analysis variables was deleted from the computations. In contrast, *pairwise* deletion involves removing cases that have missing values for either or both of the pair of variables being used. Thus, the number of observations underlying each coefficient in a correlation matrix can be different. When the correlation matrix is used as input for a multivariate procedure, the sample size calculation is an issue. The multivariate procedures in most statistical packages will find the lowest pairwise sample size and assume this for the procedure. Note that this may overstate the actual number of observations with valid data for all the analysis variables. In fact, it is possible to have zero observations with valid data for all of the analysis variables simultaneously and yet, using the correlation matrix as input, produce valid results! This approach can be used in the most severe cases when listwise deletion has yielded a very low number of usable records.

Chapter 4

Analysis Framework for Customer Satisfaction Data

Analytical Approaches to Satisfaction Data

Customer satisfaction data may be examined in many different ways. The best platform for understanding how to approach satisfaction data involves three levels of analysis: univariate, bivariate and multivariate statistics (Figure 4.1). Each has its own strengths, and in many cases our choice of analytical tack is constrained not by the availability of appropriate software or technical knowledge but by the data. All too often we have either insufficient data or data suffering from one or more pathologies. In the latter case, missing values, skewness, or ill-conditioning are often to blame. These conditions frequently preclude the most advanced statistical techniques and, unfortunately, customer satisfaction data are especially troublesome when these issues are concerned. In short, the choice of analysis level is not always unconstrained.

The three levels of data analysis each have a unique niche in customer satisfaction data analysis. This chapter will outline how each is used in the applied research setting. We will begin with a treatment of the significant role enjoyed by univariate metrics. Next, the need to understand how two univariate metrics relate to one another will be used to demonstrate the utility of bivariate measures. The main goal of this book is to introduce and review the application of multivariate statistical procedures to customer satisfaction data. Thus, the majority of this chapter provides a multivariate framework for analysis and briefly introduces a series of techniques that will be discussed in subsequent chapters.

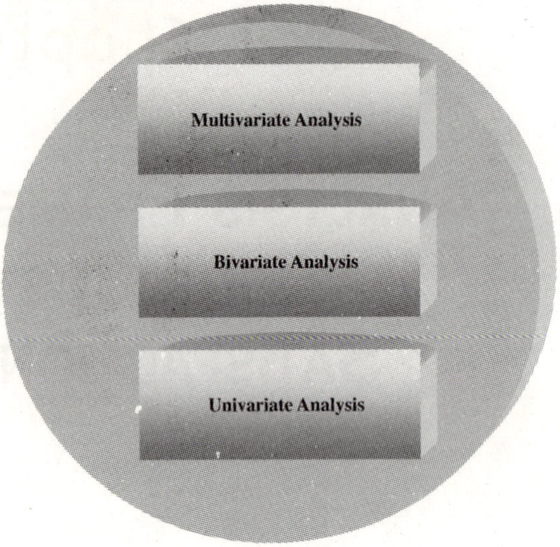

FIGURE 4.1 Levels of customer satisfaction data analysis.

The initial treatment of univariate and bivariate techniques has several advantages. First, it demonstrates the power and ubiquity of univariate metrics in tracking studies. As will be described below, although univariate statistics have tremendous utility in tracking studies, they are woefully inadequate as diagnostics for guiding strategic decision making. Thus, although our objective is a detailed discussion of multivariate approaches to satisfaction data, a review of univariate and bivariate applications will serve to illustrate the power of more advanced analytical techniques.

Univariate Data Analysis

Univariate data are most frequently the metric of choice in customer satisfaction tracking studies. Either the top box or top-two boxes of the scale are summarized in a single measure, the proportion of respondents selecting (for example, either a 4 or 5 on a five-point satisfaction scale). Comparisons of performance across quarters or between operating units (for example, whether one region performs better than another) can be easily accomplished using a simple z-test for proportions.

Tracking the top box or top-two boxes in customer satisfaction research represents the norm. Proportions are easily understood by managers and accommodate statistical testing as described earlier. As an incentive tool, however, the top-box approach is somewhat problematic because it reflects only one part of the overall distribution. Indeed, the *least* satisfied customers may be neglected because they would theoretically require the most effort with respect to migrating them to the top box.

The mean score as a tracking metric is much maligned because of its lack of intuitive appeal to management. Knowing that performance is 3.7 on a five-point scale is clearly less obvious than a top-box score. Nonetheless, the mean score has an advantage. It accommodates the *entire* distribution of responses. As a result, input from the least satisfied customers counts, and there is now an incentive to increase their satisfaction even if it is from a 1 to a 2 on the five-point scale.

A variety of "robust" univariate metrics offer an attractive alternative to the top-box and average satisfaction ratings. Robust estimators include **trimmed means,** medians, and the **trimean.** The objective of these metrics is to minimize the effect outlier observations have on the tracking metric. Despite their desirable properties, metrics such as these have not been well-received in applied situations; we are unaware of a customer tracking system that employs robust estimators.

The choice of univariate tracking metric is in reality not a statistical decision but all too often a *political* one. In the final analysis, organizations choose metrics with which they are comfortable and familiar. This is often determined by more mature reporting systems in operations management or information systems. A manufacturing organization that tracks the *average* daily number of units produced may be more likely to consider the mean for customer satisfaction tracking. Nonetheless, it seems clear that in North America, the top box or top-two boxes are overwhelmingly preferred.

Bivariate Data Analysis

Bivariate analysis has an arguably limited role in customer satisfaction research. When we refer to bivariate analysis, the relationship between two variables is implied. Thus, bivariate analysis most generally involves establishing the extent to which two variables *covary* and determining whether the level of association is statistically significant.

When numeric data (that is, interval or ratio-level) are involved, we most frequently encounter parametric summary measures of association such as the Pearson correlation coefficient. Correlations and covariances represent measures of pairwise association—the extent to which two variables covary. As will be discussed later, correlation and covariance represent fundamental building blocks for more sophisticated multivariate techniques such as structural equations and factor analysis.

Although the Pearson, Kendal, and Spearman correlation coefficients are most widely recognized, there are other less well-known coefficients intended to accommodate situations that do not involve two numeric variables. Phi and the point-biserial correlation coefficient are appropriate when both distributions are binary (phi) or when one is binary and the other continuous (point-biserial). The former case represents a nonparametric measure of association between *categorical* (nominal-level) variables. The biserial correlation (r_b) accommodates another unique situation: when one variable is continuous and the remaining variable is recorded as binary but characterized by underlying continuity and normality. Such may be the case when a continuous variable has been dichotomized. Other measures of association appropriate for categorical data include the Cramér coefficient C and the Spearman and Kendall rank-order correlation coefficients.

Bivariate measures are frequently—perhaps erroneously—used in the derivation of attribute importance with respect to some critical dependent variable. Most typically, this involves gauging the level of covariation between a specific service or product quality issue and a dependent measure such as overall satisfaction or repurchase intent. As a measure of importance, however, the correlation coefficient is quite inadequate. An exception to this involves the partial correlation coefficient, which is technically a *multivariate measure.* The role of pairwise association in the derivation of importance is discussed in chapter 5.

Multivariate Data Analysis

This book focuses on *multivariate statistical techniques* and their applications in customer satisfaction research. Having briefly treated both univariate and bivariate techniques in the preceding sections, we now turn our attention to an overview of multivariate data analysis. The nature of customer satisfaction and loyalty data frequently compels us to employ multivariate techniques. Not infrequently we encounter data sets composed of dozens of variables—sometimes logically ordered and sometimes not. Multivariate statistical approaches for analyzing service quality data can be decomposed into three broad classes. As shown in Figure 4.2, these involve *dependence models, interdependence models,* and *hybrid models.* The former are characterized by their ability to demonstrate how a set of predictor variables affects one or more outcome variables. The thrust is *dependence.* In a sense, causality is implied but by no means established, as will be discussed in chapter 7, which introduces structural equation modeling and the criteria for establishing cause-and-effect relationships. The nature of the dependence of the outcome variable(s) on the predictor variables is of great interest in applied customer satisfaction research. With limited exceptions, we will generally assume that the outcome variable(s) within a dependence model framework involves some overall assessment of satisfaction, loyalty, commitment to the relationship, or even repurchase propensity. The predictor variable set will generally be considered to include a wide variety of specific service or product quality performance ratings.

Dependence models may be further classified based upon the nature and number of outcome variables. With a single *numeric* outcome variable multiple regression analysis or **Kruskal's Relative Importance** approach are appropriate. The difference between these two techniques—particularly with respect to iil-conditioned data—will be described in great detail in chapter 5. When the outcome variable is categorical, techniques such as **discriminant analysis** or logistic regression are in order. As will be discussed later, there are some important differences between discriminant analysis and logistic regression that are well worth noting. Finally, when multiple *outcome* variables are associated with multiple *predictor* variables, canonical correlation analysis is relied upon.

In contrast to dependence models, interdependence models in customer satisfaction data analysis generally involve dimension reducing techniques. Although other interdependence models exist, they generally have somewhat limited utility in customer satisfaction and loyalty modeling. Among interdependence models, factor and principal components analysis are the most frequently used in customer satisfaction research. The techniques—although mathematically somewhat divergent—yield parallel results. Both have the same objective: to reveal the underlying dimensions of customer satisfaction perceptions.

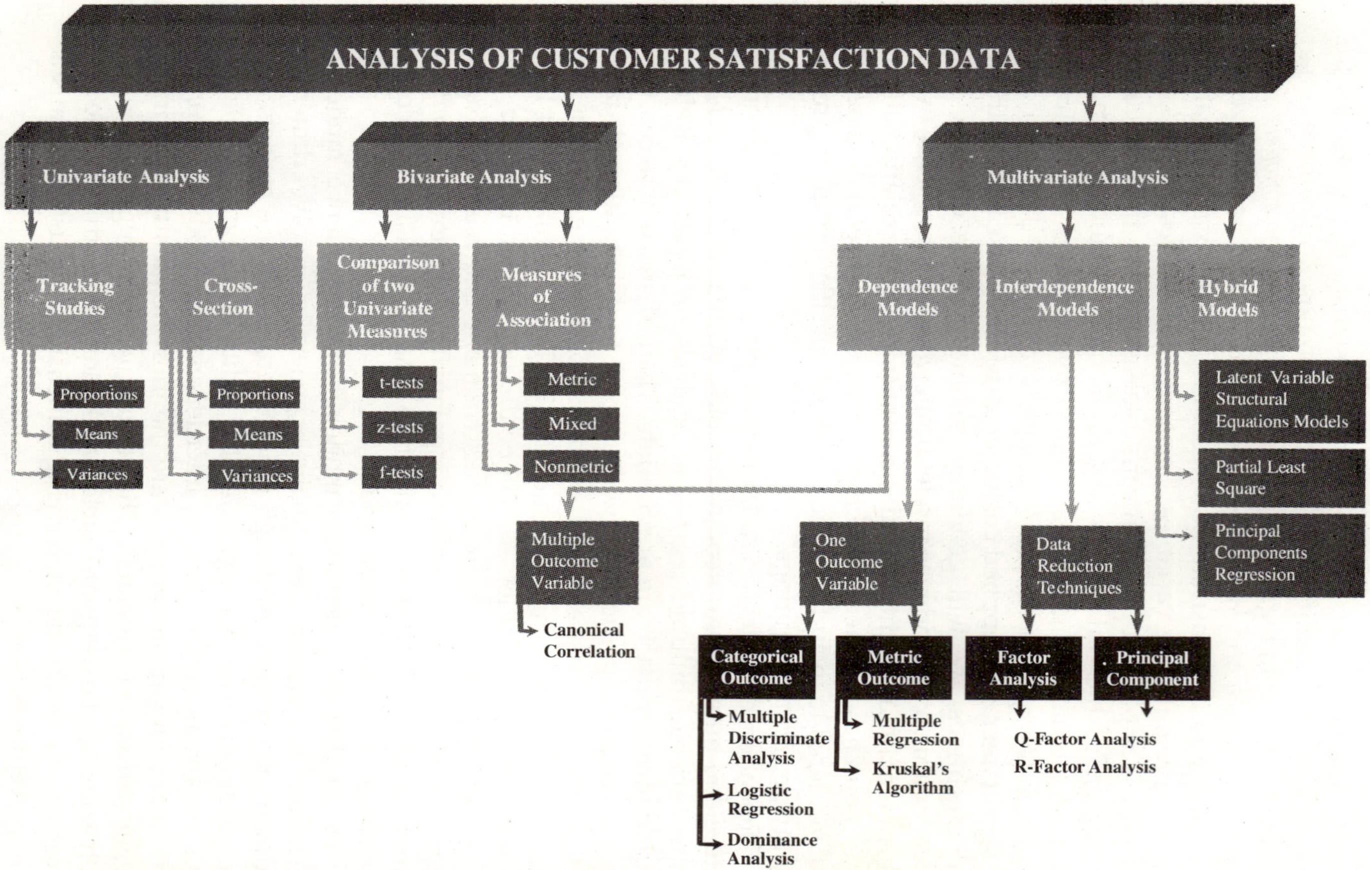

FIGURE 4.2 Framework for customer satisfaction data analysis.

Several hybrid models that are frequently applied to customer satisfaction data are introduced in the final chapter. The term *hybrid* is used because these powerful techniques incorporate both interdependence and dependence model characteristics. The approaches that we introduce include latent variable structural equation models, principal components regression, and latent variable path modeling with partial least squares. In each case, both dependence and interdependence are addressed simultaneously. These models are extremely useful in customer satisfaction research and are discussed in greater detail in chapter 9.

KEY DRIVER ANALYSIS

Despite its onerous technical term, the multivariate dependence model is probably most familiar to researchers engaged in customer satisfaction programs and is known generally as **key driver analysis.** Typically, one outcome variable is presumed to be dependent on a series of predictor variables, as shown in Figure 4.3. Multiple regression is the basis for virtually all key driver analysis. It is also at the core of the semantic and conceptual confusion surrounding the nature of *importance* in customer satisfaction research.

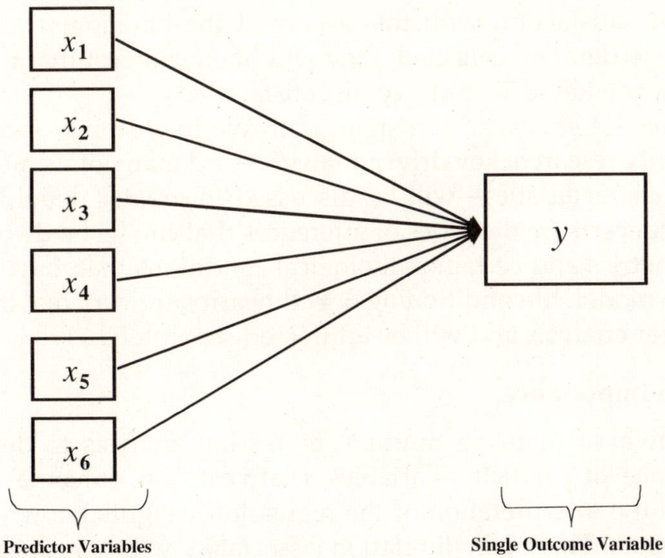

FIGURE 4.3 Multiple regression analysis.

To articulate the difference between *stated* importance and *derived* importance, we frequently cite the airline safety example. In a stated importance framework, wherein respondents are *asked* what is important to them, safety emerges as most critical. After all, what rational consumer would indicate that food quality is more important than their safety when it comes to air transportation? In a key driver analysis, airline safety almost never is identified as important. The reason is that *variance* is necessary in key driver analysis for a predictor variable to be isolated as "important." More accurately, *covariance* between the predictor variable and the outcome variable (overall satisfaction) is necessary to establish this form of importance. Because consumers overwhelmingly experience safe air travel, it is understandable that their satisfaction with this issue tends to be unrelated to their overall satisfaction and loyalty. Semantic confusion arises over the word *importance,* which, in the case of key driver analysis, implies strong covariation with an outcome variable.

Derived importance modeling is a powerful tool for allocating *marginal resources.* In essence, the key driver analysis reveals where you'll get the biggest "bang for the buck" when investing marginal resources. Key driver analysis should *not* be used as a resource *reallocation* tool. This approach would simply result in a new set of key drivers. For example, reducing the budget for teller service in a bank because it did not emerge as a key driver would most likely reduce customer satisfaction with this aspect of the banking relationship. When new data are collected, they will likely suggest that teller service is now a key driver of overall satisfaction.

Because it enjoys such a significant role in customer satisfaction and loyalty research, key driver analysis—and many of its most problematic characteristics—will be discussed in greater detail later. Of special concern are the types of inferences that can be made from key driver metrics and certain pathological conditions that may interfere with the model. Ill-conditioning or collinearity are very real threats to key driver analysis and will be addressed separately.

Relative Importance

One drawback of using multiple regression analysis to derive the importance of predictor variables relative to an outcome variable involves the interpretation of the regression weights known as **beta coefficients.** The main limitation associated with unstandardized beta weights is that they are *ordinal-level* metrics. As such, only infer-

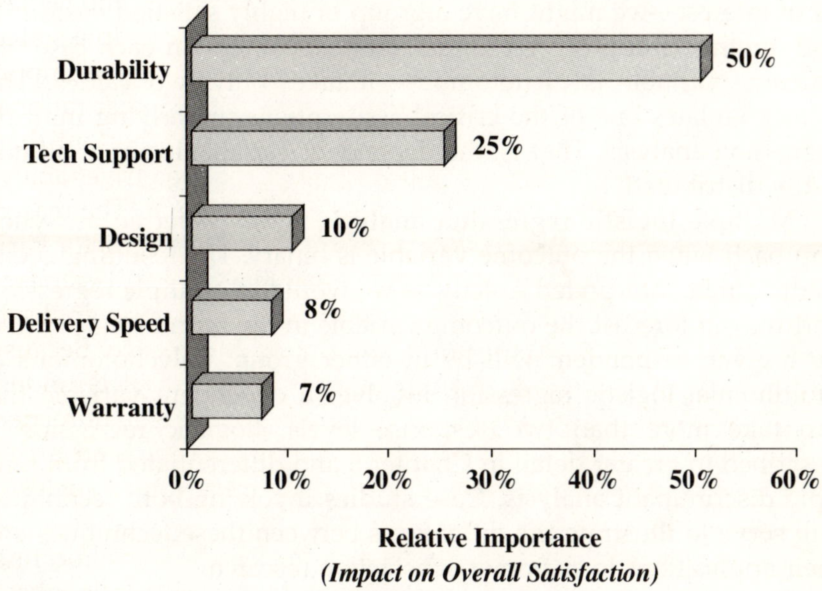

FIGURE 4.4 Example of relative importance measure.

ences concerning their rank order can be made. We cannot, for example, conclude from multiple regression analysis that one variable is *twice* as important as another—only that one is a *stronger* predictor than another.

A very sophisticated means of derived importance modeling is introduced in chapter 5. The technique, known as Kruskal's Relative Importance algorithm, yields importance metrics that have *ratio-level* properties. Although computationally intensive, Kruskal's technique permits us to conclude that, for example, product durability is five times more important than design, as shown in Figure 4.4. This is a powerful advance in data interpretation and is explained thoroughly in chapter 5 and illustrated with a case study.

Other Dependence Models

Key driver analysis in the form of multiple regression is characterized by a series of predictor variables and a single, numeric outcome variable (typically overall satisfaction). When the nature of the outcome variable changes, so must our analytical approach. Frequently we encounter outcome variables that are *binary.* For example, either a customer purchased a product or did not. Group membership might be of interest—we might have a group of highly satisfied customers and another group of very dissatisfied customers. In each case, the outcome variable is dichotomous—it takes only two values. This clearly violates one of the critical assumptions underlying multiple regression analysis. That is, the dependent variable is not at all normally distributed!

Multiple **logistic regression analysis** is the preferred analytical approach when the outcome variable is binary. The resulting coefficients can be interpreted exactly as we would in multiple regression, and we can forecast the outcome variable in the form of the *probability* a given respondent will be in either group. Polychotomous or multinomial logistic regression involves a dependent variable that can take more than two response levels. Logistic regression is described in greater detail in Chapter 5 and differentiated from multiple discriminant analysis. Case studies involving both techniques will serve to illustrate the differences between these techniques and their applications in customer satisfaction research.

Sometimes we encounter scenarios characterized by *more than one outcome variable.* For example, suppose we want to relate a series of predictor variables like product quality, brand image, and price to a *group of outcome variables.* These might include overall satisfaction, repurchase intent, and loyalty. In this case, we have three predictor variables and three outcome variables, as depicted in Figure 4.5. This

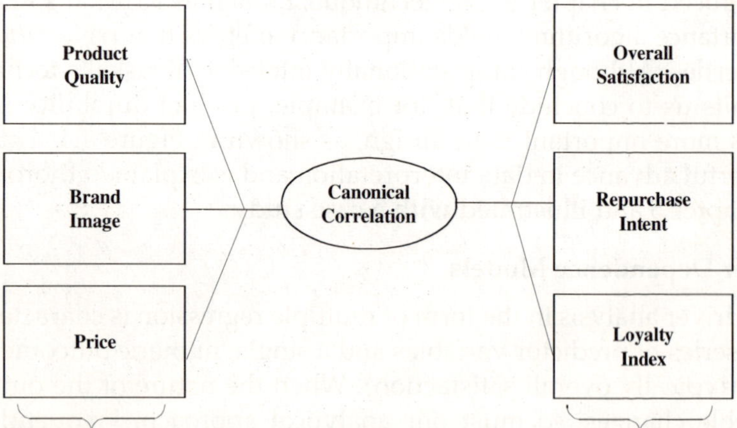

FIGURE 4.5 Canonical correlation analysis.

scenario requires us to rely upon **canonical correlation** analysis. Described in greater detail later, this technique is a powerful means of relating two sets of variables in a dependence model framework.

Multivariate Interdependence Models

While dependence models describe how an outcome variable is related to a set of predictor variables, *multivariate interdependence models* reveal how we naturally group variables into conceptually distinct sets. In customer satisfaction research, the most frequently employed interdependence model is a broad family of techniques known collectively as **factor analysis.** Note that this term is frequently misapplied and that we should clearly delineate *common factor analysis* from its close cousin, **principal components analysis (PCA).** Although the two techniques are very similar with respect to their intended objective, they are quite different in terms of underlying assumptions.

Customer satisfaction data are well-suited either to common factor analysis or to PCA. An example will help illustrate how PCA and factor analysis are used. Suppose 500 consumers are asked to rate a new automobile using a questionnaire with 30 items. The questionnaire might contain items relating to style, appearance, durability, power, torque, speed, interior comfort, and so on. Even though the questionnaire contains 30 items, it should be clear that, in general, people do not use this many criteria to evaluate a car. Instead, they use a few broad dimensions such as style and functionality. A PCA (or factor analysis) of the hypothetical automobile ratings might reveal three dimensions underlying the consumers' ratings: performance, style, and efficiency. This reduction would assign all 30 items in the questionnaire to one of the three dimensions, as shown in Figure 4.6.

Dimension reducing techniques such as common factor analysis and PCA are also frequently used to circumvent one of the most troublesome problems in multiple regression (that is, key driver) analysis. Most customer satisfaction surveys have a wealth of questions! Regressing a single outcome variable on more than 12 to 15 predictor variables frequently results in collinearity problems. To avoid this problem, we frequently advocate the use of factor analysis or PCA to reduce a large predictor variable set into a smaller set of factors or components. The principal components regression technique along with case studies and limited technical discussions will be introduced also.

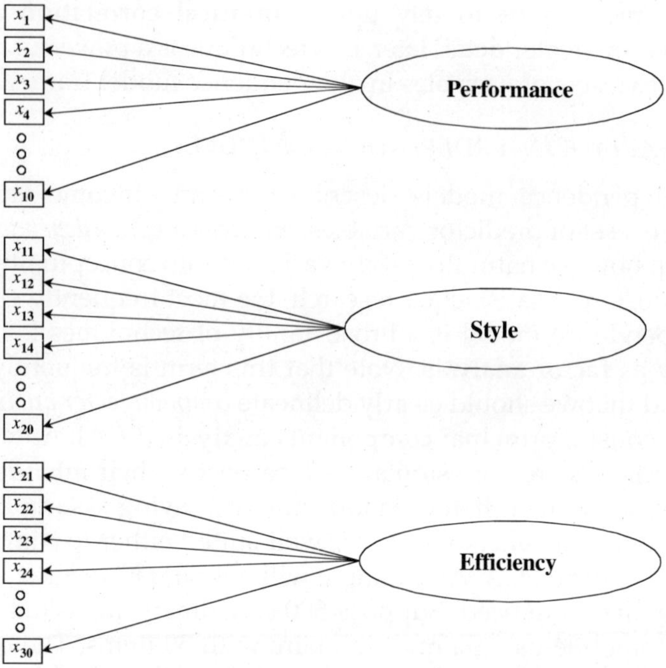

FIGURE 4.6 Data reduction example.

MULTIVARIATE HYBRID MODELS

The multivariate hybrid model accommodates both dependence and interdependence frameworks simultaneously. Chin (1998, 296) refers to this class of models as second-generation multivariate techniques. Among the most exciting developments in customer satisfaction research has been the application of a family of techniques known collectively as **causal modeling.** Perhaps the most familiar of these is LISREL, which technically is a software package. LISREL has become synonymous with a technique known generally as **structural equation modeling** with **latent variables.** Numerous statistical packages (for example, SAS, **EQS,** SPSS, and LISREL-8) accommodate this family of analysis, but they are still frequently referred to as LISREL models. There are actually journals devoted exclusively to issues, problems, and extensions to this family of analysis (for example, *Structural Equation Modeling: A Multidisciplinary Journal*).

Much of the mystique associated with this technique is attributable to the wide variety of names used to describe it. Among them are

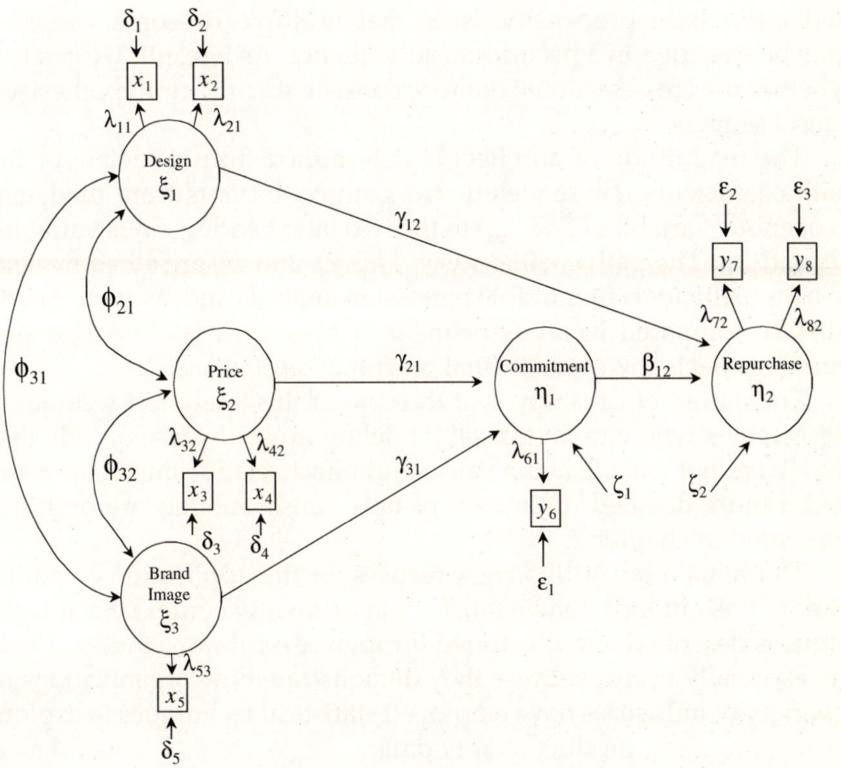

FIGURE 4.7 Structural equation model with latent variables.

latent variable path modeling, structural equations with latent variables, LISREL, and *covariance analysis of latent structures.* No other technique used in customer satisfaction has been known by so many different names.

The real appeal of causal models is that they permit customer satisfaction researchers to test hypotheses involving causal sequences and the dimensionality of key constructs such as loyalty and satisfaction simultaneously. Figure 4.7 presents an example of a "latent variable" causal model. In simplified terms, the technique permits us to simultaneously build dependence and interdependence models. The latent variables are factors as derived through confirmatory factor analytic techniques. The relationship among these factors is the dependence portion of the model. Figure 4.7 suggests there are three latent predictor variables (satisfaction with design, price, and brand image) that affect *two* latent outcome variables: brand commitment and repurchase propensity. Note that multiple outcome variables may be specified in a pseudocausal sequence. As a result, we can test whether the cross-sectional data are consistent with our hypothesized causal sequences.

The magnitude of an effect is determined from a review of the path coefficients. These include the path coefficients from the latent exogenous variables (ξ_1, ξ_2, ξ_3) to the two latent endogenous variables (η_1 and η_2). The path coefficients γ_{12}, γ_{21}, γ_{31}, and β_{12} are all equivalent to beta coefficients in multiple regression analysis and, as such, can be directly compared in an assessment of how each latent exogenous variable affects the model's final outcome: repurchase.

The nature of causality is at the core of this analytical technique. Researchers who employ causal modeling must always concede that they have not established a cause-and-effect relationship. This issue and a more detailed discussion of how causal models are built are presented in chapter 7.

The remainder of this book focuses on the application of multivariate tools in a customer satisfaction or loyalty context. Each technique is described and illustrated through several case studies. These are especially useful because they demonstrate how organizations in a variety of industries have employed statistical techniques to explore their service and product quality data.

The analysis framework established in this book will enhance the reader's ability to recognize that virtually all analytical problems in customer satisfaction research involve either dependence or interdependence. Within each of these broad categories exist numerous specialized techniques to accommodate a variety of data types. A full understanding of how these techniques may be applied and leveraged to mold strategic decision making will greatly enhance your data's value.

Chapter 5

DEPENDENCE MODELS: TOWARD RELATIVE IMPORTANCE

INTRODUCTION

Dependence models are a customer satisfaction research mainstay. Although most frequently encountered as multiple regression applications, dependence models take a variety of other forms. For example, although multiple regression will accommodate a variety of predictor variable types (for example, dichotomous variables), the dependence model can take other forms. Most notable among these involves alternative *outcome variable* forms. Dichotomous outcome variables such as group membership or purchase status flagrantly violate critical assumptions underlying multiple regression analysis—namely, that the dependent variable is normally distributed. Logistic regression is the alternative to multiple regression when the outcome variable is dichotomous.

In other cases, we might encounter situations with *multiple* outcome variables. Clearly, neither multiple regression nor logistic regression can accommodate more than one dependent variable. This special case requires the use of canonical correlation analysis, which is intended to quantify the relationship between a set of predictor variables and a set of outcome variables. Other special situations will also be described and illustrated in this chapter. Much of our emphasis, however, is on the derived importance framework and our quest for a metric that will permit inferences concerning **relative importance.**

THE NATURE AND DERIVATION OF IMPORTANCE

Derived importance models represent a cornerstone of customer satisfaction research. The *derivation* of attribute importance currently represents the norm in the customer satisfaction research industry.

Few, if any, consultants advocate the **stated importance** framework today. Its shortcomings have been illustrated with the airline safety example in which stated and derived importance metrics lead to disparate conclusions. In the airline safety example, we contrast the importance of five issues:

1. Food quality
2. Cleanliness
3. Safety
4. Attendant courtesy
5. Comfort

When *asked* which of these issues is most important to them, most consumers will indicate that safety is their primary concern. After all, who would respond that food quality is more important than their safety? As most who are familiar with this example will recall, the derived importance framework employs multiple regression to mathematically determine the impact of each issue on a single outcome variable: overall satisfaction with the airline.

There is some confusion surrounding the implication of the word *importance* in the dependence model (for example, multiple regression) context. Take, for example, the reaction of product managers at a world-class manufacturing company when told that product quality was not important. Their initial inclination was to dismiss the results and walk out! The simple fact is that the use of the term *importance* tends to cloud the true meaning of what we are trying to convey. In the regression context, importance implies the magnitude of impact on an outcome variable such as overall satisfaction or repurchase propensity. Once they understood this, the managers and engineers at this manufacturing company were actually quite pleased. Their products were—and still are—considered "best in class" and enjoy stellar customer satisfaction scores.

Marginal Resource Allocation Models

So, exactly what are we conveying when we say something is important in a dependence model context? It should be clear that derived importance results provide managers with road maps for *maximizing* an outcome variable such as overall satisfaction. In order to achieve the greatest increase in overall satisfaction (or any other outcome variable), we focus on the predictor variable(s) that have the greatest

TABLE 5.1 Hypothetical key drivers.

Service/Product Satisfaction	Quarter 1 Key Driver Status	Quarter 4 Key Driver Status
Teller courtesy	No	Yes
Competitive rates	No	No
Waiting time for teller	No	Yes
Statement accuracy	No	No
Parking space	Yes	No
Branch proximity	No	No

effect on it. More accurately, we isolate predictor variables that *covary* most strongly with the outcome variable. It is this covariation that is at the heart of derived importance models.

Derived importance models are probably erroneously labeled. A more appropriate name might be *marginal resource allocation* models. Note that it is important that we consider only marginal resources because *reallocating* existing resources based upon a derived importance model will not necessarily yield the desired results. Consider the extreme example of a retail bank that blindly reallocates existing resources based upon their key driver analysis. Assume the simplified set of key drivers in Table 5.1.

If bank management erroneously decides to reallocate resources based upon this set of *first quarter* key drivers, they may choose to reduce the number (and quality) of their teller staff in order to free funds for the acquisition of adjacent land for parking. This reallocation of resources yields a completely different set of drivers in the *fourth quarter.* The new drivers reflect the effects of management's decision to reallocate existing rather than *marginal dollars.* Because teller staffing was cut back, waiting time increased and, as a result, customers became less satisfied with this aspect of the relationship with the bank. In fact, it appears from these data that the dissatisfaction was sufficiently acute as to affect overall satisfaction. Such a turn of events underscores the *dynamic nature of key drivers.* It also illustrates why key driver analysis should really be considered as a marginal resource allocation tool.

Because it plays such a major role in the derivation of attribute importance in customer satisfaction research, a large portion of this chapter focuses on various forms of regression analysis. We begin with the bivariate case in an effort to illustrate its shortcomings and also to illustrate a fundamental problem associated with interpreting beta coefficients in more sophisticated multiple regression approaches.

Regression Techniques and Importance

Regression analysis enjoys a prominent role in customer satisfaction research today. This section presents and contrasts a series of increasingly sophisticated regression models. Each is described and discussed with respect to strengths and weaknesses. Although our focus is on *multivariate techniques,* it will be helpful to review the pitfalls of less sophisticated *bivariate* approaches first.

The implications of choosing each technique will be illustrated with a simple case study. We will focus on HugeCo, a manufacturing company interested in five critical service and product quality issues:

1. Product reliability
2. Technical support
3. Delivery
4. Price
5. Warranty

Although the number of attributes has been reduced in order to simplify the illustration, the data are real. In this case, the organization's quality management team is interested in tracking one key outcome variable: overall satisfaction. The team's goal is to maximize overall satisfaction among its customer base by leveraging information gleaned from the survey process. A 10-point scale was chosen by the team due, in most part, to their past experiences with similar scales. A sample of the actual survey is presented in Figure 5.1.

A random sample of 400 interviews was obtained using the internal customer list. Although the original survey instrument contained many more questions, we will focus exclusively on the relationship between the five predictor variables introduced earlier and our single outcome variable: overall satisfaction. This data set (six columns and 400 rows) will be the focus of a series of increasingly sophisticated derived importance techniques. We will begin by assessing the relationship of each predictor variable with the outcome variable in a bivariate sense. This is followed by analyses of the same data using simple linear regression, multiple linear regression, stepwise multiple linear regression and, finally, Kruskal's (1987) relative importance technique. The objective is to highlight the types of output each technique provides and to illustrate how they differ.

We'd like to hear from you about your experiences with HugeCo's digital widget. Please use a 10-point scale where one means you're very dissatisfied and 10 means you're very satisfied with each of the areas I'll describe. Of course, you may use any number between one and 10. Let's start. How satisfied are you with. . .

	Very Dissatisfied									Very Satisfied
1. Product reliability	1❑	2❑	3❑	4❑	5❑	6❑	7❑	8❑	9❑	10❑
2. Technical support	1❑	2❑	3❑	4❑	5❑	6❑	7❑	8❑	9❑	10❑
3. Delivery	1❑	2❑	3❑	4❑	5❑	6❑	7❑	8❑	9❑	10❑
4. Price	1❑	2❑	3❑	4❑	5❑	6❑	7❑	8❑	9❑	10❑
5. Warranty	1❑	2❑	3❑	4❑	5❑	6❑	7❑	8❑	9❑	10❑

Now, considering all aspects of your recent HugeCo product purchase, we'd like to know how satisfied you are overall, considering all these issues. Please use the same 10-point scale where one means you're very dissatisfied and 10 means you're very satisfied. Overall, how satisfied are you with HugeCo?

6. Overall satisfaction	1❑	2❑	3❑	4❑	5❑	6❑	7❑	8❑	9❑	10❑

FIGURE 5.1 Sample survey instrument with 10-point scales.

THE CORRELATION COEFFICIENT

The banal correlation coefficient actually is a tool that has a lot of utility when embarking upon a data exploration. Its implications, however, are frequently misinterpreted, and the overzealous researcher may jump to erroneous conclusions about the relative importance of the predictor variables. Its failure to accommodate multivariate data, of course, makes it largely inadequate for applied customer satisfaction research.

The abbreviated customer satisfaction data set described earlier was initially subjected to a simple bivariate analysis. Pearson correlation coefficients were calculated for the six variables and are presented in Table 5.2.

As shown in the table, the strongest linear relationship between any variables involves overall satisfaction and product reliability (r_{x1y} = 0.74). The weakest relationship with overall satisfaction involves delivery (r_{x3y} = 0.23). Note that despite the relatively modest magnitude of the latter relationship, it is still statistically significant. In fact, with a sample size of 400 and no missing values, all of the Pearson correlation coefficients in Table 5.2 are statistically significant.

Using the correlation coefficient to make inferences concerning the relationship between each predictor variable and dependent variable

TABLE 5.2 Intercorrelations among predictor and outcome variables.

	y	x_1	x_2	x_3	x_4	x_5
y. Overall satisfaction	1.0					
x_1. Product reliability	0.74	1.0				
x_2. Technical support	0.26	0.22	1.0			
x_3. Delivery	0.23	0.17	0.77	1.0		
x_4. Price	0.28	0.19	0.72	0.67	1.0	
x_5. Warranty	0.41	0.38	0.51	0.46	0.60	1.0

frequently involves ranking the correlation coefficients. Although simple, this way of determining attribute importance can be misleading, as implied earlier. One cannot make valid inferences concerning the relative magnitude of correlation coefficients. It is not appropriate to conclude that $r_{x1y} = 0.74$ is more than three times stronger than $r_{x3y} = 0.23$. What is frequently overlooked, however, is that when *squared,* the correlation coefficient is interpreted as the *proportion of variance shared by two variables.*

When squared, the relationship between overall satisfaction and product reliability ($r_{x1y} = 0.74$) suggests the two variables have about 55 percent of their variance in common. In contrast, the relationship between overall satisfaction and price ($r_{x4y} = 0.28$) suggests these two variables share only 5 percent of their variance. The difference in linear relationship between these two variables and overall satisfaction is much greater than would have been suggested by a simple comparison of the correlation coefficients.

It is easy to forget that the correlation coefficient r has a multivariate relative: the **multiple correlation coefficient.** It is most frequently encountered in multiple regression analyses as the R^2—a summary statistic that reflects the amount of variation in the dependent variable accounted for by the predictor variables. All researchers who evaluate or conduct multiple regression analyses are familiar with the **R^2 statistic.** That R^2 is the multivariate equivalent of r^2 is sometimes overlooked, however. The multiple correlation coefficient (R) will be addressed below.

It should be clear now that the squared correlation coefficient is quite a good bivariate measure of relative importance. Of special note is its ratio-level property, which permits inferences concerning *relative* importance. It would be reasonable to conclude based upon the squared correlation, for example, that one variable shares *twice as much*

TABLE 5.3 Comparison of five simple linear regressions.

Model	$\beta_1 x_k$	T	P	R^2
x_1. Product reliability	0.78	6.07	0.0001	0.55
x_2. Technical support	0.33	5.46	0.0001	0.07
x_3. Delivery	0.27	4.62	0.0001	0.05
x_4. Price	0.34	5.78	0.0001	0.07
x_5. Warranty	0.48	8.85	0.0001	0.16

variance with the outcome as another. This aspect of the correlation coefficient—that its square has some especially useful properties—will be leveraged later in this discussion when we introduce Kruskal's approach to the optimum relative importance metric.

SIMPLE LINEAR REGRESSION

Simple linear regression involves a single outcome variable being regressed on *one predictor variable.* It is a *bivariate* statistical technique as shown in Equation 5-1, which consists of just one predictor variable and one outcome variable. Remember that the term β_0 is simply the intercept term and can be considered the value of y when all the predictor variables are equal to zero.

$$y = \beta_0 + \beta_1 x_1 \quad (5\text{-}1)$$

Table 5.3 presents the results of five simple linear regressions. Both the parameter estimates and t-statistic are shown in addition to the R^2 statistic. Note that because all variables were measured on the same scale, we can compare the unstandardized parameter (beta) estimates. The t-scores and R^2 may also be directly compared.

These results are highly consistent with the exploratory bivariate analysis. Product reliability emerges unequivocally as most strongly related to overall satisfaction. It is important to note that the actual parameter estimates for the five predictor variables can only be compared in terms of their *rank order.* We cannot, for example, conclude that product reliability ($b = 0.78$) is about two times more important than technical support ($b = 0.33$). Nor can we reasonably make ratio-level inferences concerning the t-statistics associated with each simple linear regression.

A quick comparison of Table 5.3 with the correlation results will confirm that the rank orders of the five predictor variables are consistent.

That is, in both cases the results suggest that product reliability is the most significant predictor of overall satisfaction. This is followed by warranty coverage. If our management team were to conduct only the bivariate analyses presented thus far, they would surely focus their future efforts on improving satisfaction with product reliability and, to a lesser extent, warranty coverage.

MULTIVARIATE CORRELATION ANALYSIS

The term *multivariate correlational analysis* may seem like an oxymoron to some. After all, most of us are familiar with the bivariate correlation and generally do not extend this family of techniques to multivariate settings. The *partial correlation,* for example, is not frequently encountered in applied customer satisfaction research settings. Unlike the Pearson correlation coefficient, the partial correlation can tell us a great deal about the relationships underlying a set of predictor variables. In brief, the partial correlation provides us with a measure of linear relationship between two variables *once the effects of the remaining variables have been taken into account.* The symbol for the partial correlation is slightly different because we must convey both the relationship being measured and the variables that we are holding constant. For example, the term $r_{x1y.x2}$ indicates we are measuring the relationship between x_1 and y after the relationship between y and x_2 has been taken into account. This term, when *squared* provides us the unique variance common to the two primary variables (that is, y and x_1) once the effects of x_2 have been accommodated. Equation 5-2 illustrates how the partial correlation takes into account the effects of a third variable.

$$r_{12,3} = \frac{r_{12} - r_{13}r_{23}}{\sqrt{(1-r_{13}^2)(1-r_{23}^2)}} \tag{5-2}$$

The partial correlation offers an excellent alternative or supplement to a simple bivariate correlation. Its most desirable property involves its ability to take into account the effects of other variables. It is by definition, therefore, a multivariate technique.

A very useful cousin of the partial correlation is the *semipartial correlation.* Although it plays an important role in both multiple correlation analysis and common factor analysis, the semipartial correlation is not encountered frequently in exploratory customer satisfaction research. It is useful however, to understand how the partial and semipartial correlations differ. Equation 5-3 presents the formula for the semipartial correlation.

$$r_{1(2,3)} = \frac{r_{12} - r_{13}r_{23}}{\sqrt{1 - r_{23}^2}} \tag{5-3}$$

In Equation 5-3, we are interested in controlling x_3 only for x_2, not x_1. The semipartial correlation lets us hold a variable constant for only one of the two variables involved in the correlation. Why, you might ask, would we possibly want to do this? The principal reason involves the relationship between the variable we are holding constant (x_3) and the variables we are interested in (x_1 and x_2). If, for some reason, we feel that x_3 should legitimately covary with x_1, we may want to hold x_1 constant only for x_2. Again, this rarely occurs; the real reason for introducing it involves the semipartial correlation's role in factor analysis and multiple correlation analysis.

The multiple correlation coefficient is most frequently encountered in a slightly different form in multiple regression analysis. In applied customer satisfaction research, reporting the R^2 statistic associated with a key driver analysis is practically *de rigueur.* Nonetheless, few practitioners remember that this key metric is really the squared multiple correlation coefficient.

In a key driver analysis context, the multiple correlation coefficient has an important diagnostic role. When it is low ($R^2 < 0.70$) the implication is that the predictor variable set is not strongly predictive of the dependent variable. Typically, this results in additional qualitative research aimed at generating additional items for the survey instrument.

The multiple correlation has some noteworthy properties. Of greatest interest may be the fact that R will always be equal to, or exceed, the highest pairwise correlation involving the outcome and predictor variables. From Table 5.2, we know that the multiple correlation between y and the five predictor variables must be at least 0.74 (because $r_{x1y} = 0.74$) and will likely be higher barring any strong relationships among the predictor variables. It should be clear that if the predictor variables are subjected to **orthogonal rotation** (that is, have zero correlations with one another) then R^2 will be equal to the sum of the squared bivariate correlations. This is illustrated in Equation 5-4.

$$R^2_{y.123} = r^2_{yx1} + r^2_{yx2} + r^2_{yx3} \text{ when } r_{x1x2} = 0;\ r_{x1x3} = 0;\ r_{x2x3} = 0 \quad (5\text{-}4)$$

Again, Equation 5-4 is valid *only when the predictor variables are orthogonal*. When strong dependencies exist among the predictor variables, we turn to a different means of determining the total shared variance among the outcome and predictor variables. Equation 5-5 employs the semipartial correlation as described earlier and can be used to calculate the R^2 value. In effect, Equation 5-5 confirms that the R^2 is equal to the squared correlation between y and x_1 (r^2_{yx1}) plus the squared correlation between y and x_2 holding x_1 constant for x_2 ($r^2_{y(x2.x1)}$) plus the squared correlation between y and x_3 with both x_1 and x_2 held constant for x_3.

$$R^2_{y.123} = r^2_{yx1} + r^2_{y(x2.x1)} + r^2_{y(x3.x1x2)} \quad (5\text{-}5)$$

Although not immediately obvious, a closer inspection of the sequence in Equation 5-5 reveals that after the first term (which is a simple correlation), each is a successively higher order squared semipartial correlation. Each term in Equation 5-5 is contributing *unique* variance with respect to y. The reason semipartial and not *partial* correlations are used in this calculation is illustrated by considering the second term in Equation 5-5, which is contributing variance unique to x_2 once x_1 has been taken into account. In short, we use semipartial correlations because although we are interested in partialling variance on the predictor variable side, we do not want to partial this variance from the *dependent* variable.

Multiple Linear Regression

Our first two forays into HugeCo's data involved exploratory bivariate techniques. The results of these two techniques were quite consistent in terms of rank-order importance. It was clear from the correlation analysis that product reliability was strongly related to overall satisfaction ($r_{x1y} = 0.74$) whereas price was not ($r_{x4y} = 0.28$). In fact, taking the square of these correlations suggested that although product reliability and overall satisfaction shared about 55 percent of their variance, price and overall satisfaction had only 8 percent of their variance in common. Still, neither of these bivariate approaches accommodated *multivariate* data. That is, only two variables were considered at a time. Multiple linear regression will permit us to reveal the effect on overall satisfaction of all five predictor variables operating in concert.

TABLE 5.4 Multiple regression results.

Variable	Parameter Estimate	Standard Error	T for H_0 Param = 0	Prob > $\lvert T\rvert$
Intercept	0.25	0.33	0.74	0.46
x_1. Product reliability	0.72	0.04	19.26	0.00
x_2. Technical support	–0.00	0.07	–0.10	0.92
x_3. Delivery	0.02	0.07	0.32	0.75
x_4. Price	0.10	0.07	1.52	0.13
x_5. Warranty	0.11	0.05	2.13	0.03

Note: $R^2 = 0.57$.

The results of regressing overall satisfaction on our set of five predictor variables is presented in Table 5.4. The model's adjusted R^2 suggests the five variables account for a modest 57 percent of the variation in overall satisfaction. Note that R^2 is the squared multiple correlation coefficient (R) and that this value ($R = 0.75$) is only slightly higher than the correlation between product reliability and overall satisfaction ($r_{x1y} = 0.74$). Recall from the earlier discussion that R will always be *at least* as large as the correlation between y and any of the predictor variables. The implication is that after the effect of x_1 has been taken into account, the remaining variables contribute very little explanatory power.

Before examining the coefficients in Table 5.4, the reader may wish to review the correlation matrix presented in Table 5.2. A review of the predictor variable intercorrelations reveals a potential problem. This involves the relationship between technical support and both delivery ($r_{x2x3} = 0.77$) and price ($r_{x2x4} = 0.72$). In short, the relationship between technical support and these predictor variables appears to be stronger than the relationship between technical support and overall satisfaction. Further, the relationship between technical support and delivery ($r_{x2x3} = 0.77$) is stronger than the relationship between any single predictor variable and the outcome variable! The implication is that there *may* be data problems that make multiple regression analysis unstable.

The parameter estimates presented in Table 5.4 do not strongly point to a collinearity problem. We introduce this topic and the tools for its diagnosis in the next chapter. Briefly, **collinearity** involves a data condition, not a statistical condition. It occurs when two or more predictor variables are very strongly related to one another. Two of the most common and irksome manifestations of collinearity include very large standard errors around the parameter estimates and parameter estimates with the "wrong" signs. In the latter case, we might encounter a sign opposite of that revealed by a bivariate correlation. Results like these can be very troublesome because they could suggest, for example, that overall satisfaction increases as product quality decreases. Obviously, this sort of result should be cause for alarm.

Multiple Linear Regression with Stepwise Selection

Stepwise selection techniques are a mechanical means of circumventing the collinearity problem that we frequently encounter in customer satisfaction research. Stepwise selection procedures are based upon comparing the t-statistic that is computed for each predictor variable across a series of *simple linear regressions.* Recall that we conducted these separately above but that stepwise selection procedures do this in an effort to determine which of the predictors is most strongly related to the outcome variable in a purely bivariate sense. The t-statistics are compared by the program, and the predictor variable with the strongest bivariate relationship with the outcome variable is selected as the first to be included in the stepwise multiple regression.

Based upon our knowledge of the HugeCo data set, it should be clear that the first variable to be entered into the model will be product reliability (x_1). At this point, the stepwise procedure will run four multiple linear regressions. Each multiple regression pairs x_1 with one of the remaining predictors. The first will have as predictors x_1 and x_2 followed by x_1 and x_3, x_1 and x_4, and finally, x_1 and x_5. The stepwise procedure compares the results of these four multiple regressions (each with two predictor variables) and determines which predictor (that is, x_2, x_3, x_4, or x_5) is most strongly related to the outcome variable. Again, the t-statistic is used as the basis of comparison. Based upon Table 5.3, we might expect the second variable to be warranty (x_5). If this were the case, the stepwise selection procedure would complete another iteration, this time including both x_1 and x_5 in each of the three regressions. These three would involve x_1 and x_5 *plus* one of the remaining three predictor variables (x_2, x_3, or x_4). During each iteration of this process, the t-statistic is evaluated. Should a variable fail to reach statistical significance, it is dropped from the selection process. Predictor variables with insignificant t-statistics are *excluded,* and only statistically significant variables compose the final model.

TABLE 5.5 Multiple regression results with stepwise selection.

Variable	Parameter Estimate	Standard Error	F	Prob > F
Intercept	0.27	0.32	0.75	0.39
x_1. Product reliability	0.73	0.04	0.00	373.67
x_4. Price	0.11	0.05	4.54	0.03
x_5. Warranty	0.11	0.05	4.68	0.03

Table 5.5 presents the results of using stepwise selection with the HugeCo data set. As shown, the model retains three significant variables. Although the multiple regression model without stepwise selection suggested price was not a significant predictor of overall satisfaction, the model presented in Table 5.5 confirms it may very well exert a moderate effect. This seems reasonable because we know that $r_{x4y} = 0.28$ (see Table 5.2). Interestingly, however, the parameter estimates for price (x_4) and warranty (x_5) are equivalent despite substantive differences in their relations with the dependent variable ($r_{x5y} = 0.41$ while $r_{x4y} = 0.28$). We also know from the table of intercorrelations (See Table 5.2) that the two predictor variables are related to one another more strongly than either is to the dependent variable.

Kruskal's Relative Importance Approach

The notion of *relative* importance has been obscured by the variety of terms assigned to the multiple regression framework for deriving attribute importance. Multiple regression produces parameter estimates that have *ordinal*-level properties. That is, we can only make inferences concerning their rank order of covariation with the dependent variable. It was this issue that led Kruskal (1987) to pursue an approach that would permit conclusions concerning the *relative* impact of predictor variables with respect to an outcome measure.

Kruskal's approach involves the same type of mechanical process encountered in the stepwise selection procedure. It is more complex and, as a result, *much more computationally intensive.* This approach to attribute importance derivation involves calculating partial correlations for all possible combinations of predictor variables. Thus, with three predictor variables, we have a separate partial correlation equation for each of the three ($3 \times 2 \times 1 = 6$) unique combinations of predictor variables.

For each predictor variable, the *partial correlation* with the dependent variable is averaged and *squared* over all the combinations. This squared, average partial correlation is a highly robust measure that tends to overcome data problems (for example, ill-conditioning) that confound traditional regression techniques. Of special importance is its use of the partial correlation. As noted earlier, a squared correlation reflects the proportion of variance two variables have in common. The average, squared partial correlation of each predictor variable can be reasonably compared in a *relative* sense. We can conclude, for example, that x_2 is twice as important as x_1 with respect to the dependent variable.

It should be clear that when more than three or four predictor variables are of interest, this technique becomes computationally intensive. Although three predictors involves only six unique combinations, a more realistic field of 12 predictor variables involves 12! combinations. Fortunately, modern microcomputers can easily accommodate scenarios involving *billions* of computations.

Kruskal's method has two distinct advantages. First, it is much less susceptible to pathological data conditions such as collinearity because it subsumes all possible combinations of predictor variable equations. Its second desirable characteristic involves its ratio-level properties. That is, it is reasonable to conclude that one variable is *twice* as important as another.

Table 5.6 presents the HugeCo data relative importance scores. This result is consistent with previous findings and suggests that product reliability is more than *seven times* as important as any other variable with respect to overall satisfaction. Note that with this approach there is never an intercept term; Kruskal's technique does not yield a predictive equation, rather a means for understanding the extent to which each independent variable shares variance with the outcome variable.

We know from the multiple regression results presented earlier that the five predictor variables account for about 57 percent of the variance in overall satisfaction. Of this variance, more than three-quarters is attributable to product reliability (x_1). Although consistent with the other techniques used to derive attribute importance, with Kruskal's approach we enjoy the added benefit of making *ratio-level* inferences concerning *relative importance*. In short, we can conclude that product reliability is seven times more important with respect to overall satisfaction than any other predictor variable.

TABLE 5.6 Relative importance scores using Kruskal's technique.

Variable	Average Squared Partial Correlation	100% Rescaled Term
x_1. Product reliability	0.51	79.9%
x_2. Technical support	0.02	2.8
x_3. Delivery	0.01	2.0
x_4. Price	0.03	4.0
x_5. Warranty	0.07	11.4

Dominance Analysis

Kruskal's approach to the derivation of attribute importance is not without detractors. Budescu (1993), for example, proposed an alternative approach. **Dominance analysis,** according to the author, meets three important criteria for measuring relative importance. First, the technique should be defined in terms of its ability to reduce error in predicting the outcome variable. Next, it should permit direct comparison of measures within a model (that is, x_1 is twice as important as x_2). Finally, the technique should permit inferences concerning an attribute's direct effect (that is, when considered by itself), total effect (that is, when considered with other attributes), and partial effect (that is, when considered with various combinations of other predictors).

Dominance analysis was introduced as an alternative to Kruskal's approach to derived importance analysis. Rather than considering all permutations of variable combinations relative to an outcome variable, Budescu's approach considers only *pairs* of attributes and their contributions to the squared multiple correlation (R^2). The notion of "pairwise dominance" involves the pairing of all variables and consideration of how each pair affects the dependent variable. Consider Table 5.7, which summarizes the effects of three variables on a single, dependent variable.

Table 5.7 should be interpreted in the following manner. Notice that the first column is composed of the three variables individually and then in unique pairings. The column labeled R^2 presents the squared multiple correlation for each model. Thus, a simple linear regression composed of x_1 and the dependent variable yields a squared multiple correlation of 0.51. Similarly, a multiple linear regression of the dependent variable on x_2 and x_3 is associated with an R^2 of 0.49. It should come as no surprise that the correlations between

TABLE 5.7 Marginal squared multiple correlations with three predictor variables.

		Marginal R^2 Contribution		
Variable(s)	R^2	x_1	x_2	x_3
—		0.51	0.42	0.25
x_1	0.51	—	0.07	0.05
x_2	0.42	0.16	—	0.07
x_3	0.25	0.31	0.24	—
x_1, x_2	0.58	—	—	0.03
x_1, x_3	0.56	—	0.05	—
x_2, x_3	0.49	0.12	—	—

each variable and the dependent measure are $r_{y.x1} = 0.71$, $r_{y.x2} = 0.65$, and $r_{y.x3} = 0.50$. These correlations squared make up the first row of Table 5.7.

The final three columns of the table present the change in model R^2 that occurs when each variable is *added* to the models implied by the first column of the table. For example, consider the marginal contribution to the squared multiple correlation when x_1 is added to the model $y = x_2\, x_3$. The table suggests the addition of x_1 will yield a marginal increase of 0.12 to the R^2. The largest increase occurs when x_1 is added to the simple linear regression of y on x_3. That is, adding x_1 to the model $y = x_3$ will increase the model R^2 by 0.31.

Table 5.7 confirms that x_1 dominates x_3 because when it is added to the simple linear regression model $y = x_3$ the model R^2 increases by 0.31. By examining the marginal increases shown in Table 5.7, it is possible to begin developing an idea of which variables are dominant with respect to predicting the outcome variable. Budescu employed another table to summarize the relationships presented earlier. Table 5.8 presents a means of understanding the relative importance of each variable.

Note that the first row in Table 5.8 presents the squared (multiple) correlation for each variable with the dependent variable. Successive rows present the average marginal increase in R^2 when each variable is added to an existing model composed of one or two variables. For example, the third row in Table 5.8 suggests that when x_1 is added to a model composed of x_2 and x_3, the increase in R^2 is 12

TABLE 5.8 Summary of Dominance Analysis Relative Importance Metrics.

k	x_1	x_2	x_3
0	0.51	0.42	0.25
1	0.23	0.15	0.06
2	0.12	0.05	0.03
$M(C_x)$	0.27	0.19	0.16
Percent	43%	31%	26%

points. Similarly, when x_2 is added to $y = x_1\ x_3$, the result is an increase of 0.05 points.

The final two rows of Table 5.8 present each variable's marginal contribution averaged over all regression permutations. For example, x_1 has an average marginal contribution of 0.27 whereas x_2 and x_3 have marginal average contributions of 0.19 and 0.16, respectively. Notice that when summed, these numbers approximate the total R^2 for the complete model $y = x_1\ x_2\ x_3$, which is 0.61. The last line in Table 5.8 converts each variable's average marginal contribution to the squared multiple correlation to a proportion of the total. As shown, x_1 exerts the greatest marginal influence (43 percent) in this respect. These results were compared to Kruskal's output, and the results were very parallel. Using Kruskal's approach, the weight for x_1 is 47 percent, x_2 is 33 percent, and x_3 contributes 18 percent. These weights are also consistent with the magnitudes of each variable's squared correlation with the dependent measure.

Clearly, dominance analysis enjoys a unique niche in the derived importance literature. Unlike other techniques, dominance analysis focuses on the marginal impact each variable has on the regression model's predictive capacity. By considering all permutations of pairs, dominance analysis permits us to test the impact of *adding* a variable to an existing model. In this respect, dominance analysis is quite different from other approaches to importance derivation. For example, whereas Kruskal's approach provides the averaged squared partial correlation across all permutations of variables, dominance analysis focuses on the marginal impact on the squared multiple correlation in a regression context. Despite this difference, the two methods yield consistent results as discussed in the preceding.

CANONICAL CORRELATION ANALYSIS

Although encountered infrequently in applied customer satisfaction analysis, it is important, minimally, to recognize this special case of dependence model. Because the dependent variable in customer satisfaction is typically a *single item,* **canonical correlation** analysis is rarely performed in an applied setting.

In certain situations, however, there may be several outcome variables that the researcher would like to consider in combination. Consider a situation wherein *overall satisfaction, repurchase intent,* and a *loyalty index* are all dependent upon a series of six service and product quality issues. Clearly, our interest lies in how well the latter affect the set of three outcome variables. This is illustrated in Figure 5.2, which implies the three outcome variables are *dependent* upon the six predictors. Note that *causality* is typically implicit in this type of model.

The mathematics underlying canonical correlation analysis are beyond the scope of this book. A simplification will have to suffice. Readers interested in an in-depth treatment are urged to refer to Dillon and Goldstein's (1984, 337–59) discussion of both sample-based and population models. Kerlinger (1986, 562–63) also provides a brief, but readable, treatment of canonical correlation analysis.

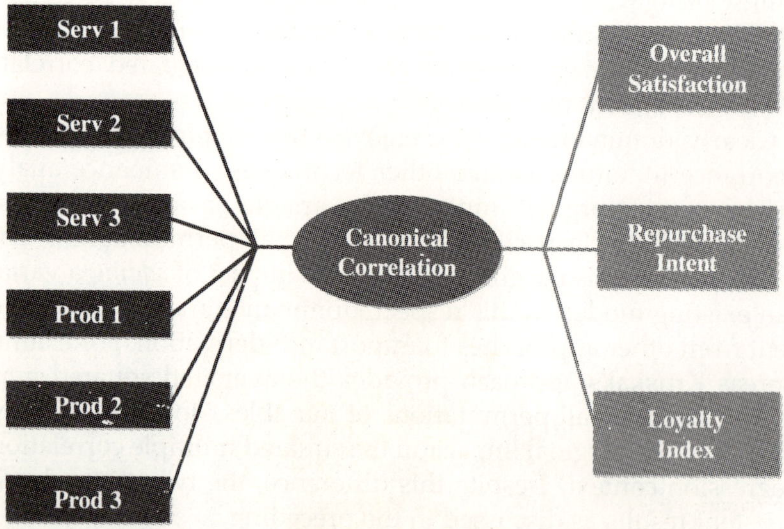

FIGURE 5.2 Simplification of canonical correlation analysis.

Multiple Logistic Regression

The classic regression analysis framework is generally used in the following manner. A series of one or more *numeric* independent variables (for example, satisfaction with service, billing, and product quality) are used to predict one *numeric* dependent variable (for example, overall satisfaction). In the present case, the dependent variable is not numeric, per se. It can take only two values. This might be the case when we want to differentiate between two groups such as high and low loyalty. Similarly, we might want to understand the differences between customers who are very satisfied and those who are very dissatisfied.

Here, we want to predict *group membership.* When a regression analysis employs a series of numeric independent variables to predict a single binary dependent variable, the classic ordinary least squares model tends to be inadequate (Hosmer and Lemeshow 1989, 5–7) based upon two important criteria. First, the conditional mean of y is constrained to take only two values—for example, 0 and 1. More technically, the conditional mean of the outcome variable $E(y \mid x)$ is limited, and as it approaches its extremes (0 or 1), it becomes increasingly curvilinear or S-shaped. The second difference between binary and interval or ratio-level dependent variables cited by Hosmer and Lemeshow involves the distribution of the error term ε. In short, the distribution of ε under the conditions of a binary outcome variable violate the assumptions associated with ordinary least squares. Based upon these violations, researchers rely upon **logistic regression analysis.**

The logit link is nonlinear and has several advantages for classification purposes. In the binary dependent variable case, the logit $g(x)$ is:

$$g(x) = \ln \frac{\pi(x)}{1 - \pi(x)} \tag{5-6}$$

and

$$\pi(x) = \frac{e^{g(x)}}{1 + e^{g(x)}} \tag{5-7}$$

where $\pi_{(x)}$ is equal to the *probability* of being a member of the highly (dis)satisfied group. The logit $g_{(x)}$ is calculated as one would if classical regression analysis were used:

$$g_{(x)} = \beta_0 + \beta_{1x1} + \beta_{2x2} + \ldots + \beta_{kxk} + e \tag{5-8}$$

We're interested in your experience flying XYZ Airlines. Please take the time to fill out the questionnaire below and return it in the postage-paid mailer.

	Very Dissatisfied									**Very Satisfied**
Food quality	1❑	2❑	3❑	4❑	5❑	6❑	7❑	8❑	9❑	10❑
Cleanliness	1❑	2❑	3❑	4❑	5❑	6❑	7❑	8❑	9❑	10❑
Safety	1❑	2❑	3❑	4❑	5❑	6❑	7❑	8❑	9❑	10❑
Attendant courtesy	1❑	2❑	3❑	4❑	5❑	6❑	7❑	8❑	9❑	10❑
Comfort	1❑	2❑	3❑	4❑	5❑	6❑	7❑	8❑	9❑	10❑

Considering all these issues, will you fly XYZ Airlines again based upon today's flight experience?

1❑ Yes 2❑ No

FIGURE 5.3 Five service and product quality issues for XYZ Airlines.

An example will facilitate an understanding of how the technique is applied. We return to the airplane safety example and its five predictor variables (Figure 5.3). Each reflects the respondents' satisfaction and was measured using a 10-point scale.

Recall that respondents were asked how satisfied they were with each of these aspects of their last flight. In the previous classic regression example, the outcome variable y was measured on an interval or ratio-level scale. In the present case, these five questions are followed by a single outcome item that elicits a binary response: "Will you fly XYZ Airlines again based upon today's flight experience?" Only two responses are possible: yes and no.

Based upon the preceding, our model takes the (somewhat) familiar form as shown in Equation 5-9:

$$g_{(x)} = \beta_0 + \beta_{1x1} + \beta_{2x2} + \ldots + \beta_{kxk} + e \qquad (5\text{-}9)$$

Note that $g_{(x)}$ is the outcome variable—technically, the logit x. Calculation of $g_{(x)}$ employs maximum likelihood analysis. An explanation of this technique is well beyond the scope of this book. Interested readers may wish to refer to Hosmer and Lemeshow's (1989) exhaustive treatment of the logistic regression analysis technique.

For the purposes of this illustration, we will retain the same five predictor variables but use the binary dependent variable. When we examine the average satisfaction scores between the two groups, it

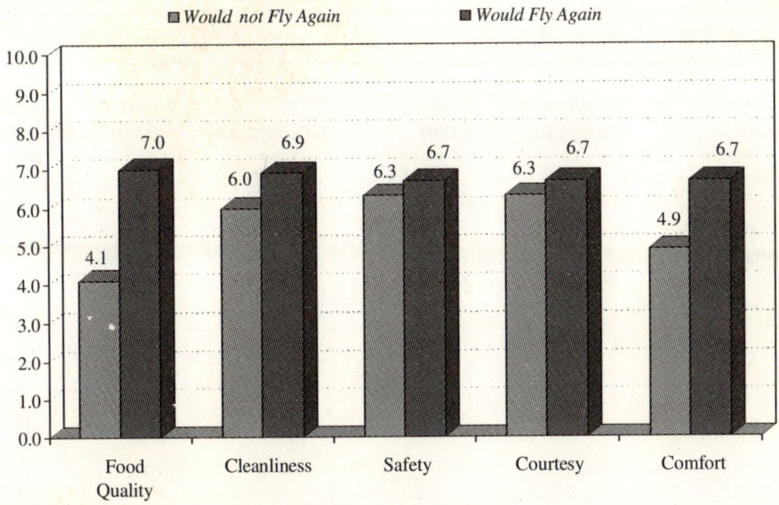

FIGURE 5.4 Differences across binary dependent variable.

becomes clear that those who indicated they would fly XYZ Airlines again were, in general, more satisfied with the five controllable business variables. This is depicted in Figure 5.4.

When multiple logistic regression is used, the dependent variable can take on two values. In the present case, they were coded "N" and "Y" indicating that the respondent would not or would travel on the airline again, respectively. Table 5.9 suggests that the food quality (x_1) has the greatest impact on the binary dependent variable. The implication of the negative sign preceding the parameter estimates β_k will be discussed below. The logistic regression analysis confirms the second best predictor of the dependent variable is comfort (x_5). These conclusions are based on the probability of the χ^2 statistic associated with the parameter estimate. Note the column in Table 5.9 labeled "Odds Ratio." Deviations from 1.0 indicate *higher* or *lower* probability of membership in the group who indicated they would *not* fly XYZ Airlines again. The reason for this will be discussed later.

Equation 5-10 represents the first step in calculating the probability of group membership. The logit $g_{(x)}$ is calculated in a manner reminiscent of ordinary regression analysis. Thus, a respondent who rated each of the five areas as a 9 would have $g_{(x)}$ value of –1.62, which by itself has little prima facie meaning. Interpreting $g_{(x)}$ requires us to return to the logit link shown in Equation 5-11.

TABLE 5.9 Results of logistic regression using XYZ Airlines data.

Variable	Parameter Estimate	Standard Error	Pr > Chi-Square	Std Estimate	Odds Ratio
Intercept	3.06	0.48	0.00		
x_1. Food quality	–0.37	0.04	0.00	–0.58	0.68
x_2. Cleanliness	–0.04	0.06	0.48	–0.06	0.95
x_3. Safety	–0.00	0.05	0.96	–0.00	1.00
x_4. Courtesy	0.00	0.05	0.91	0.00	1.00
x_5. Comfort	–0.11	0.05	0.01	–0.17	0.88

$$g_{(X)} = 3.06 - 0.37_{(X_1)} - 0.04_{(X_2)} - 0.00_{(X_3)} + 0.00_{(X_4)} - 0.11_{(X_5)} \quad (5\text{-}10)$$

$$\pi(x) = \frac{e^{g(x)}}{1+e^{g(x)}} \quad (5\text{-}11)$$

If we now insert the value of –1.62, the value of $\pi_{(x)}$ becomes 0.197 over 1.197. Thus, the value of $\pi_{(x)}$ is approximately 0.16 or, 16 percent. This means that the customer who gives all 9s on the survey has a 16 percent chance of *not* flying on XYZ Airlines again. It should come as no surprise that x_1 (food quality) has the greatest impact on customers' future flying intentions!

Different statistical packages approach the interpretation of $\pi_{(x)}$ in varying ways. Most notably, SAS considers this the probability of being in the *lower valued* binary code, which, in this case, is indicative of the "N" response. In contrast, SPSS produces the opposite output; the value of $\pi_{(x)}$ is considered the probability of membership in the *higher valued* binary code. In the present case, the data suggest that a respondent who provided all 9 ratings on the questionnaire has an 84 percent chance of flying on XYZ Airlines again in the near future. Thus, it is the nonlinear logit link presented in Equation 5-11 that permits inferences concerning the probability of group membership, purchase propensity, or any other binary states.

Logistic regression can accommodate other scenarios, as well. For example, polychotomous or multinomial logistic regression is intended for dependent variables that take more than two states. Consider the case of a dependent variable with three possible values (0, 1, and 2). A conditional probability for each state must be considered, as shown in Equations 5-12 through 5-14.

$$P(Y=0|x)=\frac{1}{1+e^{g_1(x)}=e^{g_2(x)}} \qquad (5\text{-}12)$$

$$P(Y=1|x)=\frac{e^{g_1(x)}}{1+e^{g_1(x)}+e^{g_2(x)}} \qquad (5\text{-}13)$$

$$P(Y=2|x)=\frac{e^{g_2(x)}}{1+e^{g_1(x)}+e^{g_2(x)}} \qquad (5\text{-}14)$$

This approach addresses the polychotomous logistic regression model for a nominal dependent variable that takes three values. Other models that accommodate ordinal-level multinomial dependent variables are also available. A thorough review of all types is provided by McCullagh and Nelder (1983). Hosmer and Lemeshow (1989, 216–45) also provide discussions concerning polychotomous model building strategies.

Presentation of Derived Importance Data

At this point, it should be clear that the presentation of importance data is dictated by the level of the metric in question. For example, it would be an egregious mistake to plot ordinal (or lower-level) data because most regression techniques assume—minimally—interval-level data. Plotting regression beta coefficients in a Cartesian coordinate system erroneously assumes the weights have interval-level properties.

Note that Figure 5.5 assumes a "stated importance" methodology in which respondents rate the importance of various attributes rather than the derived importance approach in which satisfaction is rated. Again, the key is that one *cannot make inferences* concerning the relative magnitude of effect on an outcome variable using nominal and ordinal data. Recall that beta coefficients derived from regression analysis are technically ordinal data and, therefore, plots of their relative effect on the outcome variable should be avoided.

Ratio-level data such as those derived from Kruskal's technique are appropriate for plots that imply relative effect with respect to an outcome variable such as loyalty or overall satisfaction. This type of data—in particular those derived using Kruskal's technique—lend themselves to a variety of graphic depictions. When *not* subjected to monotonic transformations (such as being rescaled to 100 percent),

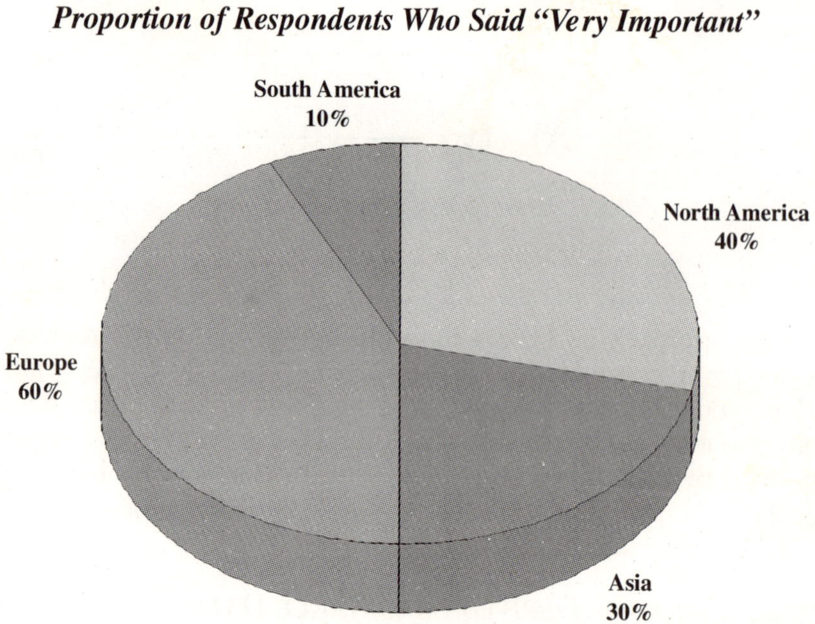

FIGURE 5.5 Pie graph used to depict differences across nominal variable categories.

Kruskal's output can be used to present information concerning model efficacy.

Figure 5.6 shows the HugeCo data (see Table 5.6). On the left side of the figure, the importance metric has been scaled to 100 percent. As a result, the percentages shown essentially convey the proportion of "explained" variance each variable is responsible for. In contrast, the right side of the figure depicts the same importance data scaled to R^2. Here we see that 36 percent of the variation in y is unaccounted for by the five predictor variables.

Integrating Performance and Importance Data

The integration of performance and importance data yields a strategic data map with significant strategic utility. Actual *satisfaction levels* are typically treated as performance in this type of approach. Figure 5.7 demonstrates how variables are mapped in a performance-importance map.

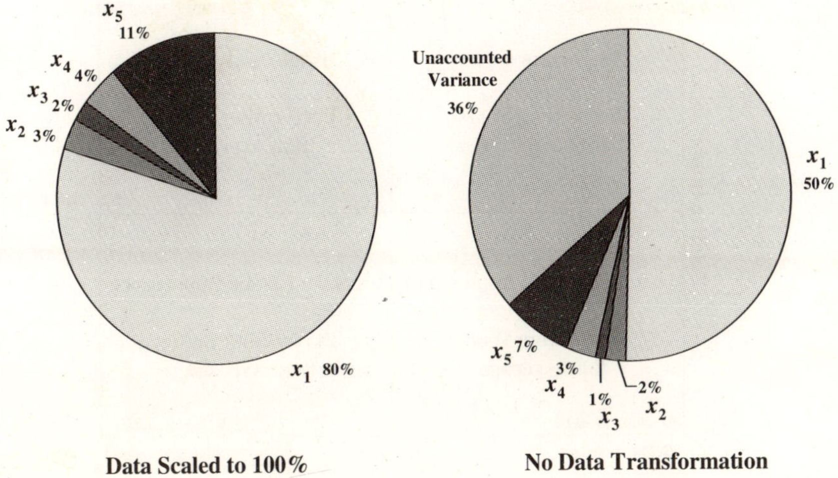

FIGURE 5.6 Scaled and raw derived importance data.

As shown in Figure 5.7, the strategic map incorporates both performance (that is, satisfaction) and importance. A variable's vertical position indicates its importance whereas horizontal positioning reflects performance. Although importance must be measured on an interval or ratio-level scale, performance (that is, satisfaction) can be depicted as a grand average of all variables, proportion such as top box score, or a corporate standard involving either.

The key to understanding the implications of a variable's position on the strategic map lies in the interaction between performance and importance. Do not lose sight of the fact that importance is *derived.* As a result, variables that tend to be higher on the y-axis have a greater impact on the outcome variable. In short, marginal resources that are allocated to variables that are "important" will yield the biggest change in the dependent variable.

The four quadrants have different strategic implications. Perhaps of greatest interest to managers are those variables that occur in the top-left quadrant. These are product or service issues characterized by lower than average performance (that is, satisfaction) and greater than average covariation with the dependent variable. These are "action areas" that demand immediate attention. In contrast, items that occur in the top-right quadrant may be equally important but enjoy higher than average levels of satisfaction.

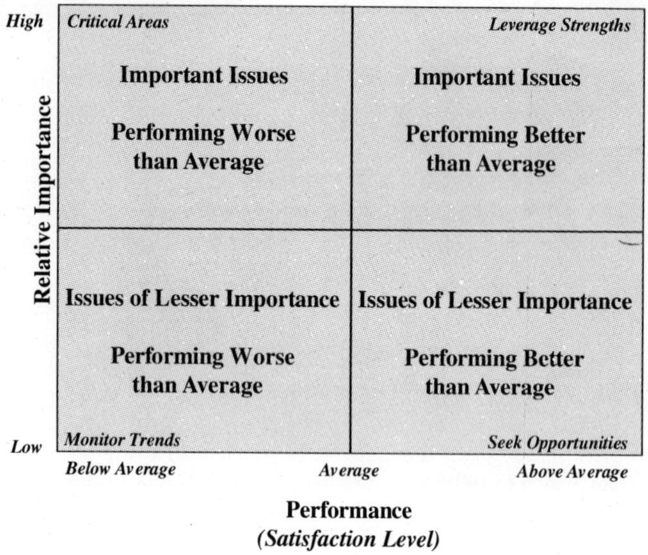

FIGURE 5.7 Integrating performance and derived importance.

Consider the top-right quadrant more carefully. Product or service issues that are placed in this quadrant are characterized by high levels of *performance* and high levels of *importance.* Note that frequently performance is *standardized.* Items appearing to the right of the center vertical line are associated with better than average performance. It is important to note that when the performance axis is standardized and not anchored with absolute scores, the strategic implications of the quadrant chart may be misleading. This is particularly true when working with an entire section of a questionnaire like *price,* which is associated with notoriously low satisfaction scores—regardless of industry.

Figure 5.8 provides absolute performance levels for the x-axis. As shown in this example, all of the items are associated with relatively low satisfaction scores. This is underscored by the addition of a corporate goal score. This type of enhancement to the performance-importance chart can greatly enhance its value.

The integration of relative importance and performance yields a powerful tool for quality managers. It provides a clear road map with

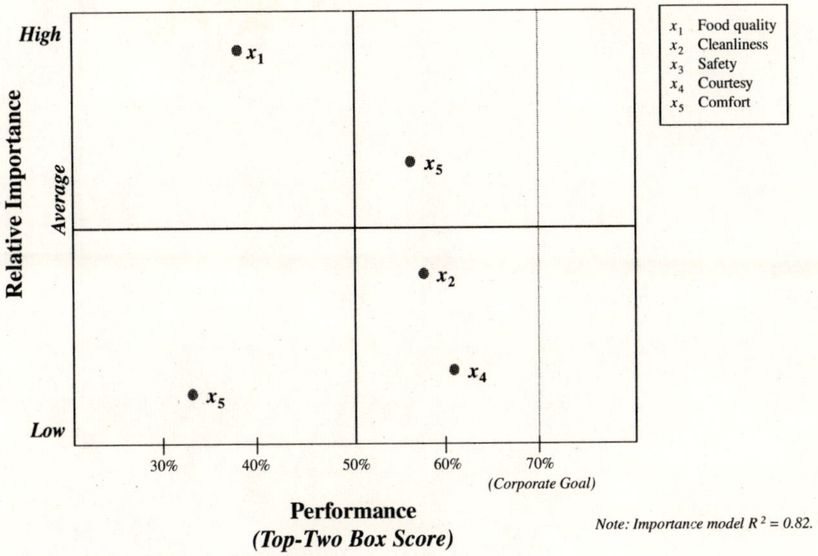

FIGURE 5.8 Performance and importance data.

respect to the service and product quality issues that must be addressed in order to increase customer satisfaction. The performance-importance quadrant chart can be further enhanced by using competitive performance. When performance is quantified relative to that of key competitors, the quadrant chart becomes an even more useful tool.

Chapter 6

Exploratory Data Analysis and Problems in Regression Analysis

Introduction

This discussion examines the role played by exploratory data analysis with respect to its multivariate predictive capabilities among dependence models. Thus, the structure of the discussion will be as follows. First, the rationale for the use of exploratory data analysis techniques will be introduced along with a number of associated robust statistics. Next, a data set will be used to illustrate the power these methods have in diagnosing problems in key driver models. Then, a number of regression diagnostics will be introduced following a univariate examination of the data. The final portions of this chapter will examine the extent to which exploratory data analysis techniques can successfully identify potentially harmful data conditions. Again, analysis of an actual data set will help to illustrate the relationship between univariate and multivariate phenomena.

Exploratory Data Analysis

Two forms of data problems tend to plague regression models. One involves the data set *rows* whereas the other involves relationships among the *columns*—specifically on the predictor variable side of the equation. Figure 6.1 illustrates this relationship. This chapter demonstrates how row and column diagnostics can complement one another and facilitate an understanding of certain data problems.

The latter data problem (collinearity) is probably most familiar to analysts working with customer satisfaction data. Specifically,

Two columns (or more) that could be strongly related

Variable	x_1	x_2	x_3	x_4	x_5	y_1
Case #1	1	1	7	7	7	7
Case #2	1	1	1	2	3	1
Case #3	1	1	3	2	1	1
⋮	⋮	⋮	⋮	⋮	⋮	⋮
Case #87	7	7	7	7	1	1
⋮	⋮	⋮	⋮	⋮	⋮	⋮
Case #120	5	5	5	5	4	3

A potentially influential case (Case #87)

FIGURE 6.1 Sources of problems in regression and other multivariate models.

collinearity involves strong relations among the predictor side of the equation. Note the term *multicollinearity* is inherently redundant because the definition of collinearity involves a strong relation between two or more variables (Belsley, Kuh, and Welsch 1980, 85). Ill-conditioned data can be most perplexing to data analysts. The condition manifests itself in a number of troublesome ways. Among the most aggravating is the statistically significant predictor variable with the wrong sign. For example, a model based on highly ill-conditioned data might suggest that increasing product quality would *lower* overall satisfaction.

Exploratory data analysis generally is not regarded as a means of addressing conditioning problems among dependence or other models. It will, however, provide some insights and perhaps reveal at this most basic level any problems that could arise during the model development effort.

Exploratory and robust data analysis as described by Hoaglin, Mosteller, and Tukey (1983) is an innovative approach in that it implores the analyst to take the data as seriously as the model used to describe it. Specifically, **exploratory data analysis (EDA)** subsumes a host of "paper-and-pencil statistics" and, more generally, a set of descriptive statistics used to reveal patterns and distribution. Measures of central tendency, dispersion, and the isolation of outlying observations are presumed to be of considerable utility in diagnosing pathological conditions associated with regression techniques.

By examining the behavior of variables in a univariate sense, EDA techniques are capable of revealing potentially problematic characteristics. EDA places substantial emphasis on various *robust* univariate measures. They are regarded as robust because of their relative insensitivity to outliers and enhanced ability to detect groupings. Rosenberger and Gasko (1983, 306) defined a set of univariate statistics called **L-estimators**. The mean is considered to be an L-estimator of a sample with size n when every observation has an equal weight $(1/n)$.

Trimmed means provide more robust insight into a data set. In essence, trimmed means simply require the removal of an equal portion from each end of the ordered data. This effectively eradicates the effects of extreme outliers at either end. Trimmed means are identified by the amount of ordered data removed. Thus, the 10 percent trimmed mean of a sample of 100 is the simple average of the remaining 80 observations.

Although not a trimmed mean per se, the trimean, according to Hoaglin, Mosteller, and Tukey (1983, 313) " . . . is motivated by the desire to include sample information farthest from the center by making use not only of the median but also of a few additional order statistics, initially the fourths along the median." Broadened medians, according to Rosenberger and Gasko (1983, 312) attempt " . . . to preserve the resistance of the median to outliers while also achieving insensitivity to rounding and grouping of the observations." This is accomplished, they suggest, by taking the average of the median and "one or two" of its neighboring order statistics. Again, note the important role played by the ordering of the data.

Broadened medians (BMED), trimmed means, trimeans, or more generally, the set of L-estimators, tend to be measures of central tendency, which remain unaffected by the force exerted by (extreme) outliers. Although the L-estimators have certainly played the greatest role in robust data analysis, both R-estimators and M-estimators offer additional utility. As Hoaglin, Mosteller, and Tukey (1983, 339) noted, the L-estimators " . . . may sacrifice resistance by giving weight to extreme observations or, conversely, they may sacrifice efficiency by placing too little weight on end observations that are not extreme, as would happen for a trimmed mean with a fixed amount of trimming." R-estimators are offered as derivations from a rank test for a shift between two samples. The rank test for a shift, is estimated by " . . . moving one sample along until the test is least able to detect a shift in estimating the location, the second sample is the mirror image of the actual sample, reflected about the estimate, so that an R-estimator of location minimizes the shift between the sample and its mirror image, as measured by the rank test." M-estimators, on the other hand, are offered as a method for the minimization of ". . . functions of the deviations of the observations from the estimate that are more general than the sum of squared deviations or the sum of absolute deviations" (Rosenberger and Gasko 1983, 340). An in-depth discussion of these statistics is beyond the scope of this discussion. An acknowledgment that the L-estimators can, at times, be problematic, as just noted, will have to suffice.

In addition to the robust central tendency measures reviewed in the preceding, EDA techniques also address a number of robust dispersion measures such as the H-spread, median absolute deviation (MAD), boxplots, and histograms. Again, these statistics and tools rely upon ordered data.

The H-spread, or "fourth-spread," according to Rosenberger and Gasko (1983, 338) gives an indication of how concentrated the data values may be. This diagnostic is simply defined as the upper-fourth minus the lower-fourth of the data. This reveals the middle half of the batch. The distance between the upper- and lower-fourths is very similar to the interquartile range but has less resistance. Other dispersion statistics, like the MAD from the median, provide similar information.

Finally, a set of graphics provides additional information about a data variable's univariate behaviors. Specifically, the histogram provides a substantial amount of information about the dispersion of a variable. This type of display provides information concerning symmetry, dispersion, isolated groupings, concentrations, and whether there are significant gaps in the data. The **boxplot** provides a similarly concise visual description of the dispersion of a data variable, which provides convenient measures of location, spread, skewness, tail length, and outlying data points. It is particularly useful in comparing several batches of data.

It should be clear that, as proponents of EDA methods argue, a substantive examination of one's data *prior* to multivariate treatments can be extremely advantageous. Further, prior knowledge of the univariate peculiarities of one's data can make diagnosing pathologic multivariate conditions considerably less difficult. In the following discussion of an actual data set, additional univariate measures will be reviewed and the ability of some of the measures discussed earlier (in particular, the histogram and boxplots) to detect outlying observations will be discussed. Next, the traditional regression analysis will be performed followed by the introduction and discussion of a number of EDA diagnostics. Finally, the extent to which an EDA examination has the capacity to predict problematic phenomena in regression analysis will be discussed.

The data set to be used as an illustration of EDA's ability to relate univariate and multivariate tendencies contains 120 observations involving consumer ratings of a new sports car. There was no theoretical thrust driving the selection of independent or dependent variables; the intent of this section is merely to assess the predictive prowess of EDA techniques with respect to univariate versus multivariate behaviors. Five independent variables are employed: satisfaction with (1) product quality, (2) design, (3) durability, (4) acceleration, and (5) technical support. The dependent variable was overall satisfaction, measured on a seven-point Likert scale.

The univariate procedures associated with most popular statistical packages provide a wealth of information. In fact, much is superfluous and not frequently employed in either applied or academic research. This is particularly true with respect to some of the statistics encountered in the 'Moments' section of the output. Readers with a special interest in some of these more exotic measures are urged to refer to either Hoaglin, Mosteller, and Tukey (1983) or Tukey (1977). Some moments worth noting, however, include skewness and kurtosis. In the former case, a distribution is positively skewed when it has a long thin tail to the right and has negative skewness when it has a long thin tail to the left. With respect to **kurtosis**, distributions can take two extreme forms. They can be either **leptokurtic distributions** or **platykurtic distributions**. In the latter case, the distribution is quite flat, whereas in the former it is very peaked. The extent to which a given distribution is skewed can be summarized with the index *s*:

$$s = \frac{\mu_3}{\mu_2^{3/2}}$$

Notice that when a distribution is perfectly symmetrical, *s* will be zero.

The following exhibits present univariate analysis for the six variables that will be treated in the case study illustration. The first, Exhibit 6.1 presents the univariate output for the dependent

Moments			
N	120	Sum Wgts	120
Mean	4.166667	Sum	500
Std Dev	1.716678	Variance	2.946779
Skewness	−0.13159	Kurtosis	−0.75721
USS	2434	CSS	350.6667
CV	41.19884	Std Mean	0.156705
T: Mean = 0	26.58922	Pr > | *T* |	0.0001
Num ^ = 0	120	Num > 0	120
M (Sign)	60	Pr > = | *M* |	0.0001
Sgn Rank	3630	Pr > = | *S* |	0.0001
W: Normal	0.921064	Pr < *W*	0.0001

Quantiles (Def = 5)			
100% Max	7	99%	7
75% Q3	5	95%	7
50% Med	4	90%	6.5
25% Q1	3	10%	2
0% Min	1	5%	1
		1%	1
Range	6		
Q3 – Q1	2		
Mode	4		

Extremes	
Lowest Obs	Highest Obs
1 (87)	7 (67)
1 (65)	7 (70)
1 (64)	7 (76)
1 (63)	7 (78)
1 (62)	7 (100)

EXHIBIT 6.1 Univariate procedure: Variable = overall satisfaction.

Histogram

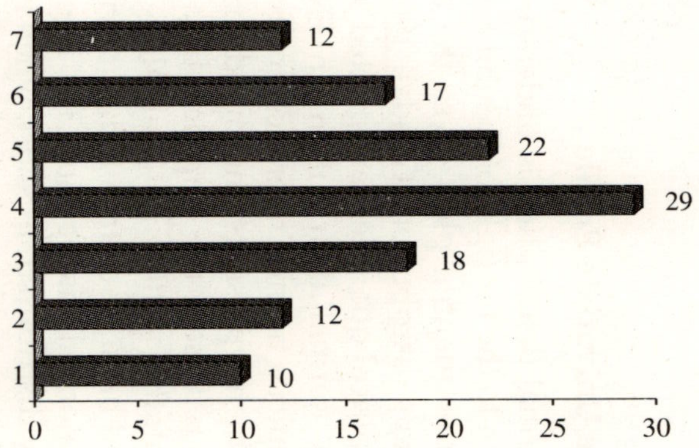

Box Plot

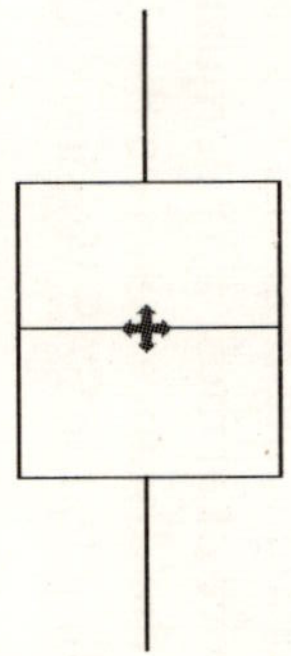

Normal Probability Plot

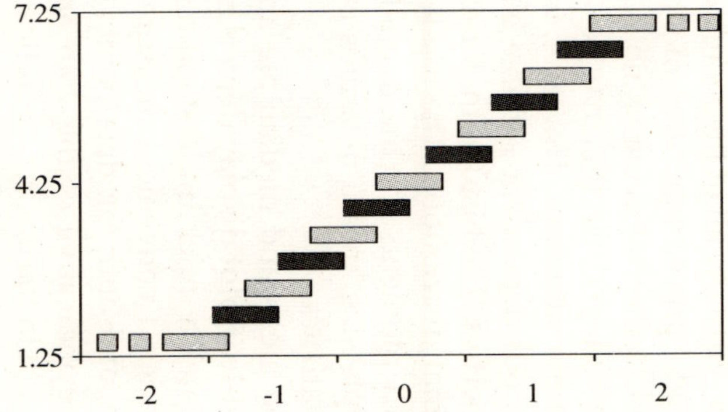

Frequency Table

Percents				Percents				Percents				Percents			
Value	Count	Cell	Cum	Value	Count	Cell	Cum	Value	Count	Cell	Cum	Value	Count	Cell	Cum
1	10	8.3	8.3	3	18	15.0	33.3	5	22	18.3	75.8	7	12	10.0	100.0
2	12	10.0	18.3	4	29	24.2	57.5	6	17	14.2	90.0				

EXHIBIT 6.1 *Continued*

variable—overall satisfaction. Virtually all of the more popular statistical packages have univariate procedures, and most contain the information that is presented in the following exhibits. This output contains a variety of univariate diagnostics that may be useful in forecasting problematic multivariate situations. However, in the present case, we can see that at least our dependent variable has some very attractive distributional properties. The histogram, for example, suggests a nearly perfectly normal distribution. The top-left portion of Exhibit 6.1 presents standard moments for the overall satisfaction variable. These include sample size, mean, measures of dispersion, and a variety of additional statistics.

The boxplot indicates the mean and median are approximately equivalent, and the **stem-and-leaf plot** display depicts a normal distribution. The boxplot facilitates a quick understanding of the data distribution because it provides a convenient measure of location, spread, skewness, tail length, and outlying data points (the top and bottom of the center box are indicative of the 25th and 75th percentiles, respectively). The + sign in the box center indicates the mean, whereas the center vertical lines extending from the box represent the data range and extend to a distance of at most 1.5 interquartile ranges. An interquartile range " . . . is the distance between the 25th and the 75th sample percentiles" according to the SAS Version 6 Users Guide (SAS Institute 1990, 617–634).

Variable Profiles

Overall Satisfaction Variable Univariate Profile

The dependent variable's normal distribution is underscored by the normal probability plot shown to the far right of Exhibit 6.1. The **normal probability plot** (quantile-quantile plot) gives the analyst an immediate picture of the data's distribution (Goodall 1983, 225). In this plot, the actual data (empirical quantiles) are plotted against the quantiles of a standardized normal distribution. In Exhibits 6.1 through 6.6, the solid bars depict a normal reference line based upon the vertical axis of the plot, which represents a normal distribution. In contrast, the crosshatch bars represent the empirical data values. If your data are roughly normal, they will tend to fall along the reference line provided by the solid bars. Of course, if they deviate drastically from the standardized normal distribution, the implication is that the data are not normally distributed. In short, when it comes to the normal probability plot, a close diagonal relationship between the two distributions is most desirable. Examination of the remaining predictor variables will serve to illustrate more problematic distributional problems as revealed by the normal probability plot.

Quality Variable Univariate Profile

Exhibit 6.2 presents the univariate profile of the quality variable. An examination of the data moments reveals considerably more variance and a far from *uniform distribution* as shown by the histogram. With respect to the boxplot, recall that the center box's top and bottom represent the 25th and 75th pecentiles of the data and that the center horizontal line represents the sample median. Of course, the central (+) sign indicates the sample mean. In the present case, therefore, the plots suggest a data distribution that is somewhat skewed toward the lower values of the variable.

Design Variable Univariate Profile

Exhibit 6.3 confirms another relatively flat distribution associated with the design variable. Note in the moments section of the exhibit the higher level of variance. That the mean is being pulled downwards by a large number of observations with low values can be verified by comparing the histogram and boxplots. This is also confirmed by the normal probability plot, which reveals a preponderance of observations at the low end of the measurement scale.

Power Variable Profile

The engine power variable is profiled in Exhibit 6.4. It suggests a slightly more normal distribution than encountered in the other predictor variables, as well as more variance. As shown in the boxplot, the mean is lower than the median. Nonetheless, the distribution of this variable—although somewhat flat—is far from problematic. Respondents were clearly less than enthusiastic when it came to the vehicle's power plant; 25 of the 120 who rated the vehicle gave its power a 2 on the seven-point scale.

Acceleration Variable Profile

In Exhibit 6.5 the 120 respondents were impressed with the test vehicle's acceleration; the mean score of 4.13 is virtually equivalent to that of the dependent variable. Well over one-quarter (27.5 percent) of the

Moments			
N	120	Sum Wgts	120
Mean	3.766667	Sum	452
Std Dev	1.926085	Variance	3.709804
Skewness	0.180057	Kurtosis	–1.1892
USS	2144	CSS	441.4667
CV	51.135	Std Mean	0.175827
T: Mean = 0	21.42261	Pr > | *T* |	0.0001
Num ^ = 0	120	Num > 0	120
M (Sign)	60	Pr > = | *M* |	0.0001
Sgn Rank	3630	Pr > = | *S* |	0.0001
W: Normal	0.895037	Pr < *W*	0.0001

Quantiles (Def = 5)			
100% Max	7	99%	7
75% Q3	5	95%	7
50% Med	4	90%	6.5
25% Q1	2	10%	1
0% Min	1	5%	1
		1%	1
Range	6		
Q3 – Q1	3		
Mode	2		

Extremes	
Lowest Obs	Highest Obs
1 (84)	7 (68)
1 (79)	7 (77)
1 (78)	7 (87)
1 (65)	7 (100)
1 (64)	7 (110)

EXHIBIT 6.2 Univariate procedure: variable = quality.

Histogram

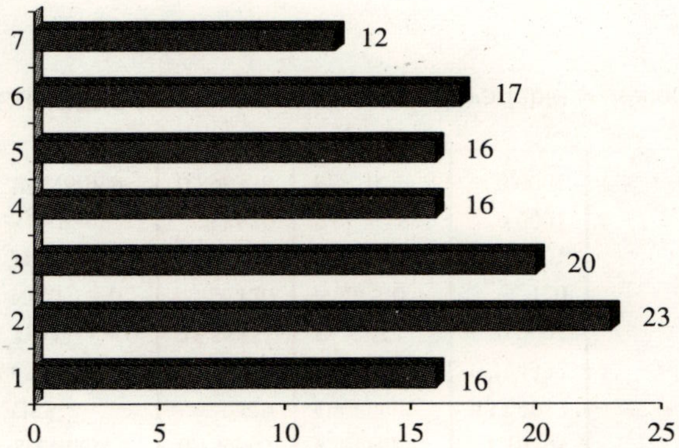

Box Plot

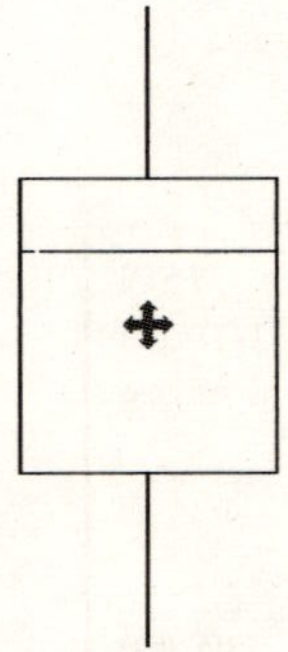

Normal Probability Plot

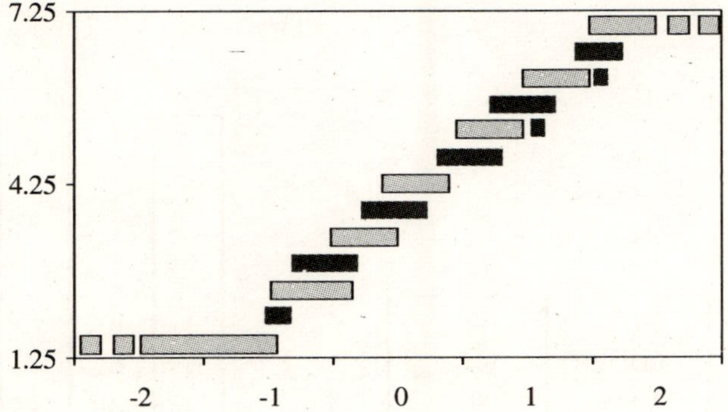

Frequency Table

Percents				Percents				Percents				Percents			
Value	Count	Cell	Cum	Value	Count	Cell	Cum	Value	Count	Cell	Cum	Value	Count	Cell	Cum
1	16	13.3	13.3	3	20	16.7	49.2	5	16	13.3	75.8	7	12	10.0	100.0
2	23	19.2	32.5	4	16	13.3	62.5	6	17	14.2	90.0				

EXHIBIT 6.2 *Continued*

Moments			
N	120	Sum Wgts	120
Mean	3.758333	Sum	451
Std Dev	1.909709	Variance	3.646989
Skewness	0.139067	Kurtosis	–1.19395
USS	2129	CSS	433.9917
CV	50.81266	Std Mean	0.174332
T: Mean = 0	21.55851	Pr > | *T* |	0.0001
Num ^ = 0	120	Num > 0	120
M (Sign)	60	Pr > = | *M* |	0.0001
Sgn Rank	3630	Pr > = | *S* |	0.0001
W: Normal	0.896336	Pr < *W*	0.0001

Quantiles (Def = 5)			
100% Max	7	99%	7
75% Q3	5	95%	7
50% Med	4	90%	6
25% Q1	2	10%	1
0% Min	1	5%	1
		1%	1
Range	6		
Q3 – Q1	3		
Mode	2		

Extremes	
Lowest Obs	Highest Obs
1 (84)	7 (68)
1 (79)	7 (77)
1 (78)	7 (87)
1 (65)	7 (100)
1 (64)	7 (110)

EXHIBIT 6.3 Univariate procedure: variable = design.

Histogram

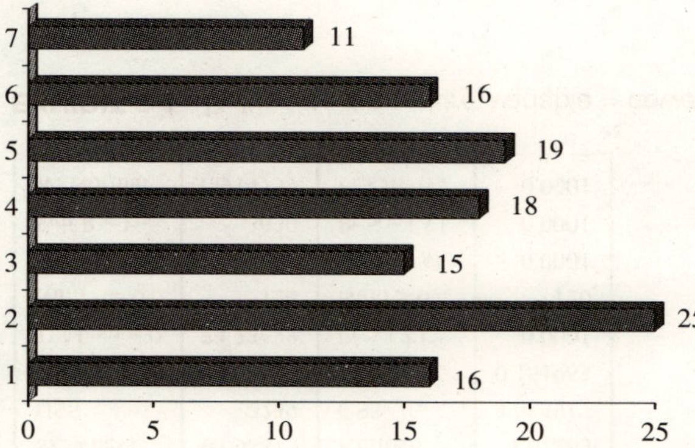

Box Plot

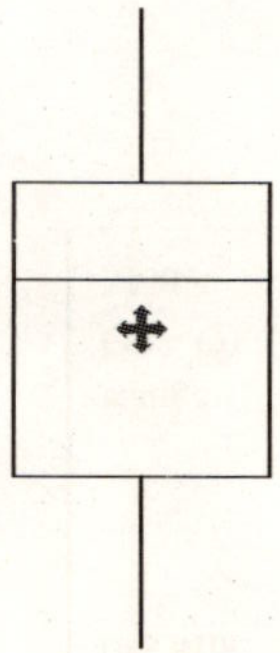

Normal Probability Plot

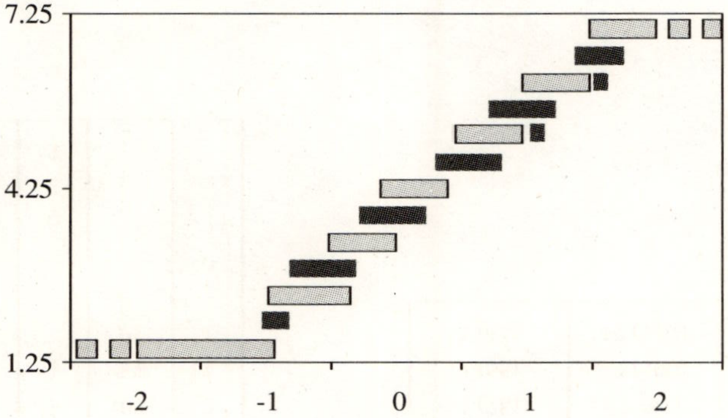

Frequency Table

Percents				Percents				Percents				Percents			
Value	Count	Cell	Cum	Value	Count	Cell	Cum	Value	Count	Cell	Cum	Value	Count	Cell	Cum
1	16	13.3	13.3	3	15	12.5	46.7	5	19	15.8	77.5	7	11	9.2	100.0
2	25	20.8	34.2	4	18	15.0	61.7	6	16	13.3	90.8				

EXHIBIT 6.3 *Continued*

Moments			
N	120	Sum Wgts	120
Mean	3.941667	Sum	473
Std Dev	1.774212	Variance	3.147829
Skewness	0.098813	Kurtosis	–1.01285
USS	2239	CSS	374.5917
CV	45.01173	Std Mean	0.161963
T: Mean = 0	24.33688	Pr > | *T* |	0.0001
Num ^ = 0	120	Num > 0	120
M (Sign)	60	Pr > = | *M* |	0.0001
Sgn Rank	3630	Pr > = | *S* |	0.0001
W: Normal	0.914759	Pr < *W*	0.0001

Quantiles (Def = 5)			
100% Max	7	99%	7
75% Q3	5	95%	7
50% Med	4	90%	6
25% Q1	3	10%	2
0% Min	1	5%	1
		1%	1
Range	6		
Q3 – Q1	2		
Mode	3		

Extremes	
Lowest Obs	Highest Obs
1 (84)	7 (68)
1 (79)	7 (77)
1 (78)	7 (87)
1 (65)	7 (100)
1 (64)	7 (110)

EXHIBIT 6.4 Univariate procedure: variable = power.

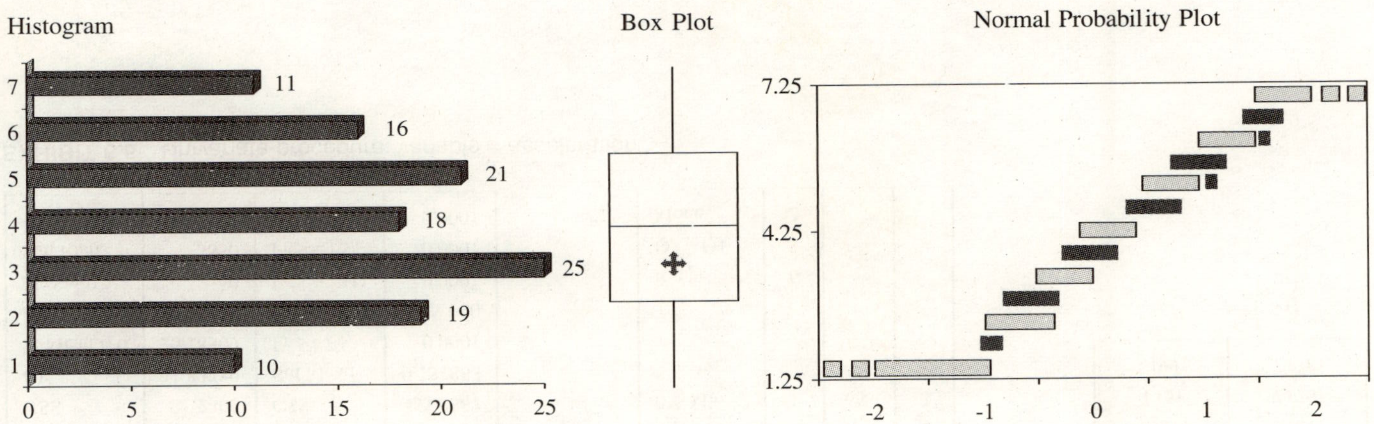

Frequency Table

Percents				Percents				Percents				Percents			
Value	Count	Cell	Cum	Value	Count	Cell	Cum	Value	Count	Cell	Cum	Value	Count	Cell	Cum
1	10	8.3	8.3	3	25	20.8	45.0	5	21	17.5	77.5	7	11	9.2	100.0
2	19	15.8	24.2	4	18	15.0	60.0	6	16	13.3	90.8				

EXHIBIT 6.4 *Continued*

Moments			
N	120	Sum Wgts	120
Mean	4.133333	Sum	496
Std Dev	1.729299	Variance	2.990476
Skewness	0.008872	Kurtosis	–1.19832
USS	2406	CSS	355.8667
CV	41.83789	Std Mean	0.157863
T: Mean = 0	26.18309	Pr > | *T* |	0.0001
Num ^ = 0	120	Num > 0	120
M (Sign)	60	Pr > = | *M* |	0.0001
Sgn Rank	3630	Pr > = | *S* |	0.0001
W: Normal	0.901513	Pr < *W*	0.0001

Quantiles (Def = 5)			
100% Max	7	99%	7
75% Q3	6	95%	7
50% Med	4	90%	6
25% Q1	3	10%	2
0% Min	1	5%	2
		1%	1
Range	6		
Q3 – Q1	3		
Mode	2		

Extremes	
Lowest Obs	Highest Obs
1 (87)	7 (50)
1 (65)	7 (61)
1 (27)	7 (67)
1 (5)	7 (76)
1 (99)	7 (78)

EXHIBIT 6.5 Univariate procedure: variable = acceleration.

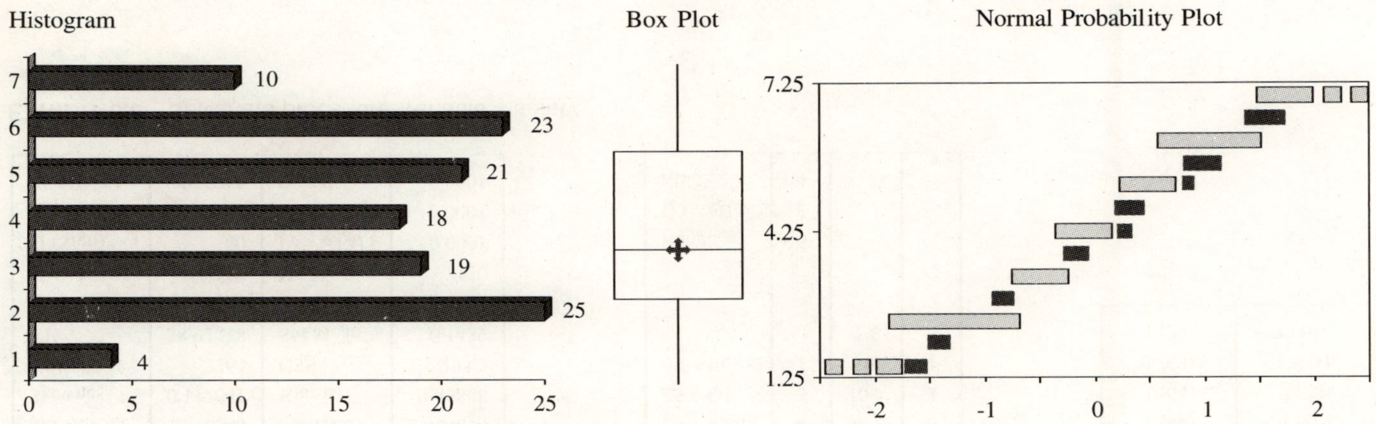

Frequency Table

Percents				Percents				Percents				Percents			
Value	Count	Cell	Cum	Value	Count	Cell	Cum	Value	Count	Cell	Cum	Value	Count	Cell	Cum
1	4	3.3	3.3	3	19	15.8	40.0	5	21	17.5	72.5	7	10	8.3	100.0
2	25	20.8	24.2	4	18	15.0	55.0	6	23	19.2	91.7				

EXHIBIT 6.5 *Continued*

Moments			
N	120	Sum Wgts	120
Mean	4.05	Sum	486
Std Dev	1.576348	Variance	2.484874
Skewness	0.112641	Kurtosis	−0.45888
USS	2264	CSS	295.7
CV	38.92218	Std Mean	0.1439
T: Mean = 0	28.1445	Pr > | *T* |	0.0001
Num ^ = 0	120	Num > 0	120
M (Sign)	60	Pr > = | *M* |	0.0001
Sgn Rank	3630	Pr > = | *S* |	0.0001
W: Normal	0.926765	Pr < *W*	0.0001

Quantiles (Def = 5)			
100% Max	7	99%	7
75% Q3	5	95%	7
50% Med	4	90%	6
25% Q1	3	10%	2
0% Min	1	5%	1
		1%	1
Range	6		
Q3 – Q1	2		
Mode	4		

Extremes	
Lowest Obs	Highest Obs
1 (87)	7 (70)
1 (84)	7 (76)
1 (64)	7 (78)
1 (63)	7 (100)
1 (24)	7 (109)

EXHIBIT 6.6 Univariate procedure: variable = safety.

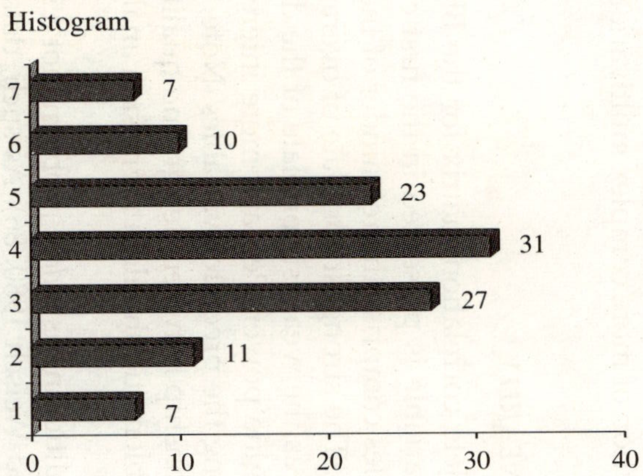

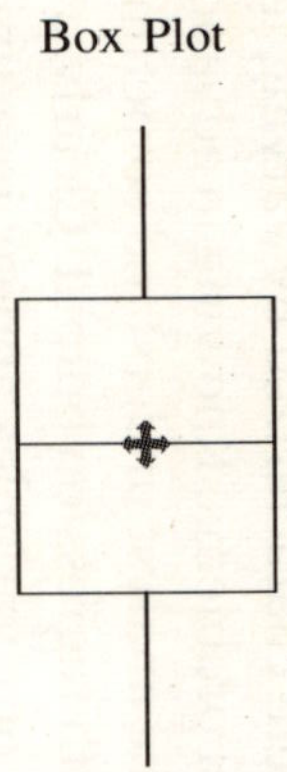

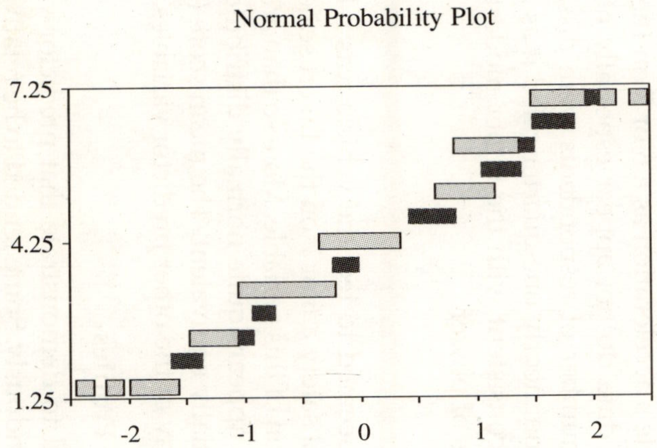

Frequency Table

Percents				Percents				Percents				Percents			
Value	Count	Cell	Cum	Value	Count	Cell	Cum	Value	Count	Cell	Cum	Value	Count	Cell	Cum
1	7	5.8	5.8	3	27	22.5	37.5	5	23	19.2	82.5	7	11	9.2	100.0
2	11	9.2	15.0	4	31	25.8	63.3	6	10	8.3	90.8				

EXHIBIT 6.6 *Continued*

respondents rated the vehicle's acceleration as a 6 or 7 on the seven-point Likert scale. Still, the data do not appear especially normally distributed. A substantive number of respondents were dissatisfied with the vehicle's acceleration; nearly one-quarter rated it as a 1 or 2 on the Likert scale. This is consistent with the rather modest scores the vehicle received in terms of power.

Safety Variable Profile

Respondents in Exhibit 6.6 seemed to feel the vehicle was relatively safe—nearly 15 percent rated safety a 6 or 7 on the Likert scale. More interestingly is the distribution of this variable. More so than any other of the predictor variables, it appears quite normally distributed. The mean and median are essentially equivalent. The mean score (4.05) is equivalent to or exceeds many of the other predictor variables.

Summary of the Univariate Profiles

The preceding was intended to demonstrate that predictor variable distributions can vary tremendously. Some tended to be relatively flat (platykurtic) whereas others were characterized by varying levels of skewness or other distributional problems. Knowing in advance what these conditions are will help the analyst understand sometimes perplexing problems associated with regression output. Clearly, a fundamental understanding of how our variables appear in a univariate sense will facilitate the resolution of more complex multivariate problems, should they emerge.

The Diagnosis of Collinearity

Table 6.1 presents the complete correlation matrix for the Big Auto Co. data set. The outcome variable is presented in the first column, and the five predictor variables comprise the remainder of the lower triangular correlation matrix. The strongest correlate of overall satisfaction is acceleration, whereas the weakest correlate of the dependent variable involves the engine power. Perhaps more interestingly are the intercorrelations among the predictor variables. Note, in particular, the very strong relationship between design and quality. This could prove to be highly problematic should a regression analysis be performed using these data.

Keep in mind that ill-conditioning is a *data* problem, not a statistical problem (Belsley, Kuh, and Welsch 1980, 86). As such, data transformations such as orthogonalization (Draper and Smith 1981, 258) and

TABLE 6.1 Intercorrelations among predictor and outcome variables (Big Auto Co. data set)

	OSAT	Quality	Design	Power	Acceleration	Safety
Quality	0.65	—				
Design	0.66	0.99	—			
Power	0.56	0.79	0.78	—		
Acceleration	0.81	0.67	0.67	0.54	—	
Safety	0.76	0.55	0.53	0.64	0.70	—

Note: Strongest correlations are highlighted.

other procedures can be employed to lessen the effects of collinearity. Partial least squares (PLS) appears to yield excellent results compared to other approaches according to Naes and Martens (1985). PLS is discussed in chapter 9 of this book. Another effective approach to circumventing the effects of collinearity involves **ridge regression** (Birkes and Dodge 1993, 173–88).

Grapentine (1997, 11–20) provides a very readable introduction to ill-conditioning. Perhaps the most vexing problem for the analyst faced with collinear data involves its diagnosis. After all, some degree of linear (or nonlinear) relationship will always be present on the predictor side of the data. The exception to this, of course, is when the predictors are orthogonal, such as in the case of factor or component scores.

The key to understanding the role of collinearity is that although always present (except in the case noted earlier), its effects are not necessarily *degrading* to the regression model. Only when the level of ill-conditioning adversely affects the model should tactics to circumvent it be employed. The manifestations of degrading collinearity take numerous forms. Most notable are excessively large standard errors associated with the parameter estimates (that is, beta coefficients). Another disconcerting effect involves the volatility of the beta coefficients. A highly collinear dataset split randomly and subjected to two separate regressions may yield very different results with respect to the impact of each predictor on the outcome variable, significant levels, and the overall model's efficacy.

When the automotive data described earlier were subjected to regression analysis, the findings were intuitively appealing despite a high-level collinearity. Table 6.2 presents basic regression output with

TABLE 6.2 Basic regression and analysis of variance output (Big Auto Co. data set).

Analysis of Variance

Source	DF	Sum of Squares	Mean Square	F Value	Prob > F
Model	5	262.04	52.40	67.42	0.00
Error	114	88.61	0.77		
C total	119	350.66			
R-square	0.75				
Adj. R-square	0.74				

Parameter Estimates

Variable	DF	Parameter Estimate	Standard Error	T for H_0: Parameter = 0	Prob > |T|
Intercept	1	0.25	0.24	1.03	0.30
Quality	1	-0.13	0.30	-0.44	0.66
Design	1	0.34	0.30	1.15	0.25
Power	1	-0.10	0.08	-1.18	0.24
Acceleration	1	0.43	0.08	5.45	0.00
Safety	1	0.43	0.08	5.18	0.00

parameter estimates, standard errors, and probability levels. As shown, the strongest predictors of satisfaction with the new vehicle were acceleration and safety. The adjusted R^2 (0.74) is quite acceptable, and the regression results are consistent with the relationships presented in Table 6.1. The adjusted R^2 takes into account the number of variables in a regression analysis and is the preferred means of comparing the efficacy of two models (Dillon and Goldstein 1984, 222).

There are numerous approaches to diagnosing collinearity. Belsley, Kuh, and Welsch (1980) and more recently Belsley (1991) provide excellent treatments of the subject. Of the measures reviewed by these authors, the **condition index** is preferred unequivocally. Although other good measures such as **variance Inflation Factors (VIF)** exist, we will focus on the condition index here. The VIF, incidentally, is calculated in the following manner

$$\mathrm{VIF}_i = 1/1 - R^2$$

where R_i^2 is the squared multiple correlation when x_i is regressed on the other predictor variables (Belsley, Kuh, and Welsch 1980, 93).

The mathematical derivation of the condition index is beyond the scope of this book. Instead of examining how the condition index is derived, our focus is on how to interpret it. Readers interested in a more in-depth treatment of collinearity, in general, and the conditioning index, in particular, are urged to reference either the Belsley (1991) or Belsley, Kuh, and Welsch (1980) book.

Although there are manifestations of collinearity that cannot be missed (for example, reversed coefficient signs), the condition index provides an objective empirical basis for inferences concerning the extent to which ill-conditioning may be degrading our model. Table 6.3 presents collinearity diagnostics for the Big Auto Co. regression analysis introduced earlier. Based upon Table 6.1, one would expect substantial levels of collinearity in this data set. The correlation between the quality and design satisfaction measures was 0.99, which is, of course, very strong.

Table 6.3 confirms that there is a harmful level of collinearity in the data set. The condition index associated with the sixth eigenvalue is greater than 50. This exceeds the somewhat arbitrary cutoff proposed by Belsley (1991, 129) of approximately 30. The simplest way to approach the type of output presented in Table 6.3 is to read down the column labeled "Condition Index" to the last and largest entry. If this exceeds 30, then ill-conditioning may be a problem.

To diagnose which variables are most responsible for the level of collinearity in a data set, we need to refer to the remaining columns of data labeled "Var Prop." These indicate the proportion of variance accounted for each variable by each of the six eigenvalues. If any two (or more) variables share more than about half of their variance with a given eigenvalue, the indication is that these are the probable source of the ill-conditioning. In the present case, we see that design and quality satisfaction both share 98 percent of their variance with the sixth eigenvalue. This suggests that the two variables are highly collinear, which, in fact, we know to be true. Their correlation is 0.99.

In the present case, there is little indication that the significant collinearity has substantively degraded our model. The two predictor variables that are most strongly correlated with the dependent variable (overall satisfaction) emerged as the strongest predictors in the regression analysis. Their signs are appropriate, and the standard errors around the estimates are not excessive. In this case, we can conclude that while potentially harmful collinearity exists, it has not degraded the quality of the model.

TABLE 6.3 Conditioning diagnostics for Big Auto Co. regression.

Number	Eigenvalue	Condition Index	Var Prop INTERCEP	Var Prop QUAL	Var Prop DESIGN	Var Prop SAFETY	Var Prop POWER	Var Prop ACCEL
1	5.67401	1.00000	0.0032	0.0001	0.0001	0.0014	0.0014	0.0015
2	0.16260	5.90717	0.2680	0.0055	0.0055	0.0358	0.0078	0.0082
3	0.07558	8.66447	0.5190	0.0003	0.0004	0.1066	0.0528	0.2679
4	0.06252	9.52683	0.1945	0.0026	0.0035	0.1845	0.3191	0.1191
5	0.02323	15.6302	0.0067	0.0100	0.0095	0.6659	0.6166	0.6021
6	0.00207	52.40661	0.0086	0.9815	0.9809	0.0058	0.0022	0.0012

INFLUENTIAL OBSERVATIONS IN REGRESSION ANALYSIS

Traditional univariate exploratory data analysis generally fails to reveal the extent to which discrepant observations may have affected regression coefficients and related statistics. A great deal of what we do in applied customer satisfaction research involves regression analysis. And yet, few practitioners are good diagnosticians when it comes to influential observations. **Influential observations** are those that exert inordinate effects on the overall regression model. Typically we employ row-deletion statistics to assess the impact of each observation on the model. Conceptually, row-deletion methods systematically exclude each observation from the analysis to gauge the effect each observation has on the overall regression.

Belsley, Kuh, and Welsch (1980) called for the increased use of a set of diagnostic measures that overcome the limitations associated with traditional univariate approaches. Specifically, several diagnostics—the hat matrix diagonal elements, studentized residuals, DFBETAS, DFFITS, and COVRATIO—when examined separately and in conjunction, can reveal a great deal about the volatility and normality of regression analyses. These statistics will be described and will be followed by a case study.

Researchers often initially turn their attentions to residuals in regression analysis. In regression analysis, residuals are the difference between the predicted and actual value of the dependent variable. The distribution of the residuals may reveal **heteroscedasticity,** a condition wherein the residuals vary over the range of the predictor variables. Regression analysis assumes **homoscedasticity**—where *homo* means "same," and *scedasticity* means "scatter." When heteroscedasticity occurs, the implication is that the errors (that is, residuals) are related to the predictor variable values. Residual examination, therefore, can reveal that the model may not perform uniformly at all levels of the predictor variable set.

Residuals on an individual observation basis can also be quite revealing. Each observation is associated with a residual. In cases where the observed value of the dependent variable is very different from the predicted value, the residual will be large. Very large residuals can actually affect the slope of the regression line and, depending upon the magnitude of their influence, pull the regression line toward them.

The studentized residual is a form of standardized residual that conforms to the well-known *t*-distribution. As such, the significance of any deviation (studentized residual) can be readily assessed. This is not the case when it comes to residuals in their raw (that is, unstandardized) form. It is considerably more difficult to determine the significance—statistical or otherwise—of raw residual scores because they are still in dependent variable units. Although it is a relatively simple matter to make inferences concerning the relative magnitude of raw residual values, there are no cutoffs or absolute values to use as a baseline for evaluation. The studentized residual, on the other hand, has a well-known distribution, and assessing the deviation of a given residual from the norm is straightforward.

The COVRATIO statistic is a row-deletion method for determining the effect one observation has on the regression. Specifically, COVRATIO, according to Belsley, Kuh, and Welsch (1980, 48), compares the data covariance matrix using all the data versus the covariance matrix if the *i*th row (observation) is deleted. Belsley, Kuh, and Welsch indicated that COVRATIO values of around 1.00 suggest that the model is relatively insensitive to the deletion of the *i*th row (observation). A reasonable critical value for COVRATIO is $1 \pm 3(k/n)$.

Another row-deletion diagnostic is DFBETAS. Large absolute values indicate influential observations with respect to each regression beta coefficient. DFBETAS is calculated with respect to each predictor variable for each observation. A size-adjusted cutoff for this influence statistic is $2/n^{1/2}$, which, in the case of a regression based upon 400 observations, would be 0.1. A related statistic for assessing the effect of individual observations on the overall regression analysis is DFFITS. Belsley, Kuh, and Welsch (1980, 15) suggest that the appropriate size-adjusted cutoff for DFFITS is $2(k/n)^{1/2}$ where k is the number of independent variables. In the case of a regression based upon 400 observations and five predictor variables, the cutoff for this influence statistic would be 0.22, approximately.

Removing the highly influential observation from the overall analysis is not a decision to be made lightly and should represent a rare occurrence. There should be solid justification for deleting an observation, especially in customer satisfaction research wherein doing so may affect scores that feed compensation or bonus systems. Reasons for removing an observation include data entry error or clear respondent error such as a data value outside the acceptable range of responses. Even if the record clearly contains erroneous and statistically influential data, the decision to remove it should be documented.

Exhibit 6.7 presents influence diagnostics for the first 30 of 120 observations in the Big Auto Co. data set. Again, overall satisfaction was regressed on five predictor variables: satisfaction with quality, design, power, acceleration, and safety. To reiterate, each observation is associated with a critical value as presented in Table 6.4. There is no critical value associated with the raw residual and COVRATIO because there is no natural standardized scaling of these values according to Belsley, Kuh, and Welsch (1980, 28).

Exhibit 6.7 presents the first 30 of 120 observations of the Big Auto Co. data set used earlier in a demonstration of collinearity diagnostics. For each of the 30 observations, a residual, studentized residual, COVRATIO, DFFITS, and DFBETAS are presented. Values that exceed the critical levels presented in Table 6.3 have been highlighted.

There is a distinct pattern associated with the highlighted values shown in Exhibit 6.7. In particular, certain observations emerge as more influential than others. Their influence is detected by virtually all of the indicators described here. Observations #18, #26, and #27 all appear to be affecting the regression analysis. Note that in each case, the raw residual is quite substantial, and there is generally consistency across the diagnostic measures.

To confirm that these highly influential observations may be anomalous, we can examine the raw data. Table 6.5 presents the raw data for the three influential observations. A review of the actual residual values shown in Exhibit 6.7 reveals that Observation #18 has a positive residual whereas Observations #26 and #27 have negative residuals. This is consistent with the regression equation presented earlier for this data set, which suggested that overall satisfaction was dependent upon the set of five predictor variables. Thus, one would expect that in the case of Observation #26, for example, overall satisfaction for this respondent would be higher because each of the five satisfaction content areas was rated a 6 (hence, the negative residual). The same is true for the remaining two observations. In the case of Observation #18, the model predicted much lower overall satisfaction because the respondent was somewhat dissatisfied with power and safety.

Earlier the implications of deleting certain observations was briefly discussed. Table 6.6 presents the Big Auto Co. regression analysis with the three observations noted earlier deleted. Of particular interest is the increase in R^2 that occurred with the removal of

EXHIBIT 6.7 Influence diagnostics (first 30 observations of Big Auto Co. data set).

Obs No.	Residual	Rstudent	CovRatio	DFFITS	Intercept DFBETA	Quality DFBETA	Design DFBETA	Power DFBETA	Accel DFBETA	Safety DFBETA
1	0.8004	0.9857	1.1810	0.4172	−0.1084	−0.0536	−0.0214	0.0319	0.2165	0.1090
2	−1.5152	−1.7704	0.9320	−0.3615	−0.2551	−0.0172	0.0068	0.1967	0.1365	−0.1514
3	−0.4462	−0.5246	1.1236	−0.1497	−0.0837	0.0063	0.0188	−0.0965	−0.0509	0.1091
4	−0.4462	−0.5246	1.1236	−0.1497	−0.0837	0.0063	0.0188	−0.0965	−0.0509	0.1091
5	−0.4482	−0.5193	1.0915	−0.1163	−0.0793	0.0059	0.0078	−0.0560	0.0282	0.0274
6	0.0666	0.0785	1.1489	0.0235	0.0125	0.0031	0.0015	−0.0198	−0.0144	0.0110
7	0.8176	0.9540	1.0643	0.2322	−0.0908	−0.0120	0.0059	0.1105	0.1239	−0.1234
8	0.2266	0.2582	1.0693	0.0345	0.0051	0.0029	0.0019	−0.0134	0.0052	−0.0059
9	0.3563	0.4078	1.0719	0.0654	−0.0241	−0.0038	0.0039	0.0231	0.0243	−0.0208
10	1.2487	1.4535	0.9841	0.3018	−0.1064	−0.0127	0.0231	0.1288	0.0543	−0.1072
11	−1.4284	−−1.6523	0.9360	-0.2590	0.0534	0.0172	0.0047	0.0092	−0.1727	0.0106
12	−1.4587	−1.6902	0.9322	−0.2780	−0.0392	0.0058	−0.0173	0.1504	0.0922	−0.2101
13	1.1618	1.3468	0.9938	0.2594	0.1391	0.0155	0.0200	−0.0228	−0.1951	0.0246
14	−0.3687	−0.4245	1.0838	−0.0826	−0.0450	−0.0091	0.0042	0.0069	−0.0285	0.0592
15	1.5801	1.8438	0.9149	0.3532	0.1688	−0.0330	−0.0144	0.2172	−0.0790	−0.0603
16	0.7162	0.8294	1.0628	0.1769	−0.0623	0.0014	0.0093	0.0132	0.0834	−0.0668
17	0.0437	0.0515	1.1458	0.0152	−0.0020	0.0011	0.0024	−0.0096	−0.0089	0.0091
18	1.5079	2.0080	1.1471	1.1756	0.2254	0.1881	0.0116	−0.7701	0.3000	−0.2987
19	−0.8448	−0.9715	1.0316	−0.1643	−0.0999	0.0079	0.0180	−0.0136	−0.0414	0.0164
20	0.1963	0.2259	1.0919	0.0443	0.0172	0.0042	0.0047	−0.0308	−0.0315	0.0245
21	−0.5194	−0.5978	1.0711	−0.1125	−0.0689	0.0025	0.0137	−0.0551	−0.0464	0.0812
22	−0.6960	−0.8054	1.0635	−0.1689	−0.0722	−0.0144	−0.0118	0.1354	0.0944	−0.1055
23	0.2695	0.3086	1.0777	0.0511	0.0359	0.0033	0.0026	−0.0148	−0.0375	0.0125
24	0.4523	0.5248	1.0941	0.1208	0.0928	0.0013	−0.0159	0.0431	0.0353	−0.0823
25	−0.6437	−0.7379	1.0506	−0.1183	0.0437	0.0068	−0.0070	−0.0418	−0.0439	0.0376
26	−2.0767	−2.4359	0.7950	−0.3861	0.2061	0.0307	−0.0488	−0.0246	−0.0055	−0.1100
27	−2.2075	−3.0508	0.9074	−1.8901	0.1884	0.2984	−0.0614	−0.9433	0.8057	−0.8428
28	1.6083	1.8734	0.9056	0.3350	0.0586	−0.0458	−0.0014	0.2402	−0.0595	−0.0242
29	1.6083	1.8734	0.9056	0.3350	0.0586	−0.0458	−0.0014	0.2402	−0.0595	−0.0242
30	0.5801	0.6682	1.0674	0.1280	0.0612	−0.0120	−0.0052	0.0787	−0.0286	−0.0219

TABLE 6.4 Critical values for influence diagnostics.

Influence Diagnostic	Critical Value	Value for $n = 120$; $k = 5$
Raw residual	None	
Studentized residual	*t*-distribution	1.96 ($\alpha = 0.05$)
COVRATIO	$1 \pm 3(k/n)$	1 ± 0.125
DFFITS	$2(k/n)^{1/2}$	0.408
DFBETAS	$2/(n)^{1/2}$	0.141

TABLE 6.5 Raw data for influential observations.

Variable	Obs #18	Obs #26	Obs #27
Quality	7	6	1
Design	7	6	1
Power	1	6	7
Acceleration	7	6	1
Safety	2	6	7
Overall satisfaction	7	4	1

TABLE 6.6 Basic regression and analysis of variance output. (Big Auto Co. data set with three influential observations deleted).

Analysis of Variance

Source	DF	Sum of Squares	Mean Square	*F* Value	Prob > *F*
Model	5	262.97	52.59	83.87	0.00
Error	111	69.60	0.62		
C total	116	332.58			
R-square	0.79				
Adj. *R*-square	0.78				

Parameter Estimates

Variable	DF	Parameter Estimate	Standard Error	*T* for H_0: Parameter = 0	*Prob* > |T|
Intercept	1	0.04	0.22	0.22	0.82
Quality	1	–0.36	0.27	–1.30	0.19
Design	1	0.38	0.27	1.40	0.16
Power	1	0.11	0.09	1.31	0.19
Acceleration	1	0.31	0.08	4.06	0.00
Safety	1	0.57	0.08	7.19	0.00

three observations. When all 120 observations were included, the adjusted R^2 was 0.74 (see Table 6.3), and when the three observations were removed this increased by four percentage points. The reason for this, of course, is that the sum of squared errors (that is, residuals) was decreased by removing the three influential observations. The second regression based upon 117 observations reflects a lower sum of squared errors (SSE). It is important to observe that this reduction is not equal to the sum of the squared residuals of the three influential observations. This is because the second regression is just that—a new analysis of the data set without the three influential observations. By removing the three influential observations, we have reduced the error contribution of *all* the observations. This is because the regression line was essentially being drawn away from them by the three influential observations. Once the influential observations were removed, the regression line was moved closer to the bulk of observations, therefore reducing their deviations from it.

The effect of an influential observation is shown in Figure 6.2, which illustrates a scenario very similar to that described earlier. Figure 6.2 demonstrates how Observation #6 has pulled the regression line toward itself. The residual value is shown. Observation #10 is also highlighted. Its residual is 4. Once the influential observation has been removed, the regression line is no longer drawn toward Observation #6 and instead tends to fall through the middle of the observations. The effect of this is not only the reduction in SSE attributable to the removal of Observation #6 but also the reduced residuals of the remaining observations now that the regression line has moved closer to them. Thus, SSE was reduced by nine when Observation #6 was removed and further reduced by the fact that, for example, Observation #10 is now closer to the regression line, and it has a lower residual value.

The value of influence diagnostics in customer satisfaction research is significant. And yet, in applied settings there is little reliance upon the statistics introduced in this chapter. When model building and accurate prediction are important, customer satisfaction researchers must be good diagnosticians. Of course, the implications of removing influential observations must be weighed heavily. Often we are in a "lesser of two evils" situation. On the one hand, we are removing valid data from an analysis, and on the other we may be faced with a model that could be vastly improved by simply removing a fraction of the data.

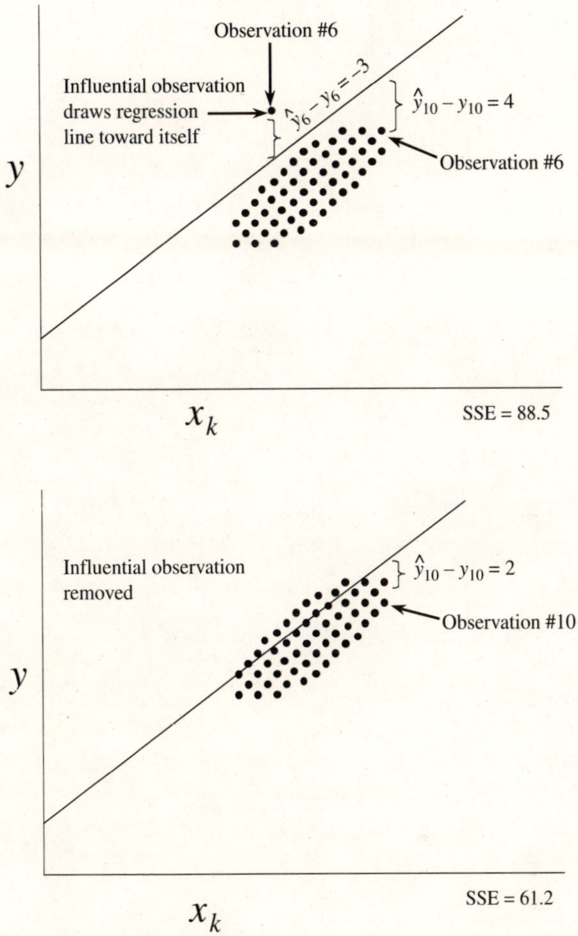

FIGURE 6.2 Effect of influential observation.

Clearly, influential observations must be retained in univariate statistical reporting. To adjust a business unit's top-box customer satisfaction score by removing outliers would be a terrible idea. On the other hand, it is possible that in the future the L-estimators will be welcomed in applied settings.

Chapter 7

Causal Modeling: Multiple Dependencies in Path Analysis

Causal Modeling

Chapter 5 focused on dependence models characterized by a single outcome variable. Ostensibly, the predictor variables *caused* fluctuations in the outcome variable—typically overall satisfaction or loyalty. That a change in one (or more) predictor variable(s) would yield an effect on the outcome variable is the presumption underlying the derived importance measurement framework. Thus, causality is implied, but it should be clear that we have established an equivocal causal relationship using *cross-sectional* data. That is, although we might demonstrate that food quality is a key driver of overall satisfaction, we have by no means established true causality, as will be described later.

This chapter introduces a technique known as **path analysis**. A substantive understanding of the data requirements, assumptions, appropriate sample sizes, and limitations is critical to fully understanding the more complex latent variable models introduced in subsequent chapters. Although only recently applied to customer satisfaction data, path analysis is by no means a recently introduced technique. In fact, it was first described in the early 1900s (Wright 1918, 1921). The contemporary preoccupation with the application of this technique in customer satisfaction research does not represent a noteworthy analytical advancement, per se. Rather, the use of path analysis among researchers involved with customer satisfaction data represents a renewed fascination with a statistical technique that has been controversial at times. It should be noted that Wright struggled with the implications of structural equations with latent (that is, factorial) variables nearly 50 years before the integration of confirmatory factor analysis and structural equation models occurred again in the late 1960s, according to Tunali (1990, 175).

THE NATURE OF CAUSALITY

Path analysis—and **causal modeling** techniques in general—have been justly criticized. The primary criticism of causal modeling involves the use of cross-sectional data to draw *causal* inferences. There are minimally three criteria that must be met to establish causation, as shown in Figure 7.1. These criteria must be met to establish a cause-and-effect relationship. Numerous authors concede that cross-sectional data do not meet these criteria. The consensus ranges from Schumacker and Lomax (1996, 28) to Asher (1983, 12). Perhaps the most cogent description of the causal inference problem is provided by Bollen (1989, 40–67). Bullock, Harlow, and Mulaik (1994) also offer specific presumptions with respect to causal inferences based on cross-sectional data.

The three criteria presented in Figure 7.1 involve temporal sequencing, concomitant variation, and the elimination of mitigating variables that might be responsible for observed causal relationships. The first involves the temporal ordering of the predictor and outcome variables. In short, one must precede the other in time. Typically, cross-sectional data—especially customer satisfaction data—fail this test. The second requirement for demonstrating causality involves concomitant variation—does the outcome variable increase as the predictor variable(s) increase? For example, is there covariation between the predictor and outcome variables? The final aspect of establishing a causal relationship is more problematic. It involves the elimination of confounding factors that might influence the observed cause-and-effect relationship. Although in theory this sounds simple enough, it is in reality a very difficult criterion to establish unequivocally, as Blalock (1964, 26) noted:

> *No matter how elaborate the design, certain simplifying assumptions must always be made. In particular, we must at some point assume that the effects of confounding factors are negligible. Randomization helps to rule out some such variables, but the plausibility of this particular kind of simplifying assumptions is always a question of degree.*

- Temporal sequencing
- Concomitant variation
- Elimination of mitigating variables

FIGURE 7.1 Minimal criteria for establishing causality.

That such a simplification may be compelled is inarguable in customer satisfaction research. It is likely that in an effort to demonstrate robust, scientifically acceptable causality, we may *never* be able to meet the third criterion in customer satisfaction research. The most critical point to be made with respect to path analysis and causal modeling in general is that cross-sectional data will *never* meet all the criteria required to demonstrate a true cause-and-effect relationship. Instead, we have made some concessions. In particular, among customer satisfaction researchers and others working with path analysis techniques, the following is generally accepted.

> Path analysis and other more advanced causal modeling techniques merely demonstrate that the relationships within the data are consistent with the hypothesized causal sequence.

It should be quite clear that cross-sectional customer satisfaction data preclude robust inferences concerning causality. This does not mean, however, that path analysis is unsuitable for customer satisfaction research projects depicting the development of other constructs such as loyalty. Indeed, the technique can produce compelling results that are both mathematically sound and intuitively appealing.

The reader may still be in somewhat of a quandary with respect to the path analysis technique. Consider the simple causal model presented in Figure 7.2. This two-variable model has one predictor variable and one outcome variable. The path coefficient (γ_{11}) is equivalent to the simple correlation (r_{x1y1}) between the two variables. This is not the case for the slightly more complex case presented in Figure 7.3. Here, we encounter three predictor variables, each of which has some level of covariance with the others. Interestingly, if the predictor variables were *orthogonal* (that is, perfectly uncorrelated) then the path coefficients would be equivalent to the simple correlations. Again,

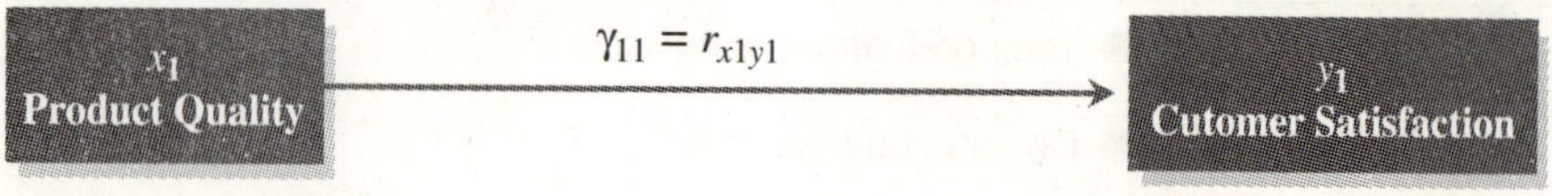

FIGURE 7.2 Simple causal relationship.

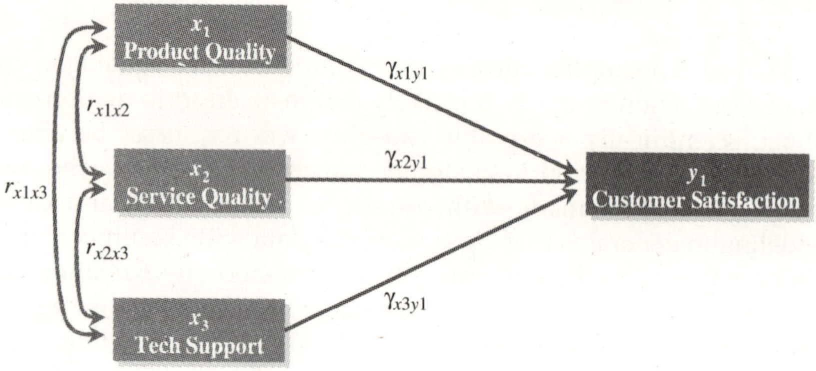

FIGURE 7.3 Multiple predictor causal model.

this would only be the case if the predictors were orthogonal, which is rarely the case. A notable exception to this involves regressing an outcome variable on a series of factors or principal components, which were extracted from the data in a manner that ensures orthogonality. This will be discussed in chapter 8.

Path analysis permits us to assess the extent to which our data are consistent with a hypothesized causal structure. It does *not* establish true causal relations because, among other things, there is no temporal ordering among the variables that compose the causal sequence. Note, too, that path coefficients between exogenous and endogenous variables are depicted using gamma (γ) whereas the effect of one endogenous variable upon another is depicted using the more familiar beta (β) sign.

Figure 7.4 depicts a relatively simple path analysis model in which five predictor variables (x_1 through x_5) affect two outcome variables. Note that the direction of causality is from left to right. Note, too, that the first outcome variable (y_1) is presumed to exert an effect on the second outcome variable (y_2). More interestingly, the five exogenous variables (x_1–x_5) are unconstrained with respect to their ability to influence one or *both* of the outcome variables. Any of the predictor variables may exert an indirect effect on loyalty (y_2)

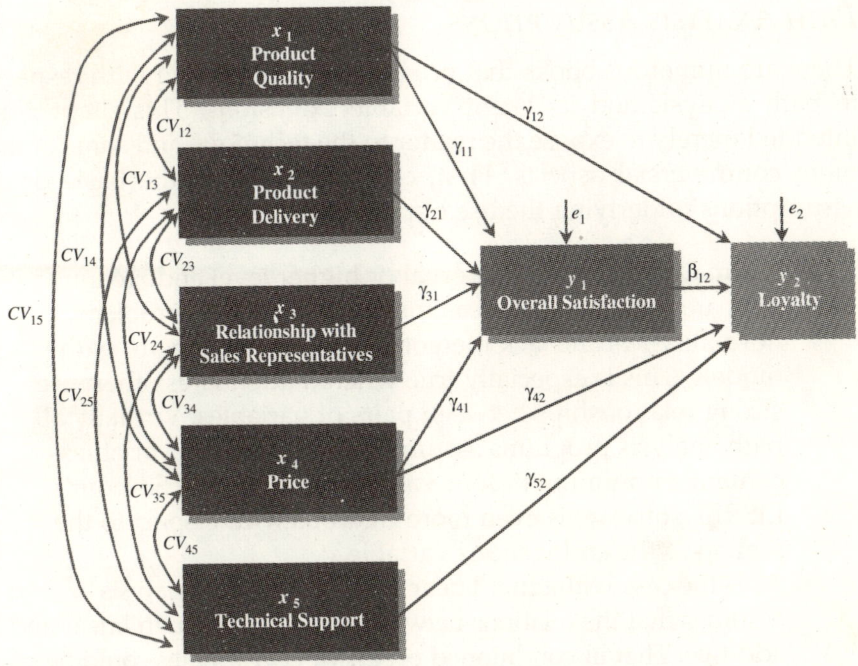

FIGURE 7.4 Path analysis model with two dependent variables.

through overall satisfaction (y_1). Thus, both direct and indirect effects are possible.

Other notable aspects of Figure 7.4 that are specific to path analysis include the covariance terms among all possible pairs of predictor variables and the *error terms* (e_1 and e_2) that affect y_1 and y_2. Finally, note that the straight lines represent path coefficients whereas curved lines indicate covariances. The term CV_{12} is an estimable parameter involving the covariation between x_1 and x_2.

As should be abundantly clear from chapter 5, customer satisfaction data are frequently plagued by ill-conditioning. Thus, only in *rare* cases are the covariances set to zero; they are typically estimated in applied customer satisfaction research.

Of special interest in path analysis is the ability of any predictor variable to affect any or all of the endogenous (y) variables. As shown in the Figure 7.4, an exogenous variable is permitted to *simultaneously* affect one, two, or even more outcome variables. This is a critical difference between regression analysis and path analysis. Nonetheless, path coefficients can be regarded as beta coefficients from regression analysis and, when compared numerically, are often very similar.

Path Analysis Assumptions

There are numerous books that provide extensive detail with respect to path analysis and its latent variable extensions. This chapter is intended merely to expose the reader to the technique and some of its more controversial aspects. First, consider some of the basic data assumptions underlying the use of path analysis:

- Normally distributed, interval or higher level endogenous data are requisite. Whereas the latter is rarely a problem; normality—or the lack thereof—can be disturbing to path models. This is especially true when it attenuates otherwise strong relationships between pairs of variables. Virtually all path analysis programs assume the endogenous variables contain a minimum of four values. Jöreskog and Sörbom's LISREL software is even more rigorous with respect to the scaling of the endogenous variable.
- As is the case with other linear techniques, path analysis assumes that the relations between variables are both linear and additive. That ill-conditioned predictor (x) variables could be problematic should also be considered seriously—particularly when the number of predictor variables exceeds 6 or 7.
- Psychometric data will always be characterized by some level of measurement error. As we know, questionnaire data are subject to a wide variety of error sources. As a result, we may never be able to fully satisfy this criterion.
- Inclusion of all nontrivial antecedents is a difficult challenge for any researcher and remains one of the most confounding aspects of social science research in general. As Hatcher (1994, 149) notes:

  "If important antecedent variables are omitted, the path coefficients for the remaining antecedents are less likely to be biased. If this requirement is met, the model is said to be self-contained *and all residual terms in the model should be noncorrelated."*

- From both applied and theoretical perspectives, we must be convinced that the "causal" side of the model is exhaustive. Researchers involved in customer satisfaction or loyalty research might, for example, seriously consider the effect of frequently overlooked variables such as employee satisfaction.

- A sufficient number of cases, as with virtually all multivariate analyses, is required to produce stable and robust path-analytic results. A wide variety of sample size prescriptions for path analysis have been offered over the past 60 years. Although "several hundred" observations has been the preferred heuristic for many years, contemporary authors have offered less equivocal prescriptions. Hatcher (1994, 149) suggests that the *minimal* number of observations be a ratio of the number of parameters to be estimated.

A review of the hypothesized model presented in Figure 7.4 will serve to illustrate Hatcher's (and others) approach to determining appropriate minimal sample sizes. The technique requires at least five observations times the total sum of estimable parameters. Note that one *could* specify a model under the conditions described later that requires fewer than 100 observations—a very dangerous proposition. Do not conduct path analysis (regardless of the number of estimable parameters) with fewer than 200 observations! The underlying covariance structures may still be too unstable to yield usable parameter estimates. Other, less stringent prescriptions have been offered by Ding, Velicer, and Harlow (1995) suggesting a *minimum* of 100 cases. On the other hand, more conservative writers such as Boomsma (1982, 1983) indicated 400 cases were necessary. Finally, Hu, Bentler, and Kano (1992, 351–62) suggested that in certain situations more than 5000 observations would be required to produce stable results!

The estimable parameters in a path analysis model include the following: the **path coefficients,** the *error variances* associated with endogenous (y) variables, and the *covariances* that will be estimated. With respect to Figure 7.4, this includes all the path coefficients (γ and β), all error (e) terms, and all (CV) covariance terms. Note that only in rare instances in which we have experiential, empirical, or theoretical reasons to justify doing so would we ever *omit* a covariance term among the exogenous variables.

First note the 10 covariance terms (CV_{12} through CV_{54}). Two error variances (e_1 and e_2) are also present because there are two endogenous variables (y_1 and y_2). Finally, we have specified a total of eight path coefficients to be estimated. Note that we are not estimating paths between product delivery (x_2) and loyalty (y_2) nor between sales rep relationship (x_3) and loyalty (y_2). Note also that technical support

TABLE 7.1 Listing of Estimable Parameters.

Covariance terms	10
Error variances	2
Path coefficients	8
Total estimable parameters	***20***

is constrained to affect loyalty (y_2) and not overall satisfaction. This, as in the other cases, is equivalent to constraining the parameters to zero. That is, our hypothesized model posits no effect will be present in the data. More specifically, with respect to Figure 7.4, we are assuming the correlation between technical support and overall satisfaction will be trivial and not statistically significant. The implications of this assumption will be described later in this section. Thus, it is *critical* to recognize we have constrained certain path coefficients to be zero. In effect, our hypothesized model does not permit either product delivery (x_2) nor sales rep relationship (x_3) to *directly* affect loyalty (y_2). In total we have 20 parameters to be estimated, as shown in Table 7.1.

Were we to embrace the sample size prescriptions proposed by some, at least 100 observations would be required to estimate the model depicted in Figure 7.1. Clearly, the prescriptions of other authors suggest that this would be a somewhat risky proposition because the resultant path model would be highly volatile.

CONFIRMATORY VERSUS EXPLORATORY MODELS

Until this point in our discussion of path analysis, the confirmatory nature of this technique has not been discussed at any length. Yet, it is the confirmatory nature of this technique that makes it so much more appealing than exploratory techniques. Examples of the latter include multiple regression analysis and PCA. In each case, a series of variables is subjected to the technique (for example, multiple regression), and the resultant output is examined for statistical significance or, in the case of PCA, rotated loading patterns.

Such is *not* the case with confirmatory techniques. Indeed, quite the opposite tack is employed. In confirmatory techniques like path analysis and its more sophisticated derivatives, which will be introduced later, the researcher first specifies the hypothesized model structure and then determines whether it is consistent with the covariance or correlation patterns in the data.

While in exploratory analysis our attention is focused on the statistical significance or contribution of individual variables, **confirmatory** analysis adopts a more holistic approach. When evaluating the suitability of a confirmatory model, we are generally concerned with how well the hypothesized model fits the relationships in the data. Consider the hypothetical model depicted in Figure 7.4 with respect to fit. In essence, (equation 7-1 and 7-2) are specified, one for each endogenous (y) variable:

$$y_1 = \gamma_{11}x_1 + \gamma_{12}x_2 + \gamma_{13}x_3 + \gamma_{14}x_4 + e_1 \tag{7-1}$$

$$y_2 = \gamma_{21}x_1 + \gamma_{24}x_4 + \gamma_{25}x_5 + \beta_{12}y_1 + e_2 \tag{7-2}$$

Note that this system of equations implicitly constrains to zero relations between x_2, x_3, and y_2 while also constraining x_5 to affect only y_2. The term β_{12}, of course, is included to demonstrate the effect of overall satisfaction on loyalty but need not *necessarily* be present. As implied earlier, model fit represents the extent to which the hypothesized model (that is, Figure 7.4) is consistent with the actual relations in the data set.

MODEL INPUT

It may be clear by now that the covariance matrix plays a substantive role in path analysis. Although correlation matrices accompanied by means and standard deviations are used, most computer programs will convert raw data into a variance-covariance matrix for analytical purposes. Nonetheless, the analyst has a variety of data input options, all of which will probably be converted to the variance-covariance matrix by the analytical software in question (Schumacker and Lomax 1996, 25).

Model "fit" simply refers to the extent to which the hypothesized model replicates the input variance-covariance matrix. Suppose, for example, that the model hypothesized in Figure 7.4 failed to recognize that technical support (x_5) exerted a *strong* effect on overall satisfaction (y_1). By not specifying this path, we are implicitly constraining the relationship between x_5 and y_1 to be zero despite the fact that it is actually quite substantial. This omission leads to "poor fit" and the regrettable conclusion that the hypothesized model must be rejected as invalid.

Fit is measured through a variety of statistics. A detailed discussion of them is beyond the scope of this book. Excellent treatments of fit statistics and model evaluations are given by Hu and Bentler

(1995, 76–99), Schumacker and Lomax (1996, 119–37) and Bollen (1989, 256–87). We will focus on the metric that is typically presented; knowledge of this will arm the reader with sufficient information to critically evaluate the fit of a causal model. The most well-known fit statistic is chi-squared. Typically, researchers are most interested when this value is sufficiently *high* that it reaches statistical significance at the 95 percent confidence level. In structural equation modeling, we are interested in the exact opposite. In effect, chi-squared measures *lack of fit;* thus, high levels that are statistically significant indicate poor fit. Chi-squared levels that do not reach statistical significance reflect hypothesized models that do not substantively depart from the relationships in the data. In short, a model is accepted if the chi-squared value is not significant.

Fortunately, although the purist may elect to discard his or her data and embrace a new hypothesized causal flow, seldom is this actually the case in practice. As shown in Figure 7.5, the model development process—although ostensibly confirmatory—frequently is quasi-exploratory and characterized by researchers who employ an iterative approach to model development.

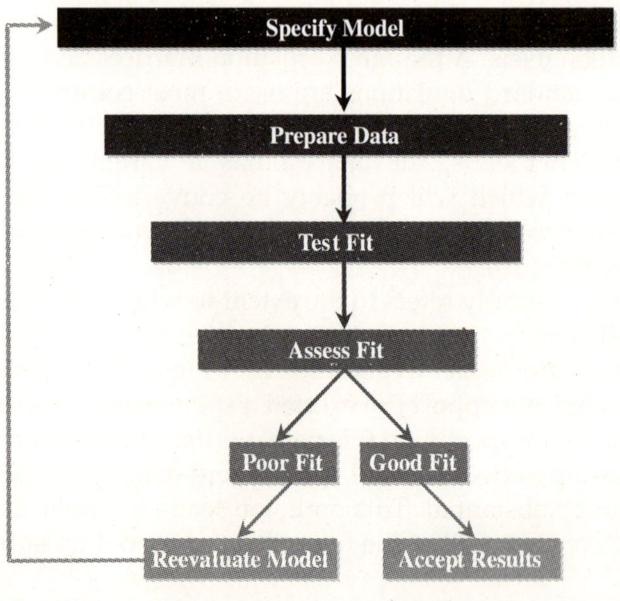

FIGURE 7.5 Quasi-confirmatory model-building approach.

CASE STUDY: DISCOUNT AUTO PARTS

This case study presents an easy-to-follow example of how path analysis works. The data includes three predictor variables—technical support, product quality, and sales service—which affect two outcome variables. The outcome variables are overall satisfaction and propensity to recommend Discount Auto Parts to a friend or colleague. The latter is assumed to be a surrogate for loyalty.

The hypothesized model is presented in Figure 7.6. As shown, the three predictor variables are presumed to affect overall satisfaction, which, in turn, may affect the loyalty measure. Note that any of the three predictor variables is permitted to exert an effect on either or both of the two outcome measures. That there is a path from each of the three predictor variables to both of the dependent variables confirms that this is a **saturated model.** A saturated model will fit the original data perfectly because none of the parameters is constrained to zero. Fit is determined by how well the hypothesized model reproduces the data covariances. A saturated model will exactly reproduce the original covariance matrix and therefore will have perfect fit.

The correlation matrix for the Discount Auto Parts data is quite revealing. As shown in Table 7.2, there are strong relationships among all the variables. The exception to this involves the third predictor variable (sales service), which is characterized by more modest intercorrelations with both outcome variables.

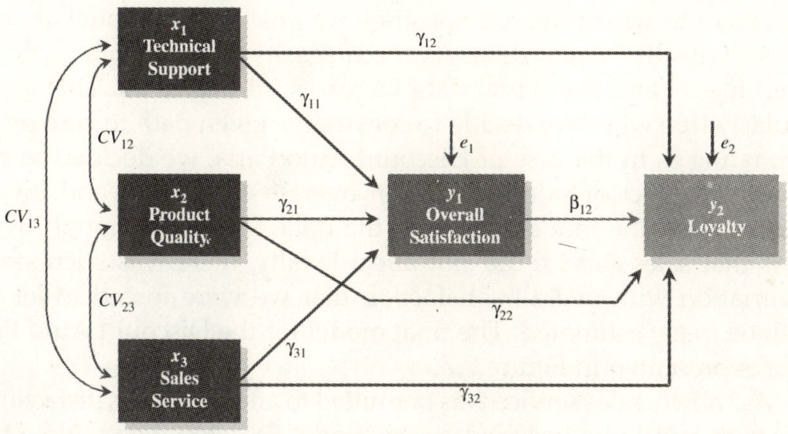

FIGURE 7.6 Saturated model for Discount Auto Parts.

TABLE 7.2 Correlation matrix for discount auto parts data.

	Overall Satisfaction	Loyalty	Tech Support	Product Quality	Sales Service
y_1. Overall satisfaction	1.00				
y_2. Loyalty	0.96	1.00			
x_1. Technical support	0.95	0.93	1.00		
x_2. Product quality	0.94	0.94	0.95	1.00	
x_3. Sales service	0.50	0.47	0.48	0.49	1.00

Indeed, sales service appears to play a minor role in the development of both overall satisfaction and loyalty. Its relationship with the other predictor variables is also quite modest. From a model development perspective, we might choose to constrain the effect of sales service on both outcome variables to zero. This means we are positing *a priori* that sales service will not affect either overall satisfaction or loyalty. There should be more than just our initial review of the correlation matrix to justify such an act; and in fact there is. Discount Auto Parts is well-known for its high-quality, polished sales tactics. As a result, we might not expect sales service evaluations to strongly covary with either of the two outcome variables. In contrast, once past the initial sales closing, Discount Auto Parts had a somewhat tarnished reputation with respect to its willingness or ability to service the parts it sells.

The notion of "fit" in causal models is an important one. It tells us the extent to which the relationships we posit in our model are consistent with the actual data. As the disparity between our hypothesized model and the actual data increases, fit decreases. This is particularly true when we decide to constrain a given path to zero by not estimating it. In the case of Discount Auto Parts, we decided to constrain the effect of sales service on overall satisfaction and loyalty. This affected the model's fit with the data. Indeed, although it was clear that sales service did not affect loyalty, there was such strong covariation with overall satisfaction that we were forced to let this path be freely estimated. The final model for the Discount Auto Parts data is presented in Figure 7.7.

As shown, sales service was permitted to affect overall satisfaction—this path had to be included or the model fit deteriorated. Note how the remaining two predictor variables affect the two outcome variables. First, product quality exerts a substantial effect on *both* overall satisfac-

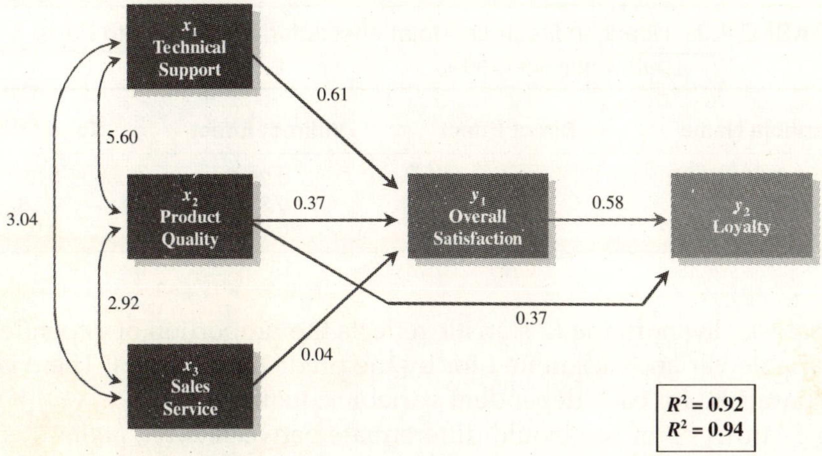

FIGURE 7.7 Discount Auto Parts path model.

tion and loyalty. In contrast, technical support affects only overall satisfaction. The model fit is excellent; the value of chi-squared is 2.8, which fails to reach statistical significance at the 95 percent confidence level. This confirms that the hypothesized model does not substantively differ from the actual relationships in the data.

There are two dependent variables in the model presented in Figure 7.7. As a result, two linear equations can summarize how satisfaction and loyalty are both interdependent and affected by the three predictor variables. Equations 7-3 and 7-4 summarize the mathematical relationships illustrated in Figure 7.7.

$$y_1 = 0.61_{x1} + 0.37_{x2} + 0.04_{x3} \tag{7-3}$$

$$y_2 = 0.37_{x2} + 0.58_{y1} \tag{7-4}$$

One of the most unique aspects of path analysis is that a dependent variable term may occur on the right side of one of the predictive equations. That is, a dependent variable is permitted to affect another dependent variable. This occurs in Equation 7-4 wherein y_2 is clearly affected most strongly by y_1, which is overall satisfaction.

Because there are two linear equations associated with the causal model depicted in Figure 7.7, it is not surprising that the explanatory power of each can also be assessed. The assessment of model efficacy in path analysis is identical to that employed in multiple regression

TABLE 7.3 Direct, indirect, and total effects for Discount Auto Parts path analysis model.

Variable Name	Direct Effect	Indirect Effect	Total Effect
Technical support	—	0.35	0.35
Product quality	0.37	0.21	0.58
Sales service	—	0.02	0.02

analysis. In short, the R^2 statistic reflects the proportion of dependent variable variance accounted for by the predictor variables. There is a separate R^2 for each dependent variable equation.

At this point we should differentiate between *direct, indirect,* and *total* effects. Each is considered with respect to the final outcome variable, loyalty. For example, product quality exerts both direct and indirect effects on loyalty. The direct effect is 0.37 whereas the indirect effect must be calculated. Indirect effects are exerted *through* a mitigating outcome variable such as, in this case, overall satisfaction. The indirect effect of product quality on loyalty is 0.37 *times* 0.58 (the effect of overall satisfaction on loyalty), which is equal to approximately 0.21. The total effect of each predictor variable is equal to the sum of its direct and indirect effects. The direct, indirect, and total effects of each predictor variable are presented in Table 7.3.

As we expected, sales service exerts the most trivial effect on the loyalty measure. Product quality, in contrast, emerged as having the strongest total effect on loyalty. Technically, because the path coefficients are equivalent to beta weights, we can make only *ordinal-level* inferences concerning their relative importance with respect to an outcome variable. The logic behind this assertion was discussed in chapter 5.

Case Study: OilTech

This case study represented a unique challenge because a variety of data sources were integrated in an effort to provide a high-level view of how employee satisfaction and customer satisfaction affected profitability. OilTech is a national retailer selling both gasoline and convenience items through their 800-store network. Since 1995, the company has made a concerted effort to collect customer satisfaction data at the store level.

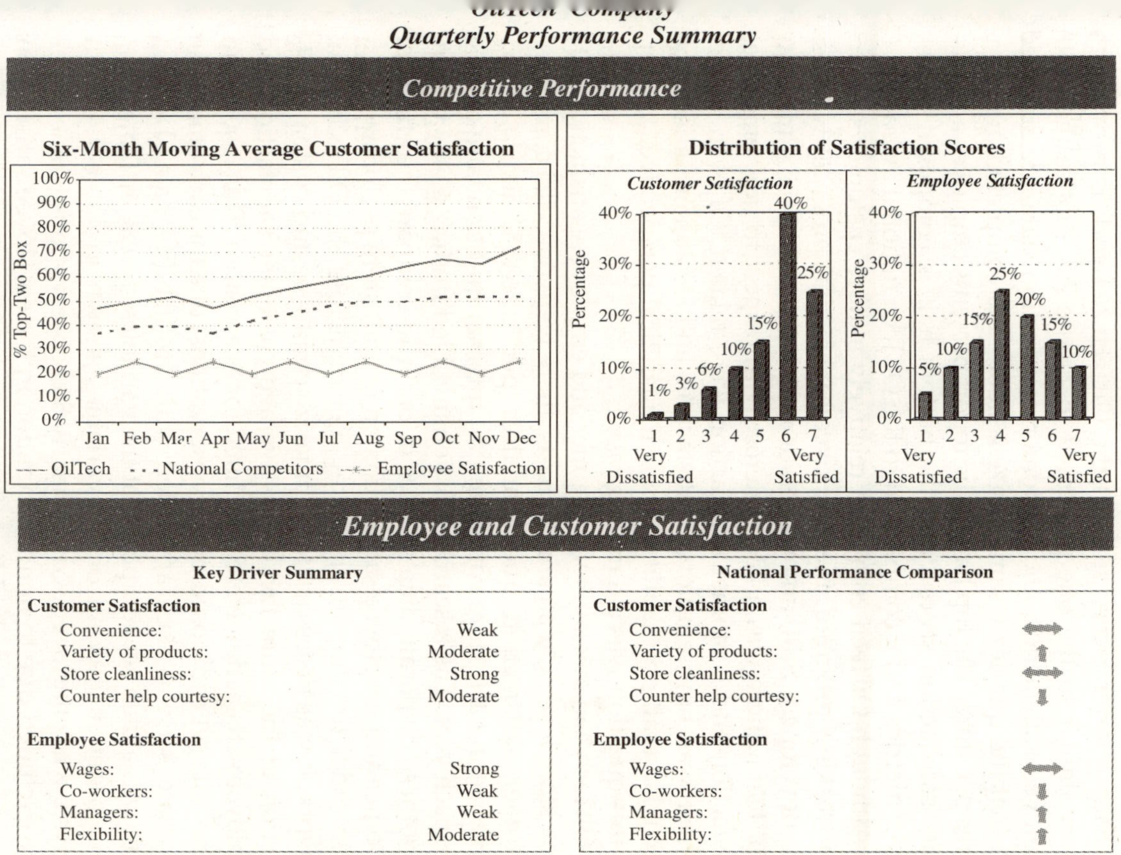

FIGURE 7.8 OilTech quarterly performance summary.

Each quarter, every store in the OilTech network is provided a report similar to the one presented in Figure 7.8. Notice that both employee satisfaction and customer satisfaction data are supplied and that the quarterly sample size is about 100 completed questionnaires per store. The top half of the report presents employee and customer satisfaction scores, and the bottom half is composed of key driver metrics and a comparison to the OilTech national average.

Although OilTech enjoyed a relatively mature customer satisfaction tracking program, the employee satisfaction program was less well developed. Still, among senior members of OilTech's management team, there was a keen interest with respect to how employee satisfaction and customer satisfaction were related. Of even greater interest was how employee satisfaction and customer satisfaction affected overall profitability. From an analytical perspective, answering this question was a daunting task.

OilTech had a wealth of consumer and employee satisfaction data at the store level. On an annual basis, there were over 400 completed customer satisfaction questionnaires per store. Similarly, every employee in each store completed an internal questionnaire at least once each year. The research question involved finding a way to integrate these disparate data sources in order to compare the effects of customer and employee satisfaction on overall store performance.

In order to compare these key metrics across the OilTech retail network, it was necessary to summarize employee and customer satisfaction at the store level. The average customer satisfaction and employee satisfaction were calculated for every store. This resulted in a new data set composed of 800 observations, one for each store. The new data set was then appended with profitability data. The end result was a data set composed of the variables shown in Table 7.4.

In order to link all of the variables shown in Table 7.4, path analysis was employed. Given nearly 800 observations (some stores were excluded due to nonparticipation in the employee satisfaction program, and others had insufficient observations for the customer satisfaction program), the path model presented in Figure 7.9 was hypothesized.

The model posited in Figure 7.9 suggests that both employee satisfaction and customer satisfaction affect profitability. In total, there are three dependent variables: employee satisfaction, customer satisfaction, and profitability. All of the variables except profitability were measured using a standard seven-point Likert scale. Profitability was provided by OilTech at the store level in actual dollars.

TABLE 7.4 OilTech key satisfaction and profit metrics.

Key Tracking Metric	Mean	Standard Deviation	Number Observations
Overall store profitability	$66,000	$9,534	800
Overall customer satisfaction	5.6	2.4	797
Convenience	6.2	0.9	797
Variety	5.5	1.4	797
Cleanliness	4.6	1.9	797
Courtesy	5.5	2.1	797
Overall employee satisfaction	5.5	2.1	783
Wages	3.2	2.6	783
Co-workers	5.9	2.4	783
Managers	3.4	2.7	782
Flexibility	6.4	1.3	783

Note: All satisfaction data measured with seven-point Likert scale.

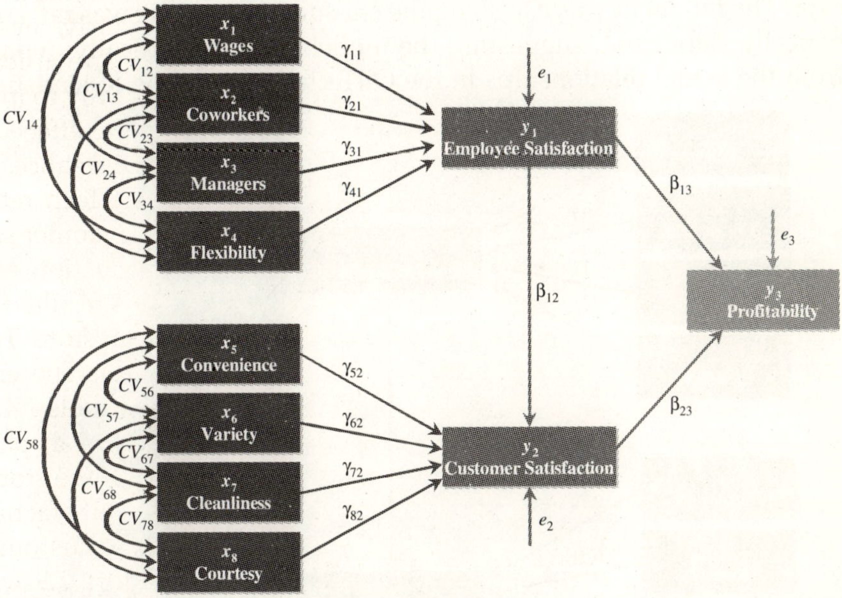

FIGURE 7.9 Hypothesized OilTech path model.

The overall model attempts to demonstrate the relative effects of employee satisfaction and customer satisfaction on store profitability. There is an arrow from employee satisfaction to customer satisfaction suggesting a causal relation between these two endogenous variables. Employee satisfaction is assumed to be a function of satisfaction with wages, co-workers, managers, and flexibility. Similarly, customer satisfaction is determined by store convenience, product variety, cleanliness, and courtesy.

Note that the exogenous variable covariances are essentially constrained within content area. That is, the four employee satisfaction variables covary with one another but not with the customer satisfaction variables. In a similar fashion, the customer satisfaction variables are constrained not to covary with the employee satisfaction variables. Whether this constraint affects model fit will be of some interest when the model is evaluated.

Figure 7.10 presents the fitted path model. As shown, all of the individual paths that were specified emerged as statistically significant. The model fit was excellent; the chi-squared statistic was not statistically significant, suggesting the model does not radically depart from the actual relationships in the OilTech data set. The R^2 statistics

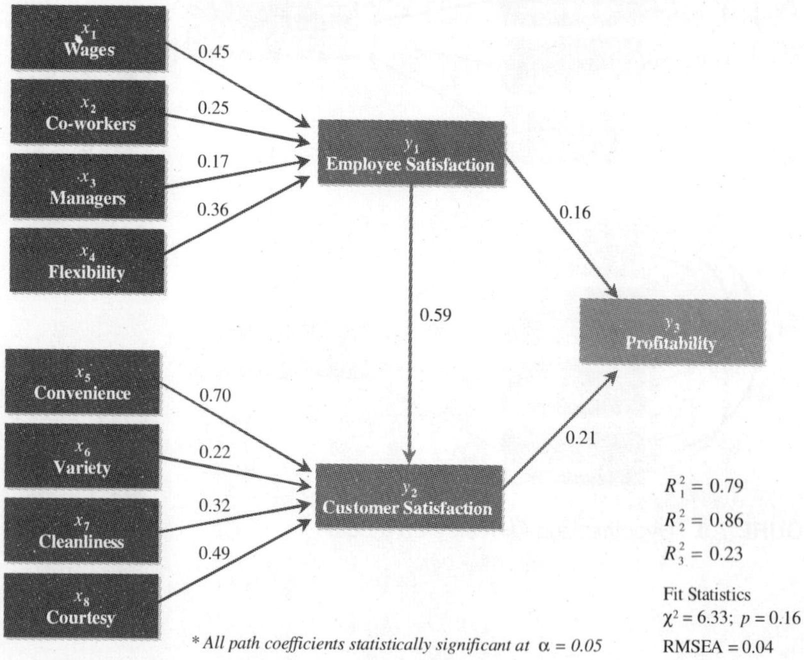

FIGURE 7.10 Final OilTech path analysis.

for each of the three dependent variables vary dramatically. Although more than three-quarters of the variance of employee satisfaction and customer satisfaction were accounted for by the exogenous variables, the model captured only 23 percent of the variance associated with the profitability variable. This is not unusual, however, because a myriad of exogenous environmental and other factors affect store profitability. In some cases, it is recommended that the profitability metric be scaled to accommodate differences in store sales volume potential or other factors that could have an effect on financial success.

The model presented in Figure 7.10 suggests that employee satisfaction and customer satisfaction, combined, account for nearly one-quarter of the variation in store profitability. The remaining variance must be attributed to other factors like accounting procedures, competitive forces, and other environmental considerations. Still, the ability to control one-quarter of the variation in store profitability is a significant finding and was of great interest to OilTech senior management. The direct, indirect, and total effects of the exogenous variables are presented in Table 7.5.

Of the eight exogenous variables in the model, store *convenience* appears to have the greatest impact on profitability. That is, the extent to which customers perceive OilTech to represent a convenient place to purchase gas or other items is associated with profitability. Subsequent analysis of this data revealed that OilTech stores placed in areas with high-population density and fewer direct competitors were most profitable. This finding was consistent with the OilTech overall business strategy that dictated placement of new stores in urban areas with high concentrations of multiunit housing. The path analysis results precipitated a management review of all OilTech stores with

TABLE 7.5. Direct, indirect, and total effects on profitability.

Variable	Direct Effect	Indirect Effect	Total Effect
Employee Satisfaction			
Wages	—	0.13	0.13
Co-workers	—	0.07	0.07
Managers	—	0.05	0.05
Flexibility	—	0.10	0.10
Customer Satisfaction			
Convenience	—	0.15	0.15
Variety	—	0.05	0.05
Cleanliness	—	0.07	0.07
Courtesy	—	0.10	0.10

respect to their demographic surroundings. Some locations once considered desirable had undergone great changes in terms of population dynamics and were eventually closed.

The second strongest predictor of overall OilTech store profitability involved an item from the employee satisfaction questionnaire: wages. Stores with employees who were more satisfied with their compensation tended to be more profitable. And of course, conversely, stores with employees who were dissatisfied with their pay tended to be much less profitable. The pay issue was easier to address in terms of a cost-benefit analysis. Because the discrepancy between OilTech employee pay and the prevailing wage rate in the area could be readily gauged, it was relatively easy to assess the relationship between this gap and employee satisfaction with wages. The resulting simple linear regression model confirmed that for every $0.25 increase in pay, employee satisfaction would increase by 0.28 points on the seven-point Likert scale. Given this model, OilTech then was able to calculate the *profit* implications of wage increases in every one of their 800 stores. In those stores characterized by wages higher than the prevailing rate, no changes were made. However, in those for which a substantive discrepancy was found, it was possible to test the impact of various wage increases on overall corporate profitability.

The OilTech case illustrates how both employee satisfaction and customer satisfaction data can be integrated at a common unit of analysis. Although these data were obtained from different sources (customers and employees), it was possible to construct a new data set at the store level. The nearly 800 observations at the store level permitted inferences that would otherwise have been precluded.

Causal modeling has greatly enhanced the value of customer satisfaction. We can now depict customer satisfaction as an *intermediate construct* that affects other variables such as loyalty or profitability. The most important aspects to retain concerning causal modeling in customer satisfaction research include the following. First, causal modeling does not prove causation—instead, this technique simply confirms that the relationships in the data are consistent with the hypothesized causal structure. Next, the model development process—although confirmatory—tends to be iterative and should be theory-driven. We also demonstrated how predictor variables exert direct, indirect, and total effects on the final outcome variable. Path analysis is a complex topic, and a detailed treatment is well beyond the scope of this book. Our intent was to provide the reader with enough information to understand the basic assumptions and outputs the technique offers.

Chapter 8

Interdependence Models: The Dimensionality of Satisfaction

Introduction

In chapter 5, a variety of dependence models were introduced. Within a customer satisfaction analysis framework, these models were shown to focus on how one (or more) outcome variables were dependent upon one or more predictor variables. **Interdependence models** involve a different type of relationship. There are neither predictor nor outcome variables. Rather, all variables and their interrelationships are considered simultaneously.

One question we frequently encounter in customer satisfaction research involves the construct's *dimensionality.* Despite the myriad aspects of products and services we ask respondents to evaluate, we know that underlying these evaluations are a few general dimensions. For example, although we might ask new car buyers about a host of issues including their satisfaction with various aspects of the sales process, delivery, vehicle condition, power, styling, and so on, it is unlikely that consumers review all of these details individually when considering a new car purchase. Rather, a few broad dimensions that subsume these specific issues are considered. Styling, power, and value might be the underlying dimensions of consumer satisfaction when automobiles are considered. Similarly, when a financial services provider is considered, the underlying dimensions may involve rates, service, and convenience.

Principal Components and Factor Analysis

To reveal the dimensions underlying customer satisfaction evaluations, we use techniques such as factor analysis and PCA. Many researchers erroneously consider them interchangeable and refer to all models in this family as "factor analysis." Factor analysis and PCA are both dimension reducing techniques but are not interchangeable. Nonetheless, they frequently produce very similar results.

PCA is an *atheoretic* approach that yields linear combinations of variables that account for successively less variance in the original data set. PCA is a dimension reducing tool that simply yields a set of factors (technically "components" or "component factors") that best account for variation in the data set.

In contrast to PCA, factor analysis is based upon a presumed, underlying causal structure. The observed variables are believed to be *caused* by some unseen latent construct. For example, the ability to perform well in a math test is caused by an unobservable construct: analytical intelligence. Conceptually, this is a very different approach compared to PCA. In the final analysis, PCA is geared toward reducing the dimensionality of a data set, whereas factor analysis seeks to reveal the latent constructs that presumably *cause* the variables we have measured.

In applied customer satisfaction research, there has been little regard for the distinction just described. Which should be used in the advanced analysis of customer satisfaction data? The answer depends somewhat on the research objectives. For example, in a dependence model framework characterized by a high degree of collinearity, we would use PCA to circumvent the problem. In this case, underlying causal structures are of no real interest. Instead, the objective is purely mathematic—to produce a data set free from the degrading effects of collinearity. On the other hand, with a battery of 25 miscellaneous items relating to satisfaction with a new product, we would be inclined to use factor analysis. In this case, we are more interested in the factors underlying our measurements, not a convenient mathematical solution to a vexing problem in regression analysis.

Exploratory versus Confirmatory Analysis

One final distinction should be kept in mind throughout this discussion. Dimension reducing analysis can be *exploratory* or *confirmatory,* as shown in Figure 8.1. In customer satisfaction research, factor analy-

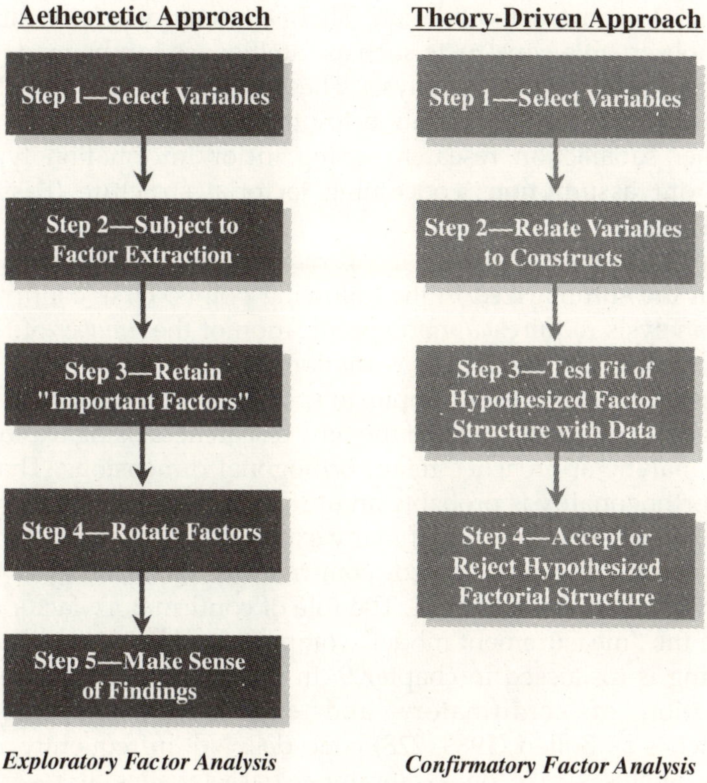

FIGURE 8.1 Exploratory versus confirmatory factor analysis.

sis is typically used in an exploratory fashion. There are no hypotheses regarding the factor structure. The approach is very much like that implicitly used in regression analysis. In regression analysis, we typically have a single outcome variable that is regressed on a series of predictor variables. We do not specify *before* running the model which predictor variables we feel will covary significantly with the outcome variable.

In exploratory factor analysis, there are no *a priori* hypotheses regarding factor composition or structure. In contrast, confirmatory factor analysis requires the explicit formulation of hypotheses regarding the underlying structure. The proposed structure is then accepted or rejected depending upon the **goodness-of-fit statistic**: the extent to which the data are consistent with the hypothesized factor structure. Heck (1998, 179–80) describes confirmatory factor analysis as one approach to construct validation. That is, inferences concerning certain unobservable constructs such as intelligence can be made based upon confirmatory factor analysis. These inferences often involve the construct's structure and relation to other constructs. In an applied customer satisfaction research setting, prior information typically drives our assumptions concerning factorial structure (Basilevsky 1994, 414–15).

The differences between confirmatory and exploratory factor analysis are summarized in the following points. First, confirmatory factor analysis requires *a priori* specification of the *number* of factors, their composition, and their covariation. In exploratory factor analysis, it is not possible, for example, to specify the degree to which two factors covary. Indeed, most of the time researchers using exploratory factor analytic approaches retain orthogonal dimensions. That construct orthogonality is probably an unrealistic assumption represents a very substantive criticism of many exploratory factor analyses.

As Heck (1998, 200) noted, confirmatory factor analysis is frequently the first stage of SEM. The role of confirmatory factor analysis and the "measurement model" component of latent variable path modeling is discussed in chapter 9. In practice, there is a less clear delineation of confirmatory and exploratory factor analytic approaches as Bollen (1989, 228) concedes. Not infrequently, confirmatory analyses take on exploratory characteristics as researchers iteratively redefine their ostensibly confirmatory analyses in a search for the model that best "fits" the data.

In reality, researchers pursuing a confirmatory approach do not simply leave their data if the hypothesized factor structure is rejected. Confirmatory analysis is iterative, as shown in Figure 8.2. Nunnally (1978, 347–48) provides a succinct description of the differences between these seemingly oppositional approaches to factor analysis.

Data Structures for Factor Analysis and Principal Components Analysis

Both factor analysis and PCA require interval- or ratio-level data. There are other dimension reducing techniques for lower-level data that are not discussed in this book. Typically, customer satisfaction data are collected at the interval level. Of some concern are data that *technically* are ordinal (for example, a fully anchored four-point scale) but are treated as interval. That many researchers subject data that are probably ordinal to both factor analysis and PCA reflects how fre-

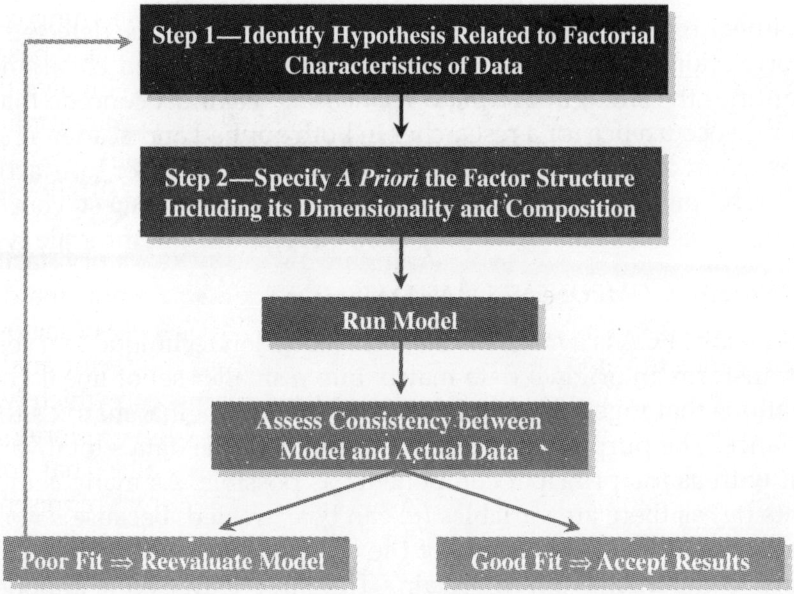

FIGURE 8.2 Iterative nature of confirmatory factor analysis.

quently misused these techniques are. Given that many marketing researchers cannot fully articulate the conceptual and mathematical differences between factor analysis and PCA, it is not surprising that this fundamental assumption is so frequently violated!

Assuming interval-level data, we must have a sufficient number of observations to yield stable and meaningful results. With customer satisfaction data, this is seldom a concern. Prescriptions concerning a minimum number of observations for either factor analysis or PCA vary from a low of about 200 to as many as 400. Note that missing values can rapidly deplete the size of your data set. It is not at all uncommon to lose more than 50 percent of a data set because of missing values. If you are not imputing missing values for your multivariate analysis, pay close attention to the number of *valid observations* because it could represent only a fraction of the complete data set.

Finally, the most widely disregarded data condition assumed by factor analysis and PCA involves normality. In short, each variable should be normally distributed. This is unfortunately rarely the case! We also must assume that all of the pairwise relationships in our data set are linear. As will be discussed later, both factor analysis and PCA operate on either a correlation matrix or covariance matrix. A strong, nonlinear relationship between two variables will not be detected by a correlation coefficient. The correlation coefficient (and covariance) quantifies the strength of a *linear relationship.* We must concede that it is a rare occurrence for a researcher in both applied and academic settings to test all of these assumptions. In applied customer satisfaction research, the matter of normality should be of greatest concern because these data are invariably skewed regardless of the scale type.

Principal Components Analysis

Technically, PCA is a multivariate data reduction technique that seeks to transform an original data matrix into a smaller set of linear combinations that together account for most of the original matrix's total variance. The purpose is to explain as much of the data's total variation with as *few* principal components as possible. As many components (m) as there are variables (p) can be extracted. Because $p = m$ is not a parsimonious reduction of the data, one must determine how many components (m) to retain. The first extracted component accounts for the most original data matrix variance. Subsequent extractions account for less and less variance until $p = m$. In short, PCA (and factor analysis) yield as many factors as there are variables. The objective is to develop a parsimonious reduction of the data matrix. This means we must account for as much of the original data variation with as few components as possible.

$$
\begin{aligned}
PC_{(1)} &= w_{(1)1}x_1 + w_{(1)2}x_2 + w_{(1)3}x_3 + \ldots + w_{(1)p}x_p \\
PC_{(2)} &= w_{(2)1}x_1 + w_{(2)2}x_2 + w_{(2)3}x_3 + \ldots + w_{(2)p}x_p \\
PC_{(3)} &= w_{(3)1}x_1 + w_{(3)2}x_2 + w_{(3)3}x_3 + \ldots + w_{(3)p}x_p \\
\vdots \quad & \quad \vdots \qquad\quad \vdots \qquad\quad \vdots \qquad\qquad\quad \vdots \\
PC_{(m)} &= w_{(m)1}x_1 + w_{(m)2}x_2 + w_{(m)3}x_3 + \ldots + w_{(m)p}x_p
\end{aligned}
$$

In this example, the first component $PC_{(1)}$ is the linear combination of the observed variables x_j, $j = 1, 2 \ldots, p$ where the weights $w_{(1)1}$, $w_{(1)2}, \ldots, w_{(1)}p$ are selected to maximize the ratio of the variance of the first component $PC_{(1)}$ to the *total* variation. The next component, $PC_{(2)}$, is the weighted linear combination of the original variables that is *uncorrelated* with the first and accounts for the maximum amount of the total remaining variation. As shown, it is possible to extract as many components as there are variables. However, the goal of PCA (and factor analysis) is to account for as much variance in the original data matrix with as *few* components as possible. Determining how many components (or factors) to retain will be discussed in detail.

PCA and factor analysis decompose correlation matrices. In PCA, the diagonal of the correlation matrix is assumed to be composed of ones, as shown in Table 8.1. The diagonal of ones in the correlation matrix makes it easy to see its symmetry. The upper triangle is a mirror image of the lower triangle. In practice, only the lower triangle is depicted in reports; it is shown here to illustrate the actual matrix and its symmetrical property.

Table 8.1 contains a hypothetical correlation matrix that has two clearly visible pockets of strong intercorrelations. The first involves the relationship between variables x_1 through x_4, which are highlighted in the upper left of the correlation matrix. The second pocket of strong correlations appears in the lower right of the matrix and involves variables x_5 through x_9. Note that other than these two areas, the matrix is characterized by relatively low correlations. It would be safe to assume that if subjected to PCA (or factor analysis), this matrix would yield a two-component solution. That is, most of the variance in the correlation matrix could be accounted for with two principal components. Furthermore, because we know PCA extracts components that account for less and less of the original data matrix variance, it would be reasonable to conclude that the first factor will involve variables x_6–x_9 because they are characterized by the strongest intercorrelations. Figure 8.3 illustrates how components (or factors) are drawn. As shown, the first component is orthogonal to the

TABLE 8.1 Sample correlation matrix.

	x_1	x_2	x_3	x_4	x_5	x_6	x_7	x_8	x_9
x_1	**1.0**	0.89	0.79	0.87	0.14	0.22	0.21	0.22	0.01
x_2	0.89	**1.0**	0.89	0.89	0.04	0.12	0.31	0.12	0.11
x_3	0.79	0.89	**1.0**	0.92	0.22	0.23	0.22	0.41	0.24
x_4	0.87	0.89	0.92	**1.0**	0.14	0.13	0.22	0.15	0.09
x_5	0.14	0.04	0.22	0.14	**1.0**	0.97	0.98	0.92	0.98
x_6	0.22	0.12	0.23	0.13	0.97	**1.0**	0.95	0.98	0.92
x_7	0.21	0.31	0.22	0.22	0.98	0.95	**1.0**	0.94	0.93
x_8	0.22	0.12	0.41	0.15	0.92	0.98	0.94	**1.0**	0.97
x_9	0.01	0.11	0.24	0.09	0.98	0.92	0.93	0.97	**1.0**

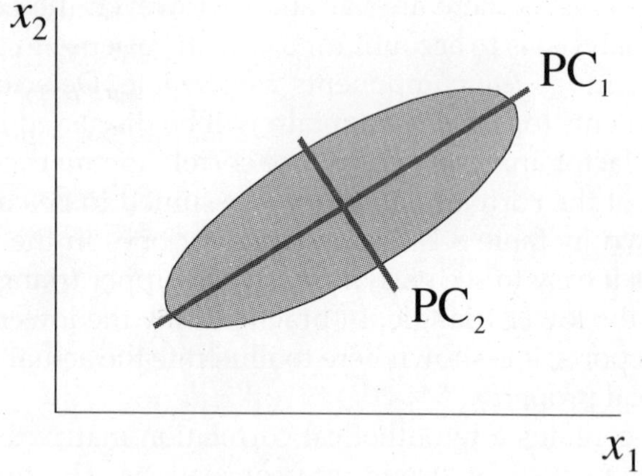

FIGURE 8.3 Principal components of bivariate data.

second and accounts for the most *variation* in the data. The second component accounts for less variation. Had this figure been presented in three dimensions, a third line would have been drawn through the z-axis of the data cluster.

That the diagonal of the correlation matrix in Table 8.1 is composed of ones differentiates this technique from factor analysis. The total variance to be accounted for in a correlation matrix subjected to the PCA technique is equal to the sum of the diagonal elements, which all happen to be ones. For the correlation matrix presented in Table 8.1, this equals nine, which is also the number of variables in the analysis because each contributes one unit of variance. As will be shown later, our objective is to account for as much of this total variance with as few components as possible.

Common Factor Analysis

Factor analysis, unlike PCA, assumes that the variables you measure are *caused* by unobservable latent constructs. We demonstrated earlier how a principal component is a linear combination of the analysis variables. In factor analysis, the *variables are considered to be linear combinations of the factors.* Jolliffe (1986, 123) summarizes the implications of this difference succinctly:

> *A final difference between principal components and common factors is that the former can be calculated exactly from x, whereas the latter typically cannot. The PCs are exact linear functions of x. The factors, however, are not exact linear functions of x; instead x is*

defined as a linear function of f (the factors) apart from an error term, and when the relationship is reversed it certainly does not lead to an exact relationship between f and x. Indeed the fact that the expected value of x is a linear function of f need not imply that the expected value of f is a linear function of x. . . ."

The preceding point is an important one and the source of considerable confusion. It should not be surprising, though, given the extent to which references to the two techniques are so loosely interchanged.

First principal component is a linear combination of the variables

Principal Components Approach

$$PC_{(1)} = w_{(1)1}x_1 + w_{(1)2}x_2 + w_{(1)3}x_3 + \ldots + w_{(1)p}x_p$$

First variable is a linear combination of the common factors

Common Factor Analysis Approach

$$x_1 = w_{(1)}(F_1) + w_{(2)}(F_2) + w_{(3)}(F_3) + \ldots + w_{(k)}(F_k) + w_{(u)}(F_u)$$

The most intriguing difference between common factor analysis and PCA involves the decomposition of each variable's variance. Factor analysis assumes that in addition to being caused by unobservable latent constructs, the variance of a variable can be separated into two parts: common and unique. Figure 8.4 depicts how a variable's variance is decomposed. As shown, 15 percent of the variable's variance is unique. This means it is not shared with any of the other variables included in our analysis data set. Note that a variable's common and unique variance is context-specific. If variables are added or removed from the analysis data set, a given variable's unique and common variance ratio will likely change.

A variable's unique variance can be further decomposed into two components: specific variance and random error. Specific variance is unique to a variable and not shared with any of the other variables in the data set. Random error variance, too, is not shared with other variables. In common factor analysis, our focus is on revealing the dimensionality of the variance *common* to the variables in the data set. In effect, we want to *exclude* specific variance. Recall that this is not the case in PCA.

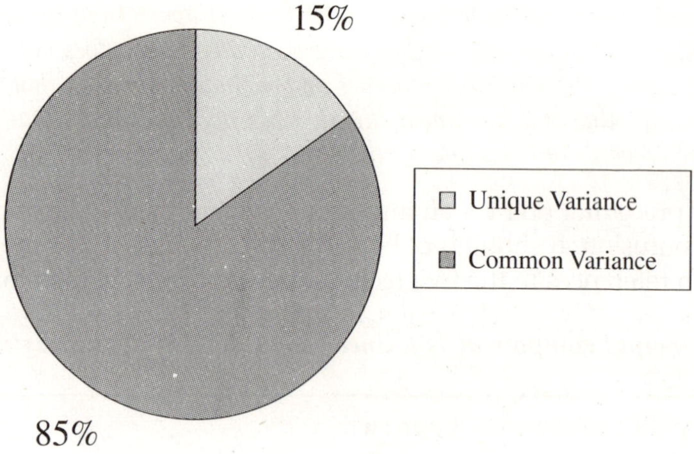

FIGURE 8.4 Common and unique variable variance.

Earlier we presented the correlation matrix for analysis with PCA and noted the diagonal was composed of ones. The implication of this is that all of each variable's variance is being included in the factor decomposition. In common factor analysis, we want to remove the unique variances and decompose only the common variance. One of the most contentious aspects of common factor analysis involves the "**communality indeterminacy.**" In effect, we must replace the ones in the diagonal of the correlation matrix with "**communalities,**" which represent each variable's *common* variance (Everitt 1998, 69). Unfortunately, these are not known until the common factors are extracted—this is the primary factor indeterminacy problem addressed by Harman (1976, 27–28), Rummel (1970, 105), and many others. As a result, common factor analysis communalities are typically estimated by using the squared multiple correlation (R^2) of each variable with the others. Thus, the diagonal of ones is replaced with these *estimates* of common variance. This represents the primary mathematical difference between common factor analysis and PCA. Again, in PCA there are no assumptions made about common and unique variance and therefore no need to generate communalities.

As described earlier, the conceptual or theoretical chasm between factor analysis and PCA is wider than the mathematical difference. In particular, factor analysis tends to be *theory-driven* whereas PCA is generally considered to be an *atheoretic* approach. Figure 8.5 presents

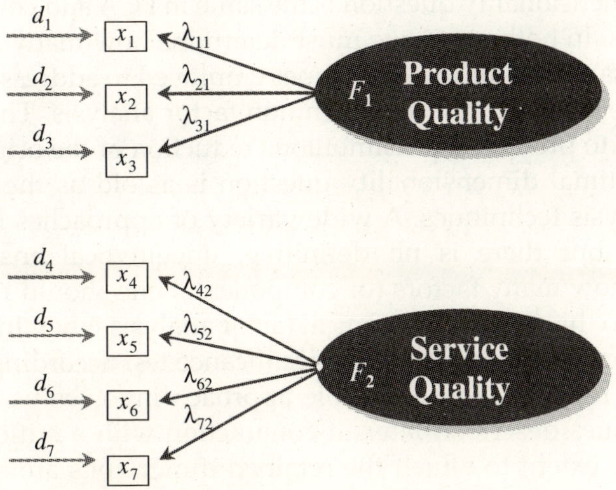

FIGURE 8.5 Common factor model.

an example of the common factor model. Note that the direction of the arrows reflects the presumption that the unseen constructs *cause* the observed variables. The greek letter lambda (λ) is typically used to denote the relationship between a factor (or component) and a variable. Thus, the symbol λ_{21} denotes the relationship between x_2 and the first factor (F_1).

How Many Factors or Components?

There are a number of heuristic and objective methods of determining how many principal components or common factors to retain. Remember that both techniques extract as many dimensions (p) as there are variables (k). Clearly, a k-factor solution is very undesirable because no data reduction has been achieved!

Both common factor analysis and PCA extract dimensions in the same fashion. That is, the first factor (or component) accounts for the most data matrix variance, the second accounts for less, and so on. Note that each successive factor (or component) is also orthogonal (that is, perfectly uncorrelated) with those that precede it. Eventually, as p approaches k, the amount of variation explained by each factor becomes trivial. Our objective is to retain only those dimensions that account for a substantive proportion of the original data matrix variance.

The dimensionality question is the same in PCA and common factor analysis. In both cases, we must determine how many factors (or components) to retain. The techniques employed to address this question are the same in PCA and common factor analysis. The primary objective is to produce a parsimonious reduction of the original data.

The optimal dimensionality question is as old as the PCA and factor analysis techniques. A wide variety of approaches have been suggested, but there is no definitive, unequivocal answer with respect to how many factors (or components) one should retain. The exception to this involves canonical factor analysis wherein the number of factors is determined by a significance test according to Rummel (1970, 169). The most sensible approach involves using one of the techniques described later in conjunction with a critical assessment of the extent to which the retained dimensions are intuitively palatable.

Approaches to the dimensionality question range from heuristic to empirical. One well-known heuristic approach involves the scree test in which the eigenvalues of the data matrix are plotted. The point at which the eigenvalue magnitude drops sharply is considered to be indicative of a drop in explanatory power.

The scree test is so named because we are interested in the breakpoint in the plot of eigenvalues. Incidentally, scree is the pile of rocks and stones at the base of a steep slope or cliff.

Figure 8.6 shows a typical eigenvalue plot used for a scree test. As shown, there is subtle change in slope between the third and fourth eigenvalues. The scree test suggests we retain three factors in the case of the data presented in Figure 8.6. Clearly, the scree test is somewhat subjective. The example in Figure 8.6 is susceptible to different interpretations—one could argue convincingly that a fourth factor should be retained.

As Jolliffe (1986, 93) observed, the most straightforward approach to determining how many dimensions to retain involves the cumulative proportion of variance accounted for. Retaining as many factors as necessary to "explain" more than 70 percent of the original data variance would be a reasonable criterion to use. This has been a popular approach to the dimensionality problem as evidenced by its use as a default selection mechanism in the most popular statistical software packages. Nonetheless, the approach has been criticized as too mechanistic (Jackson 1991, 44) by some.

It should be clear that there is no single best way to determine how many factors should be retained in either factor analysis or PCA.

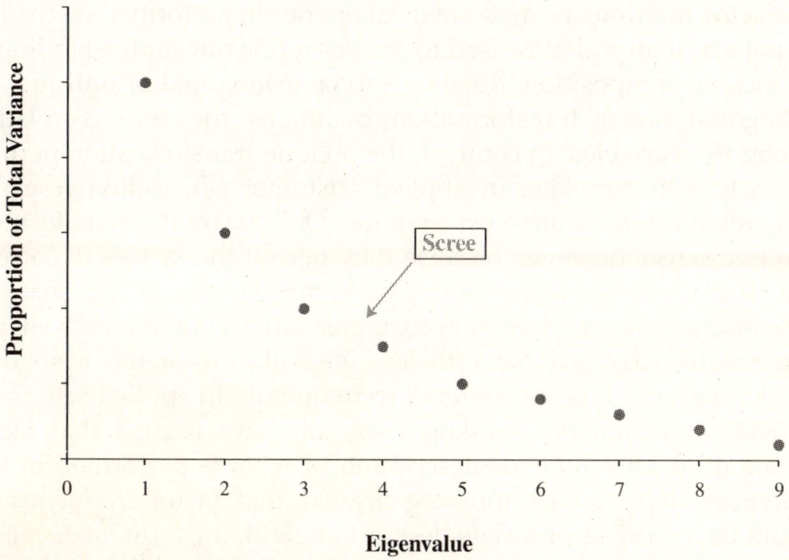

FIGURE 8.6 Example of a scree test.

Although a wide variety of heuristics have been proposed, none is unequivocal. Jackson (1991, 56) compared seven methods (Bartlett's test, Proportion of Trace Explained, Residual Variances, Scree Test, Broken Stick Test, Average Root, and Velicer's Method) using a data set with 14 variables. Using the seven approaches, he examined the extent to which they agreed with respect to the number of dimensions to retain. The seven techniques yielded widely ranging recommendations in terms of the number of factors to retain. Whereas one technique confirmed a one-factor solution, another suggested keeping 10 factors. This discrepancy across techniques simply underscores the problematic nature of the dimensionality question. Perhaps the best advice would be to combine one's own intuition with one or more of the techniques described by Jackson.

Rotating Factors or Components

Principal components (or factors) meet two mathematical criteria. First, they are all orthogonal; that is, they are perfectly uncorrelated. Further, each factor accounts for a diminishing amount of variance in the original correlation matrix. Recall that as many components (or factors) as there are variables will be produced, and that it is the researcher's job to decide how many components to retain.

Factor rotation is a mathematical operation performed on the factor pattern matrix that is used to further refine our understanding of the factors' composition. Rotation can be **orthogonal** or **oblique.** An orthogonal factor transformation maintains the zero correlation among the variables. In contrast, the oblique transformation permits the factors to correlate. In applied customer satisfaction research, orthogonal rotations are most common. Oblique rotations make more intuitive sense, however, because they permit the factors to correlation. This is a more *realistic* approach because we know that many of the constructs we work with in customer satisfaction research should be permitted to covary. Nevertheless, we will focus on the orthogonal rotation because it is encountered so frequently in applied settings.

Some researchers (Jöreskog 1963, 18) have argued that factor "rotation" is an erroneous description of what is performed in this analytical step. Rather, Jöreskog argued that factor *transformation* would be a more appropriate description. Still, the term *rotation* is so well-accepted in both academic and applied research settings it would be futile to argue for a change in terminology.

Rotation is performed in an effort to maximize some outcome. In the case of factor analysis and PCA, the objective is **simple structure.** This term was first introduced by Thurstone (1935, 156) and has three conditions:

- Each rotated pattern matrix row should have at least one zero.
- Each column of the rotated pattern matrix should have at least as many zero entries as there are retained factors.
- For every pair of columns in the rotated pattern matrix, there should be minimally *m* variables that have substantive nonzero loadings in one column but not the other.

Thurstone later (1947, 58) provided a more meaningful definition of simple structure grounded in behavioral psychology:

> *Just as we take it for granted that individual differences in visual acuity are not involved in pitch discrimination, so we assume that in intellectual tasks some mental or cortical functions are not involved in every task. This is the principle of "simple structure" or "simple configuration" in the underlying order for any given set of attributes."*

Thus, simple structure is more than a desirable mathematical characteristic—it involves the basic foundation of measurement theory. In

TABLE 8.2 Rotated factors with perfect simple structure.

Variable	*F1*	*F2*	*F3*	*F4*
X_1	1.00	0.00	0.00	0.00
X_2	1.00	0.00	0.00	0.00
X_3	1.00	0.00	0.00	0.00
X_4	0.00	1.00	0.00	0.00
X_6	0.00	1.00	0.00	0.00
X_7	0.00	0.00	1.00	0.00
X_8	0.00	0.00	1.00	0.00
X_9	0.00	0.00	1.00	0.00
X_{10}	0.00	0.00	1.00	0.00
X_{11}	0.00	0.00	0.00	1.00
X_{12}	0.00	0.00	0.00	1.00

applied customer satisfaction research and other fields involving the measurement of psychological phenomena, the search for pure constructs is closely related to establishing factor patterns with simple structure.

The key to understanding factor or component rotation is that it is performed in an effort to facilitate our understanding of the underlying structure. Perfect simple structure would yield the best possible pattern of zeros and ones. Table 8.2 presents a hypothetical case involving perfect simple structure. As shown, every variable loads on only one factor, and these loadings represent perfect (1.00) correlations.

In applied customer satisfaction research, orthogonal factor rotations are performed as a matter of course. Is the rotation step necessary? No, not really. It simply facilitates our understanding of how the factors differ. And, in this regard, it is an extremely useful step to perform. Rotation simply reallocates the variance accounted for by the retained factors. Whether one decides to perform orthogonal versus oblique rotation is beyond the scope of this introductory treatment. Suffice it to say that oblique rotations may be more realistic inasmuch as the resultant factors are permitted to correlate.

Case Study: Personal Computer Purchase Experience

This case study involves a PC manufacturer that was interested in how consumers perceived the purchase and ownership experience. The data set has been simplified to facilitate an understanding of the basic concepts underlying PCA and factor analysis. As shown in Figure 8.7, the survey instrument is composed of 10 items. The first nine can be treated as predicting the single outcome variable (overall satisfaction)

We're interested in how well we're serving you as a customer. Based upon your recent purchase of an Action PC, how satisfied are you with each aspect of the sales and ownership experience? Please use the seven-point scale provided below to rate each of the issues.

	Very Dissatisfied						Very Satisfied
1. Price of system	1 ❑	2 ❑	3 ❑	4 ❑	5 ❑	6 ❑	7 ❑
2. Price of accessories	1 ❑	2 ❑	3 ❑	4 ❑	5 ❑	6 ❑	7 ❑
3. Product reliability	1 ❑	2 ❑	3 ❑	4 ❑	5 ❑	6 ❑	7 ❑
4. Product set-up time	1 ❑	2 ❑	3 ❑	4 ❑	5 ❑	6 ❑	7 ❑
5. Product design	1 ❑	2 ❑	3 ❑	4 ❑	5 ❑	6 ❑	7 ❑
6. Product quality	1 ❑	2 ❑	3 ❑	4 ❑	5 ❑	6 ❑	7 ❑
7. Sales representative knowledge	1 ❑	2 ❑	3 ❑	4 ❑	5 ❑	6 ❑	7 ❑
8. Sales representative courtesy	1 ❑	2 ❑	3 ❑	4 ❑	5 ❑	6 ❑	7 ❑
9. Sales representative speed	1 ❑	2 ❑	3 ❑	4 ❑	5 ❑	6 ❑	7 ❑

Overall, considering all of these aspects of your ownership and purchase experience, how satisfied are you with your Action PC? Please use the same scale where 1 means you are very dissatisfied and 7 means you are very satisfied.

	Very Dissatisfied						Very Satisfied
Overall Satisfaction	1 ❑	2 ❑	3 ❑	4 ❑	5 ❑	6 ❑	7 ❑

FIGURE 8.7 Action PC questionnaire excerpt.

in a dependence model framework. In the present case, we are more interested in the first nine questions. More specifically, our focus is on the dimensions underlying these nine items because we know very few consumers use nine independent criteria in their evaluations of any product. In short, we are interested in reducing the *dimensionality* of this variable set. Note that we are only interested in the first nine variables, not the overall satisfaction measure. This is because the latter does not reflect a specific dimension of satisfaction, per se. Rather, the overall satisfaction measure is a general reflection of the nine more specific items that presumably affect it.

As reflected in Figure 8.7, Action PC was interested in how consumers perceived the product purchase and ownership experience. The *dimensions* of this experience were the focus of the analysis. This is a very different question than that addressed by the dependence model framework, which focuses on the effect of each of nine predictor variables on the single outcome variable. In the case of factor analysis or PCA, no predictor or outcome variables are identified—

TABLE 8.3 Action PC correlation matrix.

Variable Number/ Description	x_1	x_2	x_3	x_4	x_5	x_6	x_7	x_8	x_9
x_1. Price of system	1.00								
x_2. Price of accessories	0.74	1.00							
x_3. Product reliability	0.26	0.22	1.00						
x_4. Product set-up time	0.23	0.17	0.77	1.00					
x_5. Product design	0.28	0.20	0.72	0.67	1.00				
x_6. Product quality	0.41	0.38	0.51	0.46	0.60	1.00			
x_7. Tech support knowledge	–0.09	–0.03	–0.01	–0.01	–0.02	–0.03	1.00		
x_8. Tech support courtesy	–0.06	–0.04	0.01	0.03	–0.01	–0.02	0.83	1.00	
x_9. Tech support speed	–0.07	–0.05	–0.02	–0.03	–0.05	–0.07	0.85	0.88	1.00

our interest shifts to a single set of variables and the dimensions underlying them.

Both factor analysis and PCA decompose a *correlation matrix*. This is frequently transparent to the user of contemporary statistical analysis packages, of course. Packages such as SAS or SPSS simply construct the correlation matrix behind the scenes—the analyst does not explicitly direct either package towards a predefined correlation matrix—although this is certainly possible.

Table 8.3 presents the correlation matrix for the nine Action PC variables. Note that correlation coefficients with an absolute value greater than 0.45 have been highlighted. When squared, this level of correlation suggests two variables share 20 percent or more of their variance. Using this criterion for highlighting noteworthy correlations yields the pattern shown in Table 8.3. As shown, there are three clusters of variables. The first relates to price issues whereas the second and third clusters involve product and technical support issues, respectively. How many factors would you predict will emerge from a PCA?

Table 8.4 is composed of four rows and nine primary columns—one for each variable in the correlation matrix. The first row presents the eigenvalues—recall that there are as many eigenvalues as there are variables and that the sum of the eigenvalues equal the number of variables. This is because PCA was used and the diagonal of the correlation matrix was composed of ones. Had common factor analysis been employed, the diagonal of the correlation matrix would have consisted of the squared multiple correlation (SMC) of each variable with the others. This is referred to as the "reduced" correlation matrix.

TABLE 8.4 Eigenvalues of the Action PC correlation matrix.

	1	2	3	4	5	6	7	8	9
1. Eigenvalue	3.29	2.69	1.43	0.53	0.30	0.26	0.21	0.16	0.11
2. Difference	0.60	1.26	0.89	0.24	0.04	0.04	0.05	0.05	—
3. Proportion	0.36	0.30	0.16	0.06	0.03	0.03	0.02	0.02	0.01
4. Cumulative	0.36	0.66	0.82	0.88	0.91	0.94	0.96	0.99	1.00

The second row in the table presents the difference between two successive eigenvalues. The entry 0.60 under the column labeled "1" refers to the difference between the first and second eigenvalues. The third row reflects the proportion of variance each eigenvalue accounts for in the original correlation matrix. As expected, this value decreases from the first to last eigenvalue. Finally, the cumulative row shows how much variance is accounted for with each successive eigenvalue. As shown, the first three eigenvalues account for 82 percent of the correlation matrix variance.

Table 8.4 confirms that *three* factors will be retained in the PCA as a result of the minimum eigenvalue and scree test criteria described earlier. Adding the fourth dimension increases the total variance explained by a very small (6 percent) margin as shown in the table's fourth row.

The *unrotated* factor pattern is shown in Table 8.5. There are three factors (columns) and nine rows (variables). The entries in the table are analogous to correlation coefficients. Thus, in the case of this PCA, we can conclude that the correlation between product design (x_5) and the first principal component is 0.81.

Recall from an earlier discussion that the factors are initially drawn without regard to their *conceptual* implications. Rather, they meet specific *mathematical* criteria. In short, the unrotated factors are orthogonal (zero correlated) with one another and account for diminishing amounts of original data matrix variance.

Table 8.6 presents the rotated factor pattern for the Action PC PCA. As shown, the loadings are higher, and the entire pattern more closely resembles the desirable simple structure described earlier. Note how the variance "explained" by each component has also changed, but the sum of the three remains equal to approximately 7.4. This means the three components account for about 82 percent (7.4 ÷ 9) of the total variance in the original correlation matrix.

TABLE 8.5 Unrotated factor pattern for Action PC correlation matrix.

Principal Component Analysis			
Variable Number/Description	PC_1	PC_2	PC_3
x_5. Product design	0.81	0.19	−0.31
x_3. Product reliability	0.81	0.22	−0.34
x_4. Product set-up time	0.76	0.21	−0.38
x_6. Product quality	0.76	0.14	0.05
x_8. Tech support courtesy	−0.21	0.93	0.04
x_9. Tech support speed	−0.26	0.92	−0.06
x_7. Tech support knowledge	−0.23	0.91	0.04
x_2. Price of accessories	0.54	0.05	0.75
x_1. Price of system	0.60	0.03	0.70
Variance accounted for:	3.29	2.69	1.43

TABLE 8.6 Rotated factor pattern for Action PC correlation matrix (PCA with varimax rotation).

Variable Number/Description	PC_1	PC_2	PC_3
x_3. Product reliability	0.90	0.00	0.09
x_4. Product set-up time	0.88	0.00	0.04
x_5. Product design	0.88	−0.02	0.12
x_6. Product quality	0.65	−0.03	0.41
x_9. Tech support speed	−0.04	0.96	−0.02
x_8. Tech support courtesy	0.02	0.95	−0.02
x_7. Tech support knowledge	−0.00	0.94	−0.02
x_2. Price of accessories	0.11	−0.01	0.92
x_1. Price of system	0.19	−0.05	0.90
Variance accounted for:	2.83	2.71	1.86

Interestingly, when squared and summed in a columnar fashion, the loadings for any given component equal the variance accounted for by that component. In Table 8.6, this means that each entry under PC_1 can be squared and summed to equal 2.83. This is true for the remaining columns in the rotated factor pattern as well. Note that if all nine components were retained, the row-wise summation of the squared loadings would all sum to one, the amount of variance each variable contributes to the analysis.

Table 8.6 clearly shows that three dimensions underlie consumer perceptions of Action PC. These include: product issues, technical support, and price. Note that the PCA does not tell us anything about how *important* these issues are with respect to critical outcome variables such as likelihood to repurchase or overall satisfaction. Indeed, the first principal component may not be a strong predictor of overall satisfaction at all.

To demonstrate how similar factor analysis and PCA are, the Action PC correlation matrix was also subjected to common factor analysis. The rotated factor pattern is presented in Table 8.7. Although they account for somewhat different proportions of variance, the underlying structures seem highly consistent. In effect, both approaches (PCA and common factor analysis) yield a three-dimension solution. These tend to be invariant across the two analyses. That is, there is a technical support dimension, a product quality dimension, and a price dimension in each analysis. Further, the variables that compose each factor (or component) are the same.

The most noteworthy difference between the two analyses introduced earlier involves the principal diagonal of the correlation matrix. In the case of PCA, unities (1.0) were along the diagonal. Common factor analysis, on the other hand, dictated that *communalities* compose the correlation matrix diagonal entries. Recall that the best indicator of these is the squared multiple correlation coefficient (R^2), which is yielded when each variable is regressed on the others. One would therefore expect the differences between factor analysis

TABLE 8.7 Rotated factor pattern for Action PC correlation matrix (common factor analysis with varimax rotation).

Variable Number/Description	F_1	F_2	F_3
x_9. Tech support speed	0.93	–0.04	–0.03
x_8. Tech support courtesy	0.92	0.02	–0.03
x_7. Tech support knowledge	0.89	–0.01	–0.03
x_3. Product reliability	0.00	0.85	0.12
x_4. Product set-up time	0.00	0.82	0.07
x_5. Product design	–0.02	0.81	0.14
x_6. Product quality	–0.03	0.58	0.37
x_2. Price of accessories	–0.02	0.13	0.79
x_1. Price of system	–0.05	0.20	0.79
Variance accounted for:	2.51	2.44	1.43

and PCA to be significant in two instances. First, when the off-diagonal elements of the correlation matrix are very low, the presence of unities (ones) on the diagonal will tend to be problematic. Similarly, when the SMCs are low, factor analysis results will differ considerably from those derived using PCA because the latter will assume ones on the correlation matrix diagonal.

It should be clear from this example that Action PC should consider marketing communications in terms of three primary dimensions: price, product quality, and technical support. These are the fundamental building blocks upon which consumer perceptions of Action PC are based. Again, the extent to which each factor is a strong predictor of overall satisfaction is unknown.

FACTOR ANALYSIS VARIANTS

Typically, factor analysis and PCA are performed in order to group variables. This is based on their covariation. Variables that tend to be highly correlated will generally be encountered in the same factor or principal component. Figure 8.8 illustrates what has been referred to as *R*-factor analysis.

As shown in the figure, there are *k* variables and *n* cases. In a typical customer satisfaction application, each case corresponds to a completed questionnaire or telephone interview. Similarly, each variable represents, for example, a Likert scale item in the questionnaire. The *k* by *n* data matrix is reduced to a *k* by *k* correlation matrix. The

Case Number	Variables						
	x_1	x_2	x_3	.	.	.	x_k
1	x_{11}	x_{12}	x_{13}	.	.	.	x_{1k}
2	x_{21}	x_{22}	x_{23}	.	.	.	x_{2k}
3	x_{31}	x_{32}	x_{33}	.	.	.	x_{3k}
.	.	.	.	.	.	.	.
.	.	.	.	.	.	.	.
.	.	.	.	.	.	.	.
.	.	.	.	.	.	.	.
.	.	.	.	.	.	.	.
n	x_{n1}	x_{n2}	x_{n3}	.	.	.	x_{nk}

Raw Data Matrix **X**

	Variables						
	x_1	x_2	x_3	.	.	.	x_k
x_1	1.0	r_{12}	r_{13}	.	.	.	r_{1k}
x_2	r_{21}	1.0	r_{23}	.	.	.	r_{2k}
x_3	r_{31}	r_{32}	1.0	.	.	.	r_{3k}
.	.	.	.	.	.	.	.
.	.	.	.	.	.	.	.
.	.	.	.	.	.	.	.
.	.	.	.	.	.	.	.
.	.	.	.	.	.	.	.
x_k	r_{k1}	r_{k2}	r_{k3}	.	.	.	1.0

Correlation Matrix **R** of Variables

FIGURE 8.8 *R*-factor analysis approach.

correlation matrix **R** is then subjected to the factor analysis or PCA procedure. Either procedure extracts as many dimensions (factors or components) as there are variables (k). Of course, our objective is parsimonious reduction of the correlation matrix (**R**), and we retain fewer than k factors. This approach is widely used in customer satisfaction research and is useful in facilitating an understanding of the data and providing other procedures like multiple regression analysis with a new, smaller set of statistically unrelated predictor variables (that is, **factor scores**).

Another way to use factor analysis involves a reduction of the n cases rather than the k variables. This is achieved by transposing the original data matrix (**X**) and generating a correlation matrix (**R**) that relates *cases* rather than *variables*.

The transposed matrix (**X**′) has n columns and k rows as shown in Figure 8.9. If this data set represented a 20-item questionnaire and we had 200 usable surveys, the transposed data matrix (**X**′) would have 200 columns and 20 rows. A correlation matrix based on the transposed data matrix (**X**′) will have n rows and n columns. Thus, the correlation matrix will have 200 rows and 200 columns, as shown in Figure 8.10.

The correlation matrix (**R**) based on the transposed data matrix (**X**′) reflects how *respondents* covary not how *variables* covary. This approach is referred to as **Q-factor analysis** and represents another form of data reduction. In Q-factor analysis, the objective is to reveal how *respondents* may be grouped in terms of their levels of satisfac-

Case Number	Variables x_1	x_2	x_3	. . .	x_k
1	x_{11}	x_{12}	x_{13}	. . .	x_{1k}
2	x_{21}	x_{22}	x_{23}	. . .	x_{2k}
3	x_{31}	x_{32}	x_{33}	. . .	x_{3k}
.	.	.	.	. . .	.
.	.	.	.	. . .	.
.	.	.	.	. . .	.
.	.	.	.	. . .	.
.	.	.	.	. . .	.
n	x_{n1}	x_{n2}	x_{n3}	. . .	x_{nk}

Raw Data Matrix **X**

Variables	Case Number 1	2	3	. . .	n
x_1	x_{11}	x_{12}	x_{13}	. . .	x_{1n}
x_2	x_{21}	x_{22}	x_{23}	. . .	x_{2n}
x_3	x_{31}	x_{32}	x_{33}	. . .	x_{3n}
.	.	.	.	. . .	.
.	.	.	.	. . .	.
.	.	.	.	. . .	.
.	.	.	.	. . .	.
.	.	.	.	. . .	.
x_k	x_{k1}	x_{k2}	x_{k3}	. . .	x_{kn}

Transposed Data Matrix (**X**′)

FIGURE 8.9 Transposing a data matrix.

tion across the k variables. Q-factor analysis is a way to group respondents based upon their satisfaction levels.

The approach outlined here is not frequently used in applied customer satisfaction research. It represents a viable alternative to other clustering methods, however, and should be considered if there is a need to group respondents based upon their patterns of customer satisfaction. This type of approach can be useful in revealing service or product quality deficiencies.

CONFIRMATORY FACTOR ANALYSIS

In exploratory factor analysis, the researcher makes no assumptions about the data's factorial structure. Confirmatory factor analysis, on the other hand, requires this explication. The difference between confirmatory and exploratory factor analysis is analogous to the difference between multiple regression analysis and path analysis. The former requires only an assessment of which variables affect the dependent measure. In contrast, path analysis dictates that the relationships be specified before running the model. The extent to which the hypothesized causal flow is consistent with the relationships in the data reflects "goodness-of-fit" and determines whether the model is rejected or accepted.

The Action PC data were reanalyzed using confirmatory factor analysis. The correlation matrix is presented in Table 8.3 and is characterized by three pockets of strong intercorrelations. A review of the

	Case Number				
	1	**2**	**3**	**. . .**	***n***
x_1	x_{11}	x_{12}	x_{13}	. . .	x_{1n}
x_2	x_{21}	x_{22}	x_{23}	. . .	x_{2n}
x_3	x_{31}	x_{32}	x_{33}	. . .	x_{3n}
.	.	.	.	. . .	.
.	.	.	.	. . .	.
.	.	.	.	. . .	.
.	.	.	.	. . .	.
.	.	.	.	. . .	.
x_k	x_{k1}	x_{k2}	x_{k3}	. . .	X_{kn}

Transposed Data Matrix (**X**´)

	Case Number						
	1	**2**	**3**	**.**	**.**	**.**	***n***
1	1.0	r_{12}	r_{13}	.	.	.	r_{1n}
2	r_{21}	1.0	r_{23}	.	.	.	r_{2n}
3	r_{31}	r_{32}	1.0	.	.	.	r_{3n}
.	.	.	.	.	.	.	.
.	.	.	.	.	.	.	.
.	.	.	.	.	.	.	.
.	.	.	.	.	.	.	.
.	.	.	.	.	.	.	.
n	r_{n1}	r_{n2}	r_{n3}	.	.	.	1.0

Correlation matrix (**R**) based on transposed data matrix (**X**´)

FIGURE 8.10 Correlation matrix based on transposed data matrix.

TABLE 8.8 Hypothesized factor structure of Action PC data.

	Price Factor	Product Quality Factor	Tech Support Factor
x_1. Price of system	λ_{11}	0	0
x_2. Price of accessories	λ_{21}	0	0
x_3. Product reliability	0	λ_{32}	0
x_4. Product set-up time	0	λ_{42}	0
x_5. Product design	0	λ_{52}	0
x_6. Product quality	0	λ_{62}	0
x_7. Tech support knowledge	0	0	λ_{73}
x_8. Tech support courtesy	0	0	λ_{83}
x_9. Tech support speed	0	0	λ_{93}

survey instrument (Figure 8.6) confirms that there are three content areas: price, product, and sales representative performance.

From a confirmatory factor analytic perspective, our interest involves specifying the dimensionality and factorial structure of the Action PC data. This means that given our knowledge of the sample, previous experience, and instrument design, we must specify the number of factors *and* their composition and then test whether our hypothesis is correct. Using the same goodness-of-fit statistic employed in path analysis (chapter 7), we will either accept or reject the hypothesized factor pattern.

Table 8.8 presents the hypothesized factor structure for the Action PC data. We believe three factors will emerge. The two items relating to price (x_1 and x_2) are expected to load on the price factor while all other variables are constrained to zero. The second factor is expected to reflect product quality and is associated with four variables (x_3–x_6). Finally, three variables (x_7–x_9) are presumed to reflect a third underlying factor related to technical support quality.

The Greek letter lambda (λ) is used to denote factor loadings that must be estimated. For each factor, there are at least two factor loadings that must be estimated. That is, reviewing each column of Table 8.8 reveals that some of the loadings are to be estimated (λ) while others are constrained to zero. A graphic structure is presented in Figure 8.11.

As shown in Figure 8.11, there are nine manifest variables (x_1–x_9) that are "caused by" three latent factors (η_1–η_3). The manifest and latent variables are linked with paths that correspond to factor loadings (λ). Note that the three latent variables are permitted to covary, and there are explicit terms (CV_{12}, CV_{13}, and CV_{23}) to accommodate

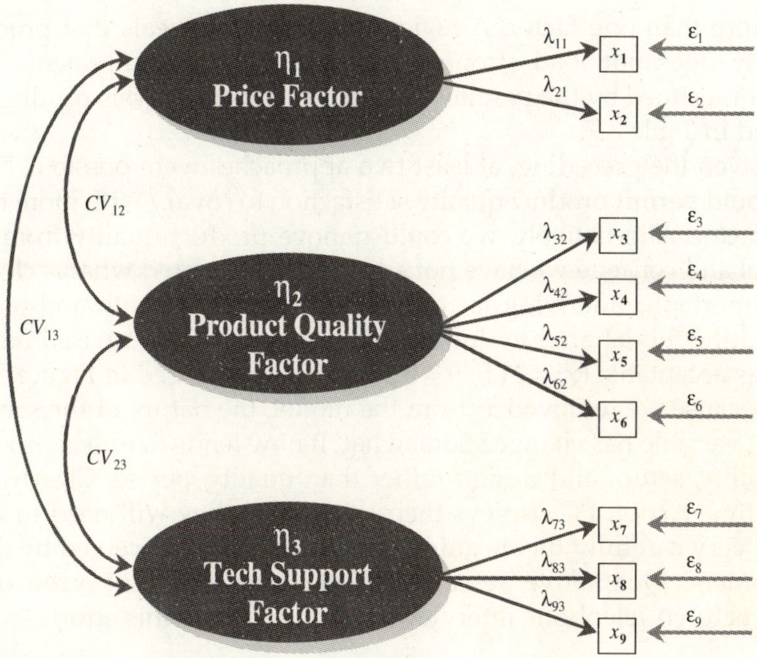

FIGURE 8.11 Confirmatory factor analysis—Action PC data.

this. In confirmatory factor analysis, we can either estimate these covariance parameters or set them to zero. The former case parallels oblique rotation in exploratory factor analysis. Clearly, setting these parameters to zero is equivalent to requiring the factors to be orthogonal as one would if, for example, varimax rotation were used.

The model presented in Figure 8.11 was tested using standard statistical software, and the results suggested a problem. Specifically, the model fit as evidenced by a significant chi-squared statistic ($\chi^2 = 96.5$; $p = 0.0001$) was unacceptable. The poor fit was attributable primarily to one variable. A review of Table 8.3 reveals that of the nine variables used in this analysis, satisfaction with product quality (x_6) has the lowest intercorrelations with the other variables. Its strongest relationship to any other variable involves satisfaction with product design (x_5), and even this correlation is relatively modest ($r_{56} = 0.60$).

Assessing the fit of a confirmatory factor analysis model and diagnosing the source(s) of poor fit is beyond the scope of this chapter. A review of standard diagnostics revealed that x_6 was characterized by factorial complexity. In short, it tended to load substantively on more than one factor. A review of Table 8.6 reveals that product quality does not load strongly on any principal component. This result is echoed by the parallel exploratory factor analysis results presented in Table 8.7.

Given the preceding, at least two approaches were possible. First, we could permit product quality satisfaction to covary with more than one factor. Alternatively, we could remove product quality from the model and concede we have not adequately measured what is clearly an important underlying factor. We chose the latter path and reestimated the model after excluding product quality. The revised model fit was acceptable ($\chi^2 = 21.5$; $p = 0.20$). It is summarized in Figure 8.12.

Because we removed x_6 from the model, the nature of the second latent variable has changed somewhat. It now tends to reflect product reliability, setup, and design rather than quality, per se. Clearly, the next time Action PC surveys their customers, they will need to consider very carefully the meaning of quality as it is perceived by their customers. Qualitative research in the form of focus groups or unstructured telephone interviews would facilitate this effort.

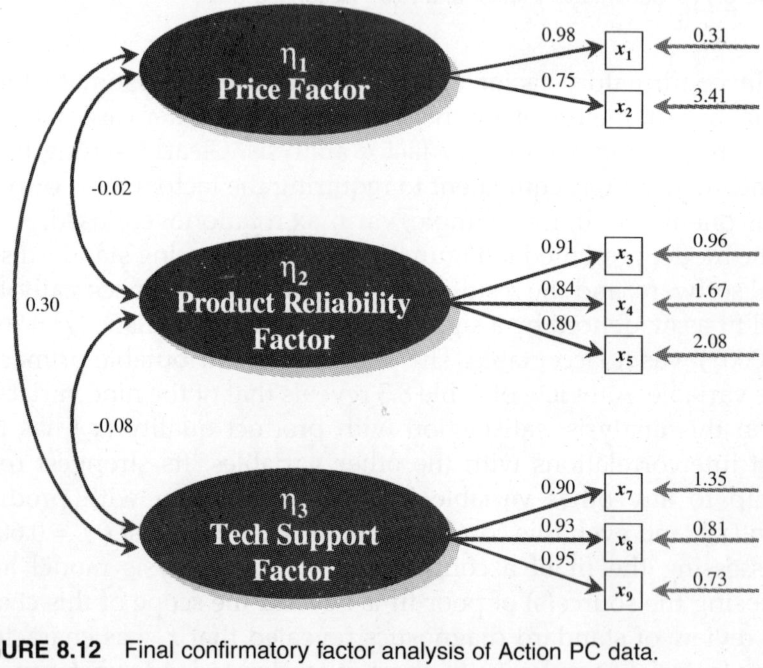

FIGURE 8.12 Final confirmatory factor analysis of Action PC data.

Dimension reducing techniques enjoy a prominent position in customer satisfaction research. Regrettably, confirmatory factor analysis remains underutilized by applied researchers. It should be clear from the Action PC case study that confirmatory factor analysis represents a powerful addition to the arsenal of analytical techniques we use to examine customer satisfaction data. It is highly flexible and permits the user to specify the magnitude of any relationship between factors and variables. Further, it is accommodating in terms of permitting a variety of oblique and orthogonal factor relationships. For example, we could have constrained the first and second factors (η_1 and η_2) to be orthogonal ($CV_{12} = 0$) while permitting the remaining factor covariances (CV_{13} and CV_{23}) to be freely estimated.

Recently, more and more applied research has taken advantage of the confirmatory factor analysis approach. Dillon, White, Rao, and Filak (1997, 24–25) acknowledged the lack of reliance on confirmatory factor analysis and concluded it was " . . . far less well-known and used in commercial marketing research studies." As more practitioners become familiar with confirmatory approaches, we may see an increased use of these techniques in applied settings.

Chapter 9

STRUCTURAL EQUATIONS WITH LATENT VARIABLES

INTRODUCTION

At this point, we have introduced path analysis in chapter 7 and latent variables (that is, factors or components) in chapter 8. With a fundamental understanding of the two, we are now prepared to merge them under one analytical umbrella. Unfortunately, for the novice, the merger of path analysis and factor analysis has been obscured by the myriad names and acronyms that this family of techniques has enjoyed. Indeed, names such as LISREL, latent variable path analysis, structural equations with latent variables, and others may sound vaguely familiar to advanced researchers in customer satisfaction research. In effect, all of these names refer to the marriage of path analytic approaches with factor analysis. Throughout this chapter, we will refer to this technique as structural equation models with latent variables. This differentiates the technique from path analysis, which, using this nomenclature, is referred to as structural equations with manifest variables. The differences will be described in greater detail later. Today, it is common practice to refer to both **manifest variable** and latent variable structural equation models under one label (SEM), which stands for **structural equation modeling**.

One of the greatest sources of confusion surrounding SEM involves the computer program known as LISREL. It has been common for researchers to refer to the SEM *technique* as LISREL, which is clearly erroneous. LISREL, like EQS, Amos, SPSS, SAS, and other software packages, is an application designed to conduct SEM. Rigdon (1998, 266–68) provides a brief but thorough review of additional SEM software packages.

Of all the techniques described in this book, no other incorporates as many Greek symbols and matrix algebraic equations. It is our intent to present an *understandable* treatment of all the techniques used in customer satisfaction research. This is especially true in the case of SEM—to the extent possible *conceptual treatments* rather than *mathematical treatments* will be presented for these models. Readers who wish to delve into the underlying matrix algebra and theoretical statistics will have no difficulty finding books that meet these requirements.

The latent variable structural equation model is best understood when decomposed into its two main components: the **measurement model** and the **structural model**. The measurement model represents the confirmatory factor analytic component. In effect, the measurement model formally explicates the relationships between manifest (observed) variables and unobservable latent constructs such as *intelligence* or *motivation.* The structural portion of the latent variable SEM model specifies the causal linkages among the latent variables. That the construct *intelligence* causes *motivation,* for example, represents the structural (or causal) relation between two latent variables.

It is easy to see how SEM represents the marriage of confirmatory factor analysis and manifest variable path analysis. Its utility for researchers interested in customer satisfaction and loyalty research cannot be overstated. A relatively contemporary technique, the introduction of the latent variable SEM approach by Jöreskog and Sörbom in the early 1970s, predates the development of intense interest in service quality research by, at best, a decade. Still, the conceptual development of this occurred in the 1960s and involved sociologists such as Blalock according to Bollen (1989, 7). He and other sociologists considered the need for a comprehensive analytical platform that would permit the integration of Sewall Wright's (1918) path analysis and confirmatory factor analysis. Although other platforms were developed in the late 1960s and early 1970s, the popularity of Jöreskog and Sörbom's LISREL software led many to conclude erroneously that the technique had eponymous software . . . or vice versa. This confusion remains today; many researchers still refer to structural equation models as LISREL models.

Matrix Algebra

The most eloquent means of describing the structural equations with latent variables model involves the use of **matrix algebra**. A full description of this branch of mathematics is beyond the scope of this book. The appendix provides a more detailed teatment. Matrix algebra involves the manipulation of scalars, vectors, and matrices. In short, a **scalar** is a single number like 37. A **vector**, in contrast, is a *row* or *column* of numbers:

$$\text{Row vector} \quad \mathbf{A} = [2 \;\; 6 \;\; 3 \;\; 4 \;\; 1]$$

$$\text{Column vector} \quad \mathbf{B} = \begin{bmatrix} 2 \\ 3 \\ 4 \\ 1 \end{bmatrix}$$

Finally, a **matrix** is a block of numbers:

$$\text{Matrix} \quad \mathbf{A} = \begin{bmatrix} 6 & 2 & 1 & 4 \\ 3 & 2 & 1 & 8 \\ 4 & 9 & 6 & 5 \end{bmatrix}$$

A matrix in most applied customer satisfaction research corresponds to a data set. The rows represent individual respondents, and the columns correspond to variables. Thus, for a typical customer satisfaction research project, the data matrix might be composed of several hundred rows (respondents) and dozens of columns (variables).

A variety of operations are possible using matrices, vectors, and scalars. The interested readers should turn to books like those by Eves (1966), Marcus and Minc (1964), Searle (1982), Schott (1997), or Steinberg (1974) for a full explication of matrix operations and their utility in statistical analysis. This brief discussion is intended only to ensure a modest level of comfort with what may well be a very unfamiliar form of mathematical notation.

Vectors and matrices are frequently referred to as being of a particular size. The convention for referencing a vector's or matrix' size involves its rows and columns. For example $\mathbf{X}_{3x6}$ is a matrix with three rows and six columns. Its elements may be noted by a_{ij} such that each entry has a unique address:

$$\mathbf{X} = \begin{bmatrix} a_{11} & a_{12} & a_{13} & a_{14} & a_{15} & a_{16} \\ a_{21} & a_{22} & a_{23} & a_{24} & a_{25} & a_{26} \\ a_{31} & a_{32} & a_{33} & a_{34} & a_{35} & a_{36} \end{bmatrix}$$

Two matrices or vectors with *exactly* the same sizes may be added:

$$\mathbf{A}=\begin{bmatrix}1 & 2\\ 3 & 4\end{bmatrix} \qquad \mathbf{B}=\begin{bmatrix}6 & 3\\ 1 & 2\end{bmatrix} \qquad \mathbf{A}+\mathbf{B}=\begin{bmatrix}7 & 5\\ 4 & 6\end{bmatrix}$$

Multiplying a matrix by a scalar is quite straightforward. Consider the matrix **T** and scalar **a** and their product:

$$\mathbf{T}=\begin{bmatrix}3 & 6\\ 3 & 1\end{bmatrix} \qquad \mathbf{a}=[2] \qquad \mathbf{Ta}=\begin{bmatrix}6 & 12\\ 6 & 2\end{bmatrix}$$

As shown, each element in **T** was multiplied by the scalar value of 2 with quite predictable results.

Next, consider the **transpose** of a matrix **A** denoted by **A′** (in some texts $\mathbf{A}^{\mathrm{T}}$ is used). The transpose of a matrix entails a reversal of its columns and rows:

$$\mathbf{A}=\begin{bmatrix}3 & 6\\ 2 & 1\end{bmatrix} \qquad \mathbf{A}'=\begin{bmatrix}3 & 2\\ 6 & 1\end{bmatrix}$$

Note that the first column of **A** is the first row of **A′**, which has great utility for some matrix operations discussed later.

Two matrices may be multiplied only if their sizes correspond.

$$\mathbf{A}_{3\times 2}=\begin{bmatrix}2 & 6\\ 1 & 4\\ 3 & 2\end{bmatrix} \qquad \mathbf{B}_{2\times 3}=\begin{bmatrix}4 & 1 & 3\\ 2 & 2 & 1\end{bmatrix}$$

$$\mathbf{AB}_{3\times 3}=\begin{bmatrix}[(2\times 4)+(6\times 2)][(2\times 1)+(6\times 2)][(2\times 3)+(6\times 1)]\\ [(1\times 4)+(4\times 2)][(1\times 1)+(4\times 2)][(1\times 3)+(4\times 1)]\\ [(3\times 4)+(2\times 2)][(3\times 1)+(2\times 2)][(3\times 3)+(2\times 1)]\end{bmatrix}$$

$$\mathbf{AB}_{3\times 3}=\begin{bmatrix}20 & 14 & 12\\ 12 & 9 & 7\\ 16 & 7 & 11\end{bmatrix}$$

Note that in order to multiply two matrices, their inner dimensions must match. The number of *columns* in the first matrix must match the number of *rows* in the second. In the example above, **A** is a 3×2 matrix, and **B** is a 2×3 matrix. Because the number of columns (2) in the former matches the number of rows (2) in the latter, the matrices may be multiplied. Note that although the product of **AB** is a 3×3 matrix, the product of **BA** is a 2×2 matrix. Matrix multiplication involves multiplying the column entries of the second matrix by the row entries of the first matrix.

$$\mathbf{B}_{2\times 3} = \begin{bmatrix} 4 & 1 & 3 \\ 2 & 2 & 1 \end{bmatrix} \qquad \mathbf{B}_{2\times 3} = \begin{bmatrix} 2 & 6 \\ 1 & 4 \\ 3 & 2 \end{bmatrix}$$

$$\mathbf{BA}_{2\times 2} = \begin{bmatrix} [(4\times 2)+(1\times 1)+(3\times 3)][(4\times 6)+(1\times 4)+(3\times 2)] \\ [(2\times 2)+(2\times 1)+(1\times 3)][(2\times 6)+(2\times 4)+(1\times 2)] \end{bmatrix}$$

$$\mathbf{BA}_{2\times 2} = \begin{bmatrix} 18 & 34 \\ 9 & 22 \end{bmatrix}$$

This illustrates one of the differences between scalar and matrix multiplication. Matrix operation **AB** is not equivalent to **BA,** nor is it always *possible.* The final matrix operation that we will briefly introduce is the **inverse** of a matrix **A**, which is denoted by $\mathbf{A}^{-1}$. The inverse of a matrix is analogous to the *reciprocal* of a scalar inasmuch as any scalar times its reciprocal equals one. For example, 10 times 1/10 equals one. This is true in matrix algebra as well and introduces the matrix **I**, which plays a special role in matrix algebra.

$$\mathbf{AA}^{-1} = \mathbf{I} \qquad \mathbf{AI} = \mathbf{A}$$

The matrix **I**, called the **identity matrix,** is composed of ones on the diagonal and zeros on the off diagonal. It is equivalent to the number one in scalar multiplication.

$$\mathbf{I} = \begin{bmatrix} 1 & 0 & 0 & 0 \\ 0 & 1 & 0 & 0 \\ 0 & 0 & 1 & 0 \\ 0 & 0 & 0 & 1 \end{bmatrix}$$

To demonstrate the simplicity of matrix algebra vis à vis the more traditional means of notation, consider the case of ordinary least squares (OLS) regression. The solutions to the *normal equations* in simple linear regression analysis yield Equation 9-1 for the slope (Draper and Smith 1966, 13–14).

$$b_1 = \frac{\Sigma X_i Y_i - [(\Sigma X_i)(\Sigma Y_i)]/n}{\Sigma X_1^2 - (\Sigma X_i)^2/n} = \frac{\Sigma(X_i - \overline{X})(Y_i - \overline{Y})}{\Sigma(X_i - \overline{X})^2} \tag{9-1}$$

Whereas the intercept is readily calculated as:

$$b_o = \overline{Y} - b_1\overline{X} \tag{9-2}$$

Now consider the simplification associated with a matrix notation approach to the OLS problem. The matrix algebraic notation for least squares is presented in Equation 9-3.

$$\boldsymbol{b} = (\boldsymbol{X'X})^{-1}\boldsymbol{X'y} \tag{9-3}$$

Equation 9-3 indicates that a column vector **b** of beta weights can be found by solving the system of linear equations $\boldsymbol{(X'X)^{-1}X'y}$. The matrix **X** represents all of the predictor variables in a regression analysis. If there are 100 observations and 14 predictor variables, then **X** is composed of 100 rows and 14 columns. As might be expected, **y** is a column vector that contains one variable (the dependent variable) and 100 rows (observations). When the matrix system of equations depicted in Equation 9-3 is solved, the column vector **b** is composed of 14 elements, one beta weight corresponding to each of the 14 variables in the matrix **X**.

Now that a very basic review of matrix algebraic nomenclature has been provided, we can turn our attention to the structural equations with latent variables model. Figure 9.1 introduces a model with three latent exogenous variables (product quality, service quality, and technical support) and two latent **endogenous variables** (customer satisfaction and loyalty).

The model presented in Figure 9.1 posits that three latent exogenous variables (product quality, service quality, and technical support) affect customer satisfaction. The latter, in turn, is presumed to affect loyalty. Table 9.1 summarizes the symbols and their implications. This form of representing latent variable path modeling is quite

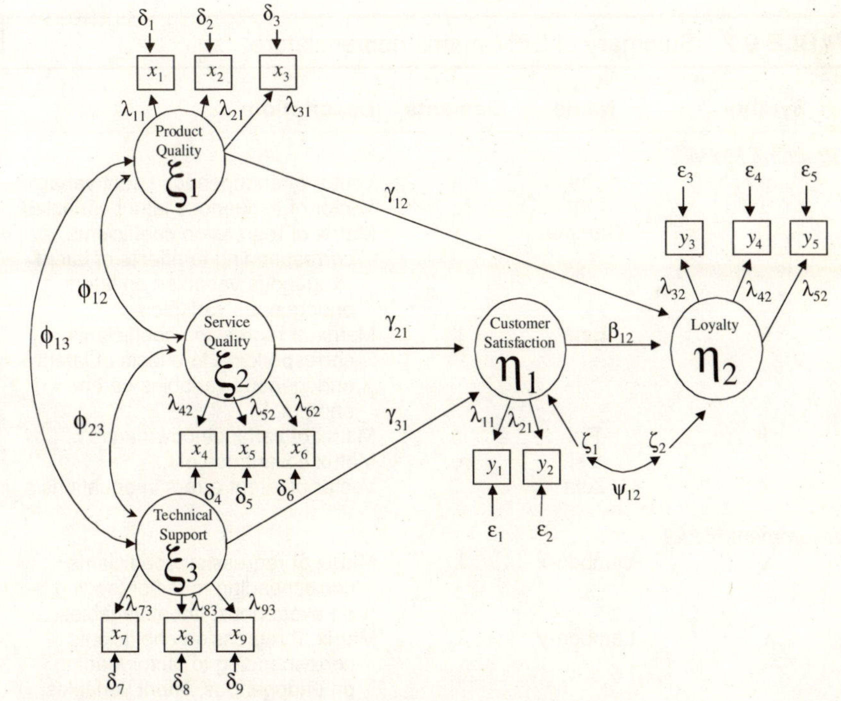

FIGURE 9.1 Structural equation model with latent variables.

TABLE 9.1

Symbol	Description
❍	Latent variable (endogenous or exogenous), a factor.
❑	Manifest variable (endogenous or exogenous), observable like a specific item in a questionnaire.
❑←❍ ❍→❑	Relationship between latent and manifest variable. The Greek letter λ_{ij} (lambda) is used to denote this path, which can be interpreted as a factor loading.
❍←❍ ❍→❍	Causal relationship between two latent variables. If the path is between an exogenous and endogenous variable, the symbol γ_{ij} is used.If the path leads from one endogenous latent variable to another, the symbol β_{ij} is used.
⤷❍ ⤷❍	The curved arrow depicts the covariance between two latent variables.

TABLE 9.2 Summary of SEM matrix nomenclature.

Symbol	Name	Elements	Description
Structural Model			
η	Eta	η	Vector of endogenous latent variables.
ξ	Xi	ξ	Vector of exogenous latent variables.
Γ	Gamma	γ	Matrix of regression coefficients corresponding to effects of latent exogenous variables on latent endogenous variables.
B	Beta	β	Matrix of regression coefficients corresponding to effects of latent endogenous variables on one another.
Φ	Phi	ϕ	Matrix of variance-covariance ξ.
Ψ	Psi	ψ	Matrix covariance of ζ.
Z	Zeta	ζ	Vector of latent errors in equations.
Measurement Model			
Λ_x	Lambda-*x*	λ_x	Matrix of regression coefficients corresponding to factor loading on exogenous, latent variables.
Λ_y	Lambda-*y*	λ_y	Matrix of regression coefficients corresponding to factor loading on endogenous, latent variables.

standard regardless of the SEM software one selects. Note that this family of techniques uses a large portion of the Greek alphabet as shown in Table 9.2. The upper-case letters denote matrices and the lower-case letters are reserved for the elements in a matrix. To illustrate the relationship between Figure 9.1 and an actual survey instrument, refer to the questionnaire presented in Figure 9.2.

The convention in SEM with latent variables is to depict manifest variables in squares and latent variables in circles. Each of the labeled squares in Figure 9.1 can be related to an actual question in the corresponding survey instrument shown in Figure 9.2. Thus, the three variables (x_1–x_3) that reflect the latent construct labeled product quality (ξ_1) involves the product's durability, finish quality, and scratch resistance. Similarly, the second latent variable (ξ_2) involves service quality and is also associated with three questions (x_4–x_6) from the survey. These three manifest variables relate to order processing speed, courtesy, and knowledge. Manifest variables x_7 through x_9 all reflect an underlying latent construct called technical support. A quick review of the survey

GIFCO Products
Customer Satisfaction Study

Dear Customer:

Thank you for purchasing a GIFCO automobile accessory. In our effort to continuously upgrade our customer service, product quality, and service to you, we ask all customers to complete this simple questionnaire. Thank you in advance for your cooperation. The GIFCO family appreciates your business.

Please tell us how satisfied you are with each aspect of your new GIFCO automobile accessory. Indicate your satisfaction with each item by using the seven-point scale where 1 means you are very dissatisfied and 7 means you are very satisfied.

A. Your GIFCO Experience

	Very Dissatisfied						**Very Satisfied**
1. Your accessory's durability	1 ❑	2 ❑	3 ❑	4 ❑	5 ❑	6 ❑	7 ❑
2. Your accessory's finish quality	1 ❑	2 ❑	3 ❑	4 ❑	5 ❑	6 ❑	7 ❑
3. Your accessory's scratch resistance	1 ❑	2 ❑	3 ❑	4 ❑	5 ❑	6 ❑	7 ❑
4. Speed your order was processed	1 ❑	2 ❑	3 ❑	4 ❑	5 ❑	6 ❑	7 ❑
5. Courtesy of rep when your order was taken	1 ❑	2 ❑	3 ❑	4 ❑	5 ❑	6 ❑	7 ❑
6. Order rep's product knowledge	1 ❑	2 ❑	3 ❑	4 ❑	5 ❑	6 ❑	7 ❑
7. Technical support rep's knowledge of your accessory	1 ❑	2 ❑	3 ❑	4 ❑	5 ❑	6 ❑	7 ❑
8. Technical support rep's courtesy	1 ❑	2 ❑	3 ❑	4 ❑	5 ❑	6 ❑	7 ❑
9. Technical support rep's problem-solving ability	1 ❑	2 ❑	3 ❑	4 ❑	5 ❑	6 ❑	7 ❑

B. Impressions of GIFCO

Now, considering GIFCO's product and service quality and our technical support personnel, please use the same seven-point scale to indicate how satisfied you are, overall, with GIFCO.

	Very Dissatisfied						**Very Satisfied**
10. Overall satisfaction with GIFCO	1 ❑	2 ❑	3 ❑	4 ❑	5 ❑	6 ❑	7 ❑
11. How likely are you to recommend GIFCO to your colleagues?	1 ❑	2 ❑	3 ❑	4 ❑	5 ❑	6 ❑	7 ❑

To what extent do you agree with the statements below?

	Strongly Disagree						**Strongly Agree**
12. GIFCO cares about me as a customer	1 ❑	2 ❑	3 ❑	4 ❑	5 ❑	6 ❑	7 ❑
13. I'd rather do business with GIFCO than another provider	1 ❑	2 ❑	3 ❑	4 ❑	5 ❑	6 ❑	7 ❑
14. I like the people at GIFCO	1 ❑	2 ❑	3 ❑	4 ❑	5 ❑	6 ❑	7 ❑

Thanks for participating in this customer survey. At GIFCO, we do everything possible to satisfy our customers. We care about you and hope to continue providing you with quality accessories.

FIGURE 9.2 GIFCO products customer satisfaction instruments.

instrument confirms that x_7 through x_9 involve technical support knowledge, courtesy, and problem-solving ability.

On the right-hand side of the model presented in Figure 9.1 are two latent endogenous variables (η_1 and η_2) which reflect overall satisfaction and loyalty, respectively. The first latent endogenous variable (η_1) represents overall satisfaction and is associated with two manifest variables. A review of the questionnaire confirms that these items request summary judgments concerning overall satisfaction and likelihood to recommend. The second latent endogenous variable is associated with three manifest variables. These represent the last three items in the survey instrument presented earlier. In each case, the items are attempting to gauge a level of psychological or emotional attachment to the company. Combined, they are presumed to reflect a latent construct called loyalty (η_2).

Structural equation models with latent variables have two distinct components as implied earlier. The *measurement model* subsumes the "composition" of the latent variables while the *structural model* depicts how the latent variables are interrelated. Equations 9-4 and 9-5 present, in matrix form, the measurement and structural components of the model.

$$y = \Lambda_y \eta + \varepsilon$$

$$x = \Lambda_x \xi + \delta \qquad (9\text{-}4)$$

$$\eta = \beta\eta + \Gamma\xi + \zeta \qquad (9\text{-}5)$$

THE MEASUREMENT MODEL

Note from our previous discussion of confirmatory factor analysis that the measurement model portion of Figure 9.1 can be depicted as Table 9.3, which confirms we have posited that the 14 variables will load on five factors: product quality, service quality, technical support, customer satisfaction, and loyalty. Note again how different this approach is from exploratory factor analysis wherein there is no *a priori* concern for dimensionality (that is, number of factors) or the factorial structure (that is, which variables are associated with which factors).

With respect to Equation 9-4, the entire measurement model associated with Figure 9.1 can be depicted in matrix notation.

TABLE 9.3 Confirmatory factor analytic representation of measurement model.

	I Product Quality	II Service Quality	III Technical Support	IV Customer Satisfaction	V Loyalty
x_1. Durability	λ_{11}	0	0	0	0
x_2. Finish quality	λ_{21}	0	0	0	0
x_3. Scratch resistance	λ_{31}	0	0	0	0
x_4. Order speed	0	λ_{42}	0	0	0
x_5. Rep courtesy	0	λ_{52}	0	0	0
x_6. Rep product knowledge	0	λ_{62}	0	0	0
x_7. Tech support knowledge	0	0	λ_{73}	0	0
x_8. Tech support courtesy	0	0	λ_{83}	0	0
x_9. Tech support problem solving	0	0	λ_{93}	0	0
x_{10}. Overall satisfaction	0	0	0	$\lambda_{10.4}$	0
x_{11}. Recommend	0	0	0	$\lambda_{11.4}$	0
x_{12}. GIFCO cares	0	0	0	0	$\lambda_{12.5}$
x_{13}. Rather do business	0	0	0	0	$\lambda_{13.5}$
x_{14}. Like the people	0	0	0	0	$\lambda_{14.5}$

$$x = \Lambda_x \xi + \zeta$$

$$\begin{bmatrix} x_1 \\ x_2 \\ x_3 \\ x_4 \\ x_5 \\ x_6 \\ x_7 \\ x_8 \\ x_9 \end{bmatrix} = \begin{bmatrix} \lambda_{11} & 0 & 0 \\ \lambda_{21} & 0 & 0 \\ \lambda_{31} & \lambda_{42} & 0 \\ 0 & \lambda_{52} & 0 \\ 0 & \lambda_{62} & 0 \\ 0 & 0 & \lambda_{73} \\ 0 & 0 & \lambda_{83} \\ 0 & 0 & \lambda_{93} \end{bmatrix} \begin{bmatrix} \xi_1 \\ \xi_2 \\ \xi_3 \end{bmatrix} + \begin{bmatrix} \delta_1 \\ \delta_2 \\ \delta_3 \\ \delta_4 \\ \delta_5 \\ \delta_6 \\ \delta_7 \\ \delta_8 \\ \delta_9 \end{bmatrix}$$

Similarly, the endogenous side of the model, which is composed of two latent variables, may also be depicted using matrix notation. Note that the variables y_1 through y_4 correspond to variables x_{10} through x_{13} in Table 9.3 and have been renamed to underscore the fact that they are on the dependent side of the *structural* model. Had a simple confirmatory factor analysis been conducted, one would not be concerned about endogenous and exogenous factors.

At this point, the entire measurement model portion of Figure 9.1 has been explicated using matrix notation. All of the matrix entries for the latent endogenous and latent exogenous variables can be found in Figure 9.1. For example, from the latent exogenous variable matrix notation above, we see the entry λ_{11} is the loading of x_1 on the first latent exogenous factor ξ_1 (product quality). Similarly, from the endogenous variable matrices, the entry λ_{22} is the loading of variable y_2 on the second latent endogenous variable η_2 (loyalty).

$$y = \Lambda_y \eta + \varepsilon$$

$$\begin{bmatrix} y_1 \\ y_2 \\ y_3 \\ y_4 \\ y_5 \end{bmatrix} = \begin{bmatrix} \lambda_{11} & 0 \\ \lambda_{21} & 0 \\ 0 & \lambda_{32} \\ 0 & \lambda_{42} \\ 0 & \lambda_{52} \end{bmatrix} \begin{bmatrix} \eta_1 \\ \eta_2 \end{bmatrix} + \begin{bmatrix} \varepsilon_1 \\ \varepsilon_2 \\ \varepsilon_3 \\ \varepsilon_4 \\ \varepsilon_5 \end{bmatrix}$$

One important aspect of the measurement model that is frequently overlooked is the direction of the arrows between the manifest and latent variables. A review of Figure 9.1 will confirm that the factor-loading arrows originate with the latent variable and point toward the manifest variable. The implications of this are important. That the arrow points from the latent variable to the manifest variable implies that the manifest variable is caused by or is a manifestation of the latent variable. An example will help clarify this relationship. Consider a student's scores on an intelligence test. The IQ score is a manifest variable. The *unobservable* construct underlying the test score is *intelligence.* Thus, the IQ score is a tangible reflection of an unobservable factor.

The Structural Model

With the measurement model complete, we can turn our attention to the structural model. The structural model specifies *dependencies* among the latent constructs. In the present case, we have five latent variables. Three of these are exogenous (product quality, service quality, and technical support), and two are endogenous (customer satisfaction and loyalty). Equation 9-5 can be expressed by the series of following matrices:

$$\eta = \beta\eta + \Gamma\xi + \zeta$$

$$\begin{bmatrix} \eta_1 \\ \eta_2 \end{bmatrix} = \begin{bmatrix} 1 & 0 \\ \beta_{12} & 1 \end{bmatrix} \begin{bmatrix} \eta_1 \\ \eta_2 \end{bmatrix} + \begin{bmatrix} 0 & \gamma_{21} & \gamma_{31} \\ \gamma_{12} & 0 & 0 \end{bmatrix} \begin{bmatrix} \xi_1 \\ \xi_2 \\ \xi_3 \end{bmatrix} + \begin{bmatrix} \zeta_1 \\ \zeta_2 \end{bmatrix}$$

Note that at this point we have been specifying a latent variable path model. The measurement model subsumes five latent constructs, and the structural model specifies dependencies among the latent variables. In effect, all of our efforts so far have been expended formally specifying the relationships we hypothesize to exist in our data set. We have yet to *test* whether our model is consistent with the relationships in our data set. This underscores the difference between *exploratory* and *confirmatory* data analysis.

Assessing the Model

Assessing the hypothesized latent variable model depicted in Figure 9.1 requires the use of SEM software like LISREL, EQS, AMOS, or SAS. It is important to keep in mind that the posited causal model is never unequivocally *proven.* We test to see if the relationships (both structural and measurement) hypothesized in the model are consistent with the relationships actually present in the data. To evaluate a model, its goodness-of-fit with the data is assessed. The chi-squared statistic is the oldest of the fit measures and was introduced in chapter 7 as a means of evaluating confirmatory factor analysis models. Interpreting the chi-squared measure as it relates to the goodness-of-fit of a given model is counterintuitive. Under ordinary circumstances (that is, exploratory analyses), a statistically significant value of chi-squared is generally a desirable finding. It suggests there is a significant relationship between two variables. In confirmatory analyses, however, the chi-squared statistic reflects the extent to which the hypothesized model is consistent with the data. As the two become more and more disparate, the chi-squared statistic increases, and its statistical significance is more likely. Thus, we interpret the chi-squared statistic and its significance level as indicators that our hypothesized model *significantly* departs from the relationships present in the data. In confirmatory analyses, we accept the hypothesized model if the chi-squared statistic is *not* statistically significant, as shown in Figure 9.3. Unfortunately, the chi-squared statistic is very

Step 1:	Specify model
Step 2:	Estimate free parameters
Step 3:	Is chi-square statistically significant? If yes; return to Step 1. If no; accept hypothesized model.

FIGURE 9.3 Assessing model goodness-of-fit.

sensitive to sample sizes—as the sample increases, chi-squared is more likely to be statistically significant. In the case of SEM, this is not desirable because it may lead us to erroneously reject a model that actually fits the data quite well (Hu and Bentler 1995, 77–81).

There are many goodness-of-fit measures that are not as sensitive to sample size. Among these are the root mean square error of approximation (RMSEA), which was developed by Steiger (1990) and is advocated by Jöreskog and Sörbom (1993, 124). Of course, many, many other fit indices exist. Among the more popular choices are the GFI and AGFI, Bentler's Comparative Fit Index, and Bollen's Indices.

Exhaustive reviews of fit statistics abound. Marsh, Balla, and Hau (1996) provide an excellent discussion of fit indices, as do Hu and Bentler (1995). A comprehensive discussion of fit is beyond the scope of this book. The most important aspect of goodness-of-fit is that it is the single measure that leads us to accept or reject a hypothesized causal model. In SEM, a model is either accepted or rejected; there is no "in between" as one would encounter in exploratory analyses. The case study will illustrate model formulation and evaluation.

IDENTIFICATION

In confirmatory analysis, **identification** plays a crucial role and yet is often misunderstood. As noted earlier, any structural equations model (regardless if latent variables are present) has some parameters that are fixed either explicitly or implicitly. For example, when we do not specify a path from an exogenous variable (whether manifest or latent) to an endogenous variable, covariances are free to be estimated.

With respect to identification, a model may be underidentified, just-identified, or **overidentified** (Chou and Bentler 1995, 39–41). Consider the simple relationship in Equation 9-6.

$$2a + b = 100 \tag{9-6}$$

There are an infinite number of solutions to this equation. For example, $a = 25$ and $b = 50$ or $a = 40$ and $b = 20$. The point is that there is no unique solution to Equation 9-6. The model is said to be underidentified.

If we constrain one of the model parameters in Equation 9-6 to be fixed, a unique solution is possible. For example, if we fix the value of b to be 40, then a unique solution is possible because a must equal 30. Such a model has a unique solution. Some authors refer to the just-identified model as being "saturated" (Everitt 1998, 160). In a similar fashion, if we added Equation 9-7 to our base of information, a unique solution ($a = 33.33$; $b = 33.33$) can be found.

$$a = b \tag{9-7}$$

A model is said to be overidentified when there is more information than necessary to find a unique solution. The system of linear relationships depicted in Equations 9-8 through 9-10 reflects an overidentified model. In short, there are more independent equations than there are unknown parameters. More information than necessary is available; the model is overidentified. A model that is just-identified or overidentified is identified. One that is underidentified is referred to as not identified.

$$x = y = 10 \tag{9-8}$$

$$x + 5 = 10 \tag{9-9}$$

$$3x + y = 20 \tag{9-10}$$

Of the two identified conditions, it is generally more desirable to have an overidentified model because it permits goodness-of-fit tests. The saturated, or just-identified model, represents a perfect fit with the data. In contrast, when one or more parameters is fixed (typically to zero by removing a path), the model becomes overidentified, and goodness-of-fit statistics can be calculated. This is desirable primarily due to the parsimony implied by the less complicated overidentified model. It means we can constrain certain relationships to zero (or conversely, require two variables to covary) and still have a model that accurately reflects the original data.

Identification for complex structural equation models is described in greater detail by numerous authors. Schumaker and Lomax (1996, 99–102), Chou and Bentler (1995, 39–41), and Rigdon (1998, 257–58) provide very readable treatments of identification. Bollen (1989, 88–104) offers a more in-depth technical treatment.

All of the SEM software packages (for example, AMOS, EQS, SAS PROC CALIS, and LISREL) provide the user feedback relating to identification. This information ranges from cryptic to confusing. The SAS system's PROC CALIS, for example, provides limited information concerning model identification (Hatcher 1994, 162).

Case Study: Aquarian Electric Utility

This case study utilizes a reduced survey instrument for the purposes of illustration. The customer satisfaction and loyalty measurement program of Aquarian Electric employed a postcard survey on a continuous basis. This analysis is based on 300 observations. As shown in Figure 9.4, the questionnaire is composed of eight items. Of these, six (x_1–x_6) will be considered exogenous. The last three questions (y_1–y_3) are clearly endogenous. Figure 9.5 presents the complete, hypothesized model. As shown, the six predictor variables (x_1–x_6) are presumed to reflect three underlying latent constructs: *rates, service,* and *power quality.* The three manifest dependent variables (y_1–y_3) clearly reflect two latent variables: *overall satisfaction* and *loyalty.* Thus, the measurement model posits five latent variables, three of which are exogenous.

The structural component of the hypothesized model presented in Figure 9.5 suggests that rates and service will emerge as significant predictors of overall satisfaction. In contrast, there were substantive grounds to believe that power quality would not affect overall satisfaction. With respect to loyalty, its three antecedents include *rates, power quality,* and *overall satisfaction.* In short, our model suggests that although power quality affects loyalty, it is not an antecedent of customer satisfaction.

Note the parameters that will be estimated in our latent variable path analysis. First, from the measurement model standpoint, we have posited five latent variables. The parameters to be estimated here include the actual loadings (λ) of manifest variables on the latent constructs. One loading for each latent variable is set to 1.0, which has the effect of constraining the remaining variables to the same scale. In the case of factor loadings, it is desirable for this to have an upper

Aquarian Electric Utility
Customer Satisfaction Survey

Dear Customer:

At Aquarian Electric, we try to continuously monitor and improve customer satisfaction. You have been randomly selected to participate in our study. Please spend a few minutes filling out the brief survey below. Note that the postcard is already stamped and addressed so all you have to do upon completion is drop it in the mail.

For the questions below, please use the seven-point scale to indicate your satisfaction. The scale ranges from (1) very dissatisfied to (7) very satisfied.

	Very Dissatisfied						**Very Satisfied**
1. Aquarian Electric's rate structure	1 ❑	2 ❑	3 ❑	4 ❑	5 ❑	6 ❑	7 ❑
2. Availability of alternative payment plans	1 ❑	2 ❑	3 ❑	4 ❑	5 ❑	6 ❑	7 ❑
3. Technical support service you receive	1 ❑	2 ❑	3 ❑	4 ❑	5 ❑	6 ❑	7 ❑
4. Billing support service you receive	1 ❑	2 ❑	3 ❑	4 ❑	5 ❑	6 ❑	7 ❑
5. Aquarian Electric's ability to avoid power outages	1 ❑	2 ❑	3 ❑	4 ❑	5 ❑	6 ❑	7 ❑
6. Aquarian Electric's ability to restore power following an outage	1 ❑	2 ❑	3 ❑	4 ❑	5 ❑	6 ❑	7 ❑
7. Overall, considering all these aspects of Aquarian Electric, how satisfied are you with us?	1 ❑	2 ❑	3 ❑	4 ❑	5 ❑	6 ❑	7 ❑

	Strongly Disagree						**Strongly Agree**
8. I would recommend Aquarian Electric to a colleague	1 ❑	2 ❑	3 ❑	4 ❑	5 ❑	6 ❑	7 ❑
9. I like the people at Aquarian Electric	1 ❑	2 ❑	3 ❑	4 ❑	5 ❑	6 ❑	7 ❑

~Thank You~

FIGURE 9.4 Aquarian Electric customer satisfaction instrument.

limit of one. We normally have theoretical grounds for setting a particular manifest variable loading to one. Typically this involves the researcher's belief that one variable is the purest measure of the underlying construct.

The model depicted in Figure 9.5 can be considered *nonstandard* in that one of the latent variables (η_1) is associated with only one manifest variable. As Hatcher (1994, 256–57) concedes, multiple measures of a construct are not always available. Some authors depict such variables as manifest (that is, by using a square rather than a circle in

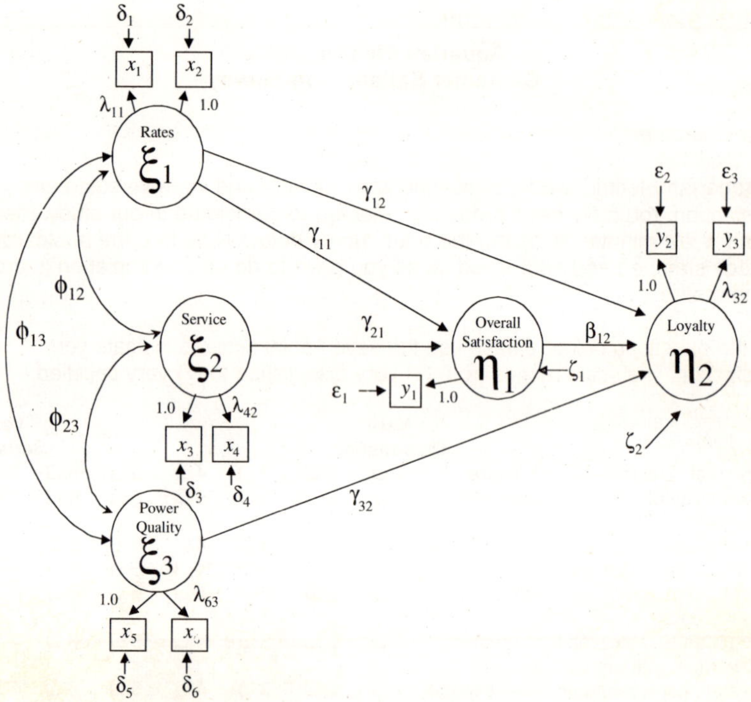

FIGURE 9.5 Hypothesized Aquarian Electric model.

the model diagram). In Figure 9.5, we have depicted η_1 as latent with a single manifest indicator. There are substantive theoretical grounds for this—one can argue compellingly that overall satisfaction may be measured with a single item.

The measurement component of Figure 9.5 also reveals that we will be estimating the covariances among the latent exogenous variables. Three such covariances are to be estimated. Note that in exploratory factor analysis with orthogonal rotation (for example, **varimax rotation**), these would normally be constrained to zero. One strength of confirmatory analyses is that we can decide whether or not to permit factors to correlate. It is possible to constrain some factors to be orthogonal while others are permitted to covary. Three latent exogenous variable covariances (ϕ_{12}, ϕ_{13}, and ϕ_{23}) will be estimated in this model although we could have set them all to zero . . . or any other level of covariance. Additionally, for each latent exogenous variable, we must estimate a variance. This is not generally depicted in SEM diagrams but is represented by the same symbol,

TABLE 9.4 Estimable parameters for Aquarian Electric model.

Description	Parameters	
Measurement Model		
Factor loadings	$\lambda_{11}, \lambda_{42}, \lambda_{32}, \lambda_{63}$	19 measurement model parameters
Endogenous manifest variable variances	$\varepsilon_1, \varepsilon_2, \varepsilon_3$	
Exogenous manifest variable variances	$\delta_1, \delta_2, \delta_3, \delta_4, \delta_5, \delta_6$	
Exogenous latent variable covariances	$\phi_{12}, \phi_{13}, \phi_{23}$	
Exogenous latent variable variances	$\phi_{11}, \phi_{22}, \phi_{33}$	
Structural Model		
Exogenous variable effects on endogenous variables	$\gamma_{12}, \gamma_{11}, \gamma_{21}, \gamma_{32}$	7 structural model parameters
Endogenous variable effects on endogenous variables	β_{12}	
Errors in equations (residuals)	ζ_1, ζ_2	

phi. The latent exogenous variable variances are represented by three parameters: (ϕ_{11}, ϕ_{22}, and ϕ_{33}).

Each manifest variable, whether on the dependent or independent side of the model, is associated with a variance term. For the three manifest dependent variables, these are ε_1, ε_2, and ε_3 whereas the six independent variables are associated with δ_1 through δ_6. As suggested by Hatcher (1994, 357) and others (Byrne 1989, 24-25) key indicator variable loadings were set to 1.0 to ensure proper scaling, leaving four **factor loadings** (λ_{11}, λ_{42}, λ_{32}, and λ_{63}) to be estimated. The measurement model, therefore, is responsible for 19 estimable parameters: four factor loadings, three latent exogenous variable covariances, three latent variable variances, and nine manifest variable variances.

The structural component of the Aquarian Electric Utility model presented in Figure 9.4 relates the latent variables. First, the errors (ζ_1 and ζ_2) in equations associated with the two dependent latent variables (η_1 and η_2) are free to be estimated. There are also four paths (γ_{12}, γ_{11}, γ_{21}, and γ_{32}) from latent exogenous to latent endogenous variables and one path (β_{12}) from the first latent endogenous variable to the second. The structural model is responsible for nine estimable parameters.

Table 9.4 summarizes the full model presented in Figure 9.5 in terms of the 26 parameters that must be estimated. The parameters presented in Table 9.4 were estimated using the SAS system's CALIS

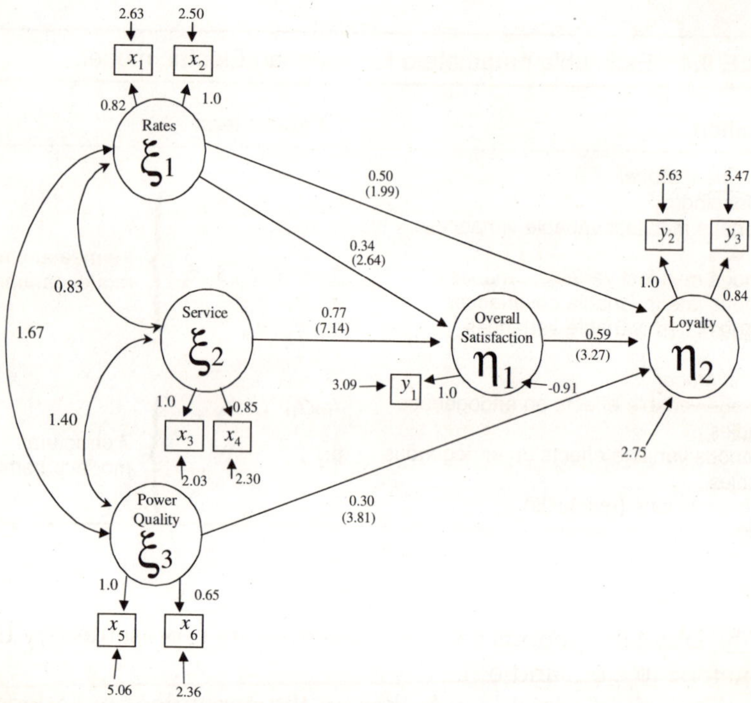

FIGURE 9.6 Aquarian Electric model.

procedure. The estimates are presented in Figure 9.6, which shows all of the measurement model and structural model coefficients. Note that under each path coefficient is a t-statistic in parentheses. As shown, all of the path coefficients are statistically significant at the 95 percent confidence level. The latent variable variances (ϕ_{11}, ϕ_{22}, and ϕ_{33}) are not depicted in the figure.

The most important aspect of the model presented in Figure 9.6 is that it represents an excellent fit with the relationships present in the data set. This is reflected in a chi-squared value (11.6) that is not statistically significant ($p = 0.89$) and a RMSEA value (0.00) that is well below the accepted cut-off criterion (0.05). Recall that with respect to the chi-square statistic, this measure reflects the extent to which the hypothesized model is consistent with the relationships presented in the data. As the two become disparate, chi-squared increases, and its statistical significance increases. A detailed discussion of fit statistics is beyond the scope of this book. As noted earlier, there are numerous resources that focus exclusively upon SEM, model development strategies, and assessment techniques.

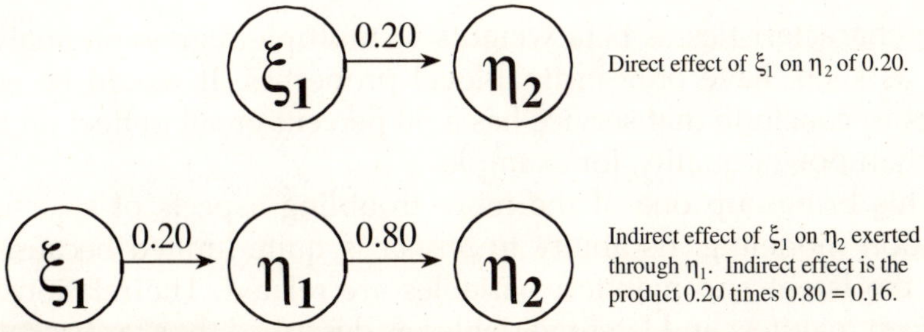

FIGURE 9.7 Direct versus indirect effects.

TABLE 9.5 Direct, indirect, and total effects of latent exogenous variables on loyalty.

Variable	Direct Effect	Indirect Effect	Total Effect
Rates	0.50	0.20	0.70
Service	0.00	0.45	0.45
Power quality	0.30	0.00	0.30

Based upon the model depicted in Figure 9.6, it is clear that rates and service have the strongest effect on the measure of loyalty. As was described earlier in our discussion of path analysis, it is very useful to differentiate between the direct, indirect, and total effects of each exogenous, latent variable. Direct effects are characterized by a single, direct path between two latent variables. The latent variables rates and power quality have direct effects on loyalty, whereas service does not. Indirect effects are exerted *through* an intervening variable. The difference between direct effects and indirect effects is illustrated in Figure 9.7. As shown, indirect effects are the product of two path coefficients. In the present case, the effects of service on loyalty are only indirect. Service first affects overall satisfaction, which in turn affects loyalty. Total effects are the sum of the direct and indirect effects each latent variable exerts on the final outcome variable: loyalty. Table 9.5 summarizes the direct, indirect, and total effects of each latent variable on loyalty.

As shown in Table 9.5, the latent exogenous variable rates exerts the strongest total effect on loyalty. It has both a direct effect (0.50) and an indirect effect (0.20). In contrast, service exerts only an indirect effect (0.45) and no direct effect whereas power quality exerts a direct effect (0.30) but no indirect effect. Note that path coefficients have the same characteristics as beta weights in multiple regression analysis and, as such, have only ordinal-level properties. It would be erroneous to conclude that service has a 50 percent greater effect on loyalty than power quality, for example.

This brings up one of the more troubling aspects of structural equation modeling. Its ability to *predict* is quite limited because of how the latent and manifest variables are related. The relationship between manifest and latent variables as described thus far has taken a factor-analytic approach. Factor loadings (that is, correlations) were presumed to link a manifest variable to a latent variable. This precludes testing the effect, for example, of a 10 percent increase in one manifest exogenous variable on a manifest endogenous variable. This has led some researchers to pursue a different and controversial course: latent variable path modeling with PLS.

Latent Variable Path Modeling with Partial Least Squares

Lately, in the applied customer satisfaction research arena, latent variable path modeling with PLS has been introduced as a competitor to the traditional LISREL approach described in the preceding section. PLS was described earlier in chapter 5 as having its roots in chemometrics. It is a dependence model technique very similar to PCR in that it combines a dimension reducing function with a dependence model. The primary difference, according to Everitt (1998, 245) is that PLS constructs a new set of predictor variables that are statistically related to the original set. In a manner reminiscent of factor analysis or PCA, each new regressor variable is statistically uncorrelated (orthogonal) with the others but maximally correlated with the dependent variable. Excellent treatments of PLS are available by Geladi and Kowalski (1986) and Helland (1988).

PLS can be performed with a variety of different software applications. At least one large-scale statistical package can perform PLS (the SAS system has an experimental procedure). PLS is really quite similar to PCR and is not, by itself, a member of the causal modeling family. The point is that SEM with latent variables can be conducted using PLS, and the assumptions about data—particularly distributions—are very different. Fortunately, the nomenclature is the same. The latent variable path model with PLS encompasses the same terms introduced earlier. Latent and manifest variables are still related in the measurement model, and latent variables are related in the structural model. The primary conceptual and mathematical difference is that PLS permits us to relate the manifest variables to latent variables in a different fashion.

Latent variable path modeling (SEM) with PLS is challenging. Indeed, none of the major statistical software packages accommodate this technique. Perhaps the most well-known software package designed specifically for latent variable path modeling with PLS was developed by Lohmöller in 1986. Lohmöller's program (LVPLS) requires considerable programming and, in this regard, is not especially different from the earlier versions of Jöreskog and Sörbom's LISREL computer application.

The most fundamental mathematical difference between the traditional approach to SEM and SEM with PLS involves the technique used to estimate the unknown parameters (for example, the factor loadings or structural model path coefficients). Recall that in the traditional SEM approach, the latent variables were assumed to be responsible for variation in their manifest indicators. For example, an IQ test score is presumed to be *caused* (at least partially) by an underlying factor called intelligence. The reversal of this causal sequence is much less appealing. To suggest that the IQ test score causes intelligence seems almost nonsensical. Nonetheless, without this type of relationship between manifest and latent variables, it is not possible to use SEM for prediction.

Clearly, there are certain types of latent variables that may *cause* manifest variables, and vice versa. Constructs such as intelligence, motivation, or job satisfaction are most appropriately modeled in the fashion described earlier. That is, it seems most reasonable to assume that the latent constructs affect their manifest indicator variables. The latter are frequently in the form of test scores. In contrast, consider latent variables such as financial performance or mortality rate. In the case of these variables, it would be prudent to consider a model that permitted us to infer that the latent variable is caused by specific manifest variables. This changes the nature of the model substantially. We interpret the relationship between manifest and latent variables in a regression framework. This permits us to model the effects of manifest variables on latent variables.

Figure 9.8 presents three ways that the relationship between manifest and latent variables can be modeled using latent variable path modeling with PLS. The first is consistent with constructs such as intelligence or motivation. Scores on manifest variables x_1 and x_2, for example, are presumed to be caused by an underlying construct, *intelligence* (ξ_1). Intelligence is presumed to affect a latent endogenous variable, *motivation* (η_1). It has two indicator variables (y_1 and y_2), which, consistent with the reflective indicator mode, are presumed to be caused by the underlying construct.

Formative indicators in PLS latent variable path modeling are appropriate when the latent construct is presumed to be directly dependent upon the manifest variables. Such would be the case if ξ_1 were a measure of advertising and public relations expenditures, and η_1 were a profitability metric. In this case, the paths between the manifest indicator variables and the latent constructs should be interpreted in a regression context. Rather than being interpreted as factor loadings, the coefficients linking manifest indicator variables to their latent constructs must be considered as path coefficients or beta weights.

The final configuration shown in Figure 9.8 presents a mixed-mode model wherein both reflective and formative indicators are

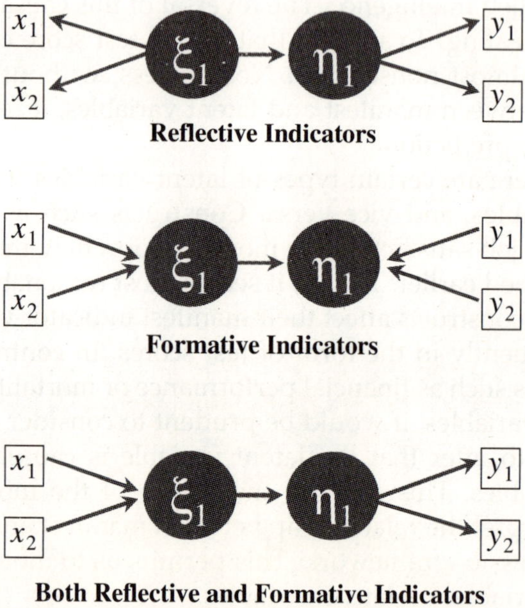

FIGURE 9.8 Reflective and formative indicators in SEM with PLS.

used. In this example, the latent exogenous variable (ξ_1) is formative, and the latent endogenous variable (η_1) is reflective. The mixed-mode model would be appropriate when, for example, the latent exogenous variable represents a composite of advertising and public relations expenditures, and the latent endogenous variable is a reflective construct such as brand loyalty or brand equity. Chin (1998, 308) suggested that this third mode is equivalent to redundancy analysis, which may be used to refine the operationalization of a construct. Redundancy in this context " . . . refers to the mean variance in the η block of indicators being predicted by the linear composite of the ξ set of indicators," where η and ξ are ostensibly measuring the same construct. The extent to which the two latent variables measure the same construct is reflected by the magnitude of the path between them.

The PLS approach to latent variable path modeling is not without detractors. Even PLS advocates concede that the LISREL approach using maximum likelihood estimation allows for more measurement error—a common phenomenon when working with psychometric data (Fornell and Bookstein 1982, 450). McDonald (1996, 240) referred to the PLS approach as " . . . difficult to describe and extremely difficult to evaluate, partly because PLS constitutes a set of ad hoc algorithms that have generally not been formally analyzed, or shown to possess any clear global optimizing properties. . . ." Clearly, latent variable path analysis with PLS is controversial. Nonetheless it remains attractive because of it predictive capabilities. The ability to predict the effect on overall satisfaction of a change in a given service or product quality issue is very appealing. Thus, it is really the *formative* indicator model that is so attractive to customer satisfaction researchers.

Latent variable path modeling has played a substantial role in both applied and academic research focusing on customer satisfaction and related constructs. Still, as Rigdon (1998, 277) notes, there are still unresolved methodological and statistical issues surrounding SEM. Most notable among these is an inability to accommodate nonlinear relationships. Further, neither the covarianced-based LISREL approach or the PLS approach to latent variable path modeling can model dynamic or time-dependent variables. There are still controversies over fundamental methodological issues, and a resolution does not appear to be forthcoming in the near future.

Other areas of concern involve the requirement for very large sample sizes (although this is not such a problem using the PLS approach) and unrealistic assumptions. Although not as problematic for PLS users, LISREL approaches to latent variable path modeling assume multivariate normality—something that is rarely encountered in applied customer satisfaction research. Finally, Rigdon (1998, 278) suggests that the complexity of the SEM approach virtually requires users to be comfortable with advanced matrix algebra in order to fully understand the implications of results.

Despite these apparent shortcomings, SEM with latent variables is likely to remain a popular technique in customer satisfaction research. The ability to demonstrate a causal sequence that involves specific product and service quality issues, overall satisfaction, and other constructs such as loyalty is very appealing. In general, the causal latent variable sequences depicted in SEM are well-suited to the needs of researchers involved in customer satisfaction research.

Appendix A

Matrix Algebra in Statistics

Matrix algebra represents a very useful shorthand for statistical data analysis. There are numerous texts that provide excellent treatments of the subject. Some of the better books on matrix algebra include Searle (1982), Steinberg (1974), and Eves (1966). A more technical treatment is provided by Perlis (1991). The use of matrix algebra to convey statistical analysis is now commonplace in both books and journals. This appendix provides a brief overview of matrix algebra and its role in the statistical analyses used in customer satisfaction research.

The three objects manipulated in matrix algebra are scalars, vectors, and matrices. Scalars are simply numbers like 1, 32, or 1/5. On the other hand, vector and matrices are sets of numbers. In both cases, the size of a given matrix or vector is referred to in terms of its dimensions. The dimension of a matrix or vector is given by its *rows* and *columns.*

$$\mathbf{a} = \begin{bmatrix} 3 \\ 6 \\ 2 \end{bmatrix} \qquad \mathbf{b} = \begin{bmatrix} 6 & 1 & 4 & 8 \end{bmatrix}$$

For example, the column vector $\mathbf{a}_{3 \times 1}$ is a 3×1 vector; it has three rows and one column. In contrast, the row vector $\mathbf{b}_{1 \times 3}$ has one row and four columns.

Vectors are actually a special form of matrix. The matrix $\mathbf{C}_{3 \times 4}$ that follows has three rows and four columns. Note that we differentiate matrices and vectors with upper- versus lowercase letters, respectively.

$$\mathbf{C}_{3 \times 4} = \begin{bmatrix} 1 & 3 & 6 & 2 \\ 2 & 1 & 4 & 8 \\ 3 & 8 & 1 & 6 \end{bmatrix}$$

Any single element of **C** can be identified based on its coordinates. For example, the element in the third row and second column is 8. The elements of **C** can be uniquely identified by their row and column addresses. Thus, the value of c_{32} is 8.

$$\mathbf{C} = \begin{bmatrix} c_{11} & c_{12} & c_{13} & c_{14} \\ c_{21} & c_{22} & c_{23} & c_{24} \\ c_{31} & c_{32} & c_{33} & c_{34} \end{bmatrix}$$

A matrix that has as many rows as columns is referred to as a square matrix. For example, the matrix **D** is square because it has two rows and two columns. Note that in most texts and journal articles, matrices are denoted with bold capital letters, and their elements are assigned lowercase italic equivalents.

$$\mathbf{D} = \begin{bmatrix} d_{11} & d_{12} \\ d_{21} & d_{22} \end{bmatrix}$$

MATRIX AND VECTOR OPERATIONS

Matrices and vectors can be added and subtracted from one another if their dimensions are exactly the same.

$$\mathbf{a} = \begin{bmatrix} 3 \\ 2 \\ 1 \end{bmatrix} \qquad \mathbf{b} = \begin{bmatrix} 1 \\ 1 \\ 2 \end{bmatrix}$$

$$\mathbf{a} - \mathbf{b} = \mathbf{c} \qquad \mathbf{c} = \begin{bmatrix} 2 \\ 1 \\ -1 \end{bmatrix}$$

The column vector **b** can be subtracted from **A** because they both have three rows and one column. Similarly, the matrices **F** and **G** may be added to produce a new matrix (**H**) of the same dimension.

$$\mathbf{F} = \begin{bmatrix} 1 & 2 & 3 \\ 2 & 3 & 1 \end{bmatrix} \qquad \mathbf{G} = \begin{bmatrix} 6 & 1 & 4 \\ 2 & 8 & 3 \end{bmatrix}$$

$$\mathbf{H} = \mathbf{F} + \mathbf{G} \qquad \mathbf{H} = \begin{bmatrix} 7 & 3 & 7 \\ 4 & 11 & 4 \end{bmatrix}$$

Each element of **H** equals the sum of the corresponding elements in **F** and **G.** For example, $h_{12} = 3$, which is the sum of $f_{12} = 2$ and $g_{12} = 1$. The matrix **H,** therefore, is simply the sum of the matrices **F** and **G.**

$$\begin{bmatrix} f_{11} + g_{11} & f_{12} + g_{12} & f_{13} + g_{13} \\ f_{21} + g_{21} & f_{22} + g_{22} & f_{23} + g_{23} \\ f_{31} + g_{31} & f_{32} + g_{32} & f_{33} + g_{33} \end{bmatrix}$$

A scalar can be added to a matrix of any size. It involves adding the scalar value to every element of the matrix. This operation can be performed regardless of the dimensions of a given matrix or vector.

$$\mathbf{a} = 6 \quad \mathbf{B} = \begin{bmatrix} 2 & 3 \\ 4 & 8 \end{bmatrix} \qquad \mathbf{a} + \mathbf{B} = \begin{bmatrix} 8 & 9 \\ 10 & 14 \end{bmatrix}$$

$$\mathbf{a} + \mathbf{B} = \begin{bmatrix} b_{11} + 6 & b_{12} + 6 \\ b_{21} + 6 & b_{22} + 6 \end{bmatrix}$$

$$\mathbf{C} = \begin{bmatrix} 3 \\ 1 \\ 3 \\ 1 \end{bmatrix} \qquad \mathbf{a} + \mathbf{C} = \begin{bmatrix} c_1 + 6 \\ c_2 + 6 \\ c_3 + 6 \\ c_4 + 6 \end{bmatrix}$$

MATRIX MULTIPLICATION

Of the operations performed in matrix algebra, matrix multiplication is one of the most powerful. Matrix multiplication requires that the matrices be compatible. In order to multiply two matrices, the number of *columns* in the first must be the same as the number of rows in the second.

Dimension of new matrix

$$\mathbf{R}_{2\times 3}\mathbf{S}_{3\times 2} = \mathbf{T}_{2\times 2}$$

Must be identical

$$\mathbf{R}_{2\times 3} = \begin{bmatrix} 1 & 2 & 3 \\ 4 & 2 & 1 \end{bmatrix} \qquad \mathbf{S}_{3\times 2} = \begin{bmatrix} 6 & 1 \\ 4 & 2 \\ 1 & 3 \end{bmatrix}$$

$$\mathbf{RS} = \begin{bmatrix} (r_{11}s_{11})+(r_{12}s_{21})+(r_{13}s_{31}) & (r_{11}s_{12})+(r_{12}s_{22})+(r_{13}s_{32}) \\ (r_{21}s_{11})+(r_{22}s_{21})+(r_{23}s_{31}) & (r_{21}s_{12})+(r_{22}s_{22})+(r_{23}s_{32}) \end{bmatrix}$$

Although **RS** yields a new 2×2 matrix **T,** we cannot assume that **SR** will equal **T** also. Indeed, unlike scalar mathematics in which 2×3 is the equivalent of 3×2, such is not the case in matrix algebra. Although the product of **RS** was $\mathbf{T}_{2\times 2}$, product **SR** may not even exist. In the present case, we can find the product of **SR,** however.

$$\mathbf{SR} = \mathbf{V}_{3\times 3}$$

$$\mathbf{V}_{3\times 3} = \begin{bmatrix} (s_{11}r_{11})+(s_{12}r_{21}) & (s_{11}r_{12})+(s_{12}r_{22}) & (s_{11}r_{13})+(s_{12}r_{23}) \\ (s_{21}r_{11})+(s_{22}r_{21}) & (s_{21}r_{12})+(s_{22}r_{22}) & (s_{21}r_{13})+(s_{22}r_{23}) \\ (s_{31}r_{11})+(s_{32}r_{21}) & (s_{31}r_{12})+(s_{32}r_{22}) & (s_{31}r_{13})+(s_{32}r_{23}) \end{bmatrix}$$

$$\mathbf{V}_{3\times 3} = \begin{bmatrix} 10 & 14 & 10 \\ 12 & 12 & 14 \\ 13 & 8 & 6 \end{bmatrix}$$

Clearly, **SR** yields a very different matrix than **RS.** To differentiate between these two matrix products, we use the terms *premultiply* and *postmultiply*. Matrix $\mathbf{V}_{3\times 3}$ is the result of premultiplying **S** with **R.** Conversely, matrix $\mathbf{T}_{2\times 2}$ is the result of postmultiplying **S** with **R.**

Vectors present a unique opportunity in matrix algebra. Consider the two vectors **a** and **b.** Note that **a** is a row vector, and **b** is a column vector. We can calculate **ab** because the number of rows in **a** equals the number of columns in **b.** This operation (**ab**) will yield a scalar equal to the sum or the products of the elements in the matrices.

$$\mathbf{a}_{1\times 4} = \begin{bmatrix} 3 & 2 & 5 & 6 \end{bmatrix} \qquad \mathbf{b}_{4\times 1} = \begin{bmatrix} 2 \\ 2 \\ 1 \\ 1 \end{bmatrix}$$

$$\mathbf{ab} = \begin{bmatrix} 21 \end{bmatrix}$$

In contrast, the matrix **BA** has a total of 16 elements.

$$\mathbf{BA} = \begin{bmatrix} 6 & 6 & 3 & 3 \\ 4 & 4 & 2 & 2 \\ 10 & 10 & 5 & 5 \\ 12 & 12 & 6 & 6 \end{bmatrix}$$

The transpose of a matrix **A** is denoted as **A′**. The transpose operation simply involves exchanging the rows and columns in a matrix. For example, the matrix **A** and its transpose **A′** illustrate the effects of transposing a matrix.

$$\mathbf{A}_{3\times 2} = \begin{bmatrix} 2 & 1 \\ 3 & 3 \\ 4 & 6 \end{bmatrix} \qquad \mathbf{A'}_{3\times 2} = \begin{bmatrix} 2 & 3 & 4 \\ 1 & 3 & 6 \end{bmatrix}$$

Assume that the matrix **A** is composed of three observations and two variables. When we calculate a new matrix **A′A** it has some interesting properties.

$$\mathbf{A'A} = \begin{bmatrix} 29 & 34 \\ 34 & 46 \end{bmatrix}$$

The matrix **A′A** is referred to as the uncorrected sums of squares and cross products (SSCP). In the case of **A′A**, we know that the diagonal elements are equal to the sum of squared values for the first of our two hypothetical variables. That is $29 = (2^2) + (3^2) + (4^2)$. Similarly, $46 = (1^2) + (3^2) + (6^2)$. The off-diagonal elements of **A′A** are equal to the sum of cross products between the two hypothetical variables. Note that the upper-right and lower-left entries are equal; both are equal to 34, which is the sum of cross products for our two variables. So,

34 = (2 × 1) + (3 × 3) + (4 × 6) is the sum of cross products. In general, the SSCP matrix takes the following form.

$$\mathbf{X'X} = \begin{bmatrix} \sum_{i=1}^{n} x_{i1}^2 & \sum_{i=1}^{n} x_{i1}x_{i2} & \cdots & \sum_{i=1}^{n} x_{i1}x_{ik} \\ \sum_{i=1}^{n} x_{i1}x_{i2} & \sum_{i=1}^{n} x_{i2}^2 & \cdots & \sum_{i=1}^{n} x_{i2}x_{ik} \\ \vdots & \vdots & & \vdots \\ \sum_{i=1}^{n} x_{i1}x_{ik} & \sum_{i=1}^{n} x_{i2}x_{ik} & \cdots & \sum_{i=1}^{n} x_{ik}^2 \end{bmatrix}$$

Note that the diagonal elements of **X′X** are the sums of squares for each variable. The off-diagonal elements are the sums of cross products for each variable pairing. Finally, notice that **X′X** is symmetric. That is, **A′A** = (**A′A**)′, which underscores the fact that the top-right element is the same as the bottom-left element.

The SSCP matrix has little intrinsic value. It is not standardized; it reflects raw measurement units and is difficult to interpret. The SSCP matrix must be centered in order to produce the mean corrected SSCP matrix **S.** The mean corrected SSCP is the basis for developing the covariance matrix **C** and correlation matrix **R.**

In order to produce **S**, we must find the mean for each variable in **A.** Because our data matrix is so small, it is a simple matter to calculate that $\bar{x}_1 = 3$ and $\bar{x}_2 = 3.33$. In matrix algebra, we can use a row vector of ones (1′) and the sample size (n) to begin the centering process.

$$\mathbf{A}_{3\times 2} = \begin{bmatrix} 2 & 1 \\ 3 & 3 \\ 4 & 6 \end{bmatrix}$$

$$\overline{\mathbf{A}} = \frac{1}{N}\mathbf{1'A}$$

$$\bar{\mathbf{a}} = \frac{1}{3}\begin{bmatrix} 1 & 1 & 1 \end{bmatrix}\begin{bmatrix} 2 & 1 \\ 3 & 3 \\ 4 & 6 \end{bmatrix}$$

$$\bar{\mathbf{a}} = \frac{1}{3}\begin{bmatrix} 9 & 10 \end{bmatrix}$$

$$\bar{\mathbf{a}} = \begin{bmatrix} 3 & 3.33 \end{bmatrix}$$

The next step in the centering process is to generate a new matrix with elements that are centered with respect to the matrix $\bar{\mathbf{a}}$. This entails finding the matrix **S**.

$$\mathbf{S} = \mathbf{A}'\mathbf{A} - \frac{1}{n}(\mathbf{A}'\mathbf{1})(\mathbf{1}'\mathbf{A})$$

For the two-variable situation, **S** is calculated in the following fashion.

$$\mathbf{S} = \begin{bmatrix} 2 & 3 & 4 \\ 1 & 3 & 6 \end{bmatrix} \begin{bmatrix} 2 & 1 \\ 3 & 3 \\ 4 & 6 \end{bmatrix} - \frac{1}{3}\left(\begin{bmatrix} 2 & 3 & 4 \\ 1 & 3 & 6 \end{bmatrix} \begin{bmatrix} 1 \\ 1 \\ 1 \end{bmatrix} \right) \left(\begin{bmatrix} 1 & 1 & 1 \end{bmatrix} \begin{bmatrix} 2 & 1 \\ 3 & 3 \\ 4 & 6 \end{bmatrix} \right)$$

$$\mathbf{S} = \begin{bmatrix} 29 & 35 \\ 35 & 46 \end{bmatrix} - \frac{1}{3}\left(\begin{bmatrix} 9 \\ 10 \end{bmatrix} [9 \quad 10] \right)$$

$$\mathbf{S} = \begin{bmatrix} 29 & 35 \\ 35 & 46 \end{bmatrix} - \frac{1}{3}\begin{bmatrix} 81 & 90 \\ 90 & 100 \end{bmatrix}$$

$$\mathbf{S} = \begin{bmatrix} 29 & 35 \\ 35 & 46 \end{bmatrix} - \begin{bmatrix} 27 & 30 \\ 30 & 33.33 \end{bmatrix}$$

$$\mathbf{S} = \begin{bmatrix} 2 & 5 \\ 5 & 12.66 \end{bmatrix}$$

With the mean corrected SSCP matrix, the calculation of a covariance matrix **C** is a simple matter. Note that **C** contains variances on the diagonal and covariances on the off-diagonal. **C** is a symmetric matrix in that it equals its transpose **C** = **C**′.

$$\mathbf{C} = \frac{1}{n-1}\mathbf{S}$$

$$\mathbf{C} = \frac{1}{2}\begin{bmatrix} 2 & 5 \\ 5 & 12.66 \end{bmatrix}$$

$$\mathbf{C} = \begin{bmatrix} 1 & 2.50 \\ 2.50 & 6.33 \end{bmatrix}$$

The correlation matrix **R** can be calculated using either the covariance matrix **C** or the mean corrected SSCP matrix. **C** contains valuable information concerning the dispersion of the two variables. The diagonal is especially useful because it is composed of variances. This can be verified using a calculator.

If we define a new matrix $\mathbf{V}^{-½}$ consisting of the reciprocal square roots of the variances for x_1 and x_2 and use it to pre- and postmultiply the covariance matrix **C**, we find the correlation matrix **R.**

$$\mathbf{V}^{-½} = \begin{bmatrix} \frac{1}{\sqrt{\mathbf{S}_1^2}} & 0 \\ 0 & \frac{1}{\sqrt{\mathbf{S}_2^2}} \end{bmatrix}$$

$$\mathbf{V}^{-½} = \begin{bmatrix} 1 & 0 \\ 0 & 0.397 \end{bmatrix}$$

$$\mathbf{R} = \mathbf{V}^{-½}\mathbf{C}\mathbf{V}^{-½}$$

$$\mathbf{R} = \begin{bmatrix} 1.0 & 0.993 \\ 0.993 & 1.0 \end{bmatrix}$$

This analysis reveals a very strong level of linear dependence between x_1 and x_2. Of course, **R** was based upon only three observations for the purposes of illustration. Larger data matrices can be subjected to the same analysis. However, it would be advisable to use software capable of manipulating matrices. For example, SAS, IML, and MATLAB both permit these types of matrix operations.

Least Squares Regression

Matrix algebra notation greatly simplifies how we convey least squares regression. Performing regression analysis using matrix algebra requires the introduction of an additional operation: the matrix inverse. The inverse of a matrix is analogous to the reciprocal in scalar mathematics. For example, although $1 \times 1/10 = 1$, $\mathbf{AA}^{-1} = \mathbf{I}$. **I** is the symbol for the identity matrix; it has many of the characteristics that the number 1 has in scalar mathematics. Any matrix pre- or postmultiplied by the identity matrix equals itself.

$$\mathbf{I}_{4\times 4} = \begin{bmatrix} 1 & 0 & 0 & 0 \\ 0 & 1 & 0 & 0 \\ 0 & 0 & 1 & 0 \\ 0 & 0 & 0 & 1 \end{bmatrix}$$

$$\mathbf{AI} = \mathbf{A}$$

$$\mathbf{IA} = \mathbf{A}$$

The following example confirms that just as 1×10 equals 10, so too does **IA** or **AI** equal **A**.

$$\mathbf{A} = \begin{bmatrix} 4 & 3 \\ 2 & 1 \end{bmatrix} \quad \mathbf{I} = \begin{bmatrix} 1 & 0 \\ 0 & 1 \end{bmatrix}$$

$$\mathbf{AI} = \begin{matrix} [(4\times 1)+(3\times 0) & (4\times 0)+(3\times 1)] \\ [(2\times 1)+(1\times 0) & (2\times 0)+(1\times 1)] \end{matrix}$$

Another operation used extensively in matrix algebra is the inverse. The inverse of **A** is $\mathbf{A}^{-1}$. The inverse of a matrix also has a scalar analogue: the reciprocal. Just as $10 \times 1/10 = 1$ in scalar mathematics, a matrix pre- or postmultiplied by its inverse is equal to the identity matrix **I**, which is composed of ones on the diagonal and zeros on the off-diagonal.

$$\mathbf{AA}^{-1} = \mathbf{I}$$

$$\mathbf{A} = \begin{bmatrix} 3 & 2 & 3 \\ 1 & 4 & 6 \\ 8 & 2 & 4 \end{bmatrix} \quad \mathbf{A}^{-1} = \begin{bmatrix} 0.4 & -0.2 & 0.0 \\ 4.4 & -1.2 & -1.5 \\ -3.0 & 1.0 & 1.0 \end{bmatrix}$$

$$\mathbf{A}^{-1}\mathbf{A} = \begin{bmatrix} [(3\times 0.4)+(2\times 4.4)+(3\times -3.0)] & [(3\times -0.2)+(2\times -1.2)+(3\times 1.0)] \\ [(1\times 0.4)+(4\times 4.4)+(6\times -3.0)] & [(1\times -0.2)+(4\times -1.2)+(6\times 1.0)] \\ [(8\times 0.4)+(2\times 4.4)+(4\times -3.0)] & [(8\times -0.2)+(2\times -1.2)+(4\times 1.0)] \end{bmatrix.$$

$$\left. \begin{matrix} [(3\times 0)+(2\times -1.5)+(3\times -1.0)] \\ [(1\times 0.0)+(4\times -1.5)+(6\times -1.0)] \\ [(8\times 0)+(2\times -1.5)+(4\times -1.0)] \end{matrix} \right]$$

$$\mathbf{A}^{-1}\mathbf{A} = \begin{bmatrix} 1.0 & 0 & 0 \\ 0 & 1.0 & 0 \\ 0 & 0 & 1.0 \end{bmatrix}$$

A matrix term that is closely related to the inverse operation is the determinant of a matrix. The determinant indicates whether an inverse exists for a given matrix. When an exact linear dependency exists between two variables, the determinant is zero, which indicates an inverse does not exist.

The inverse of (**X′X**) plays a pivotal role in regression analysis. If it does not exist (that is, there is an exact linear dependency involving two or more predictor variables), the regression analysis cannot be conducted. Of course, this represents the most egregious case. All too often we encounter instances in which the determinant of (**X′X**) *approaches* zero. This indicates potentially harmful levels of collinearity.

Least squares regression analysis in matrix algebra involves the following system of linear equations.

$$\mathbf{b} = (\mathbf{X'X})^{-1}\mathbf{X'y}$$

This simply indicates that a vector **b** of beta coefficients is equal to the inverse of **X′X** times **X′y** where **y** is a vector of dependent variable values.

Consider the following example involving three predictor variables in **X** and a single dependent measure **y.** The three predictor variables reflect responses to a brief questionnaire that subsumes three service quality issues: responsiveness, courtesy, and timeliness. The single outcome measure depicted in **y** reflects the respondents' overall satisfaction. To find the three beta coefficients that correspond to the predictor variables, we solve $\mathbf{b} = (\mathbf{X'X})^{-1}\,\mathbf{X'y}$.

$$\mathbf{X} = \begin{array}{c} \begin{matrix} x_1 & x_2 & x_3 \end{matrix} \\ \begin{bmatrix} 4 & 1 & 5 \\ 5 & 1 & 3 \\ 4 & 2 & 5 \\ 4 & 1 & 4 \\ 6 & 3 & 6 \\ 1 & 2 & 3 \\ 1 & 6 & 1 \\ 2 & 3 & 6 \\ 5 & 2 & 5 \\ 6 & 3 & 6 \end{bmatrix} \end{array} \qquad \mathbf{y} = \begin{bmatrix} 6 \\ 5 \\ 6 \\ 4 \\ 6 \\ 3 \\ 3 \\ 1 \\ 5 \\ 6 \end{bmatrix}$$

$$\mathbf{X'X} = \begin{bmatrix} 176 & 81 & 184 \\ 81 & 78 & 98 \\ 184 & 98 & 218 \end{bmatrix}$$

$$(\mathbf{X'X})^{-1} = \begin{bmatrix} 0.048 & 0.002 & -0.042 \\ 0.002 & 0.029 & -0.015 \\ -0.042 & -0.015 & 0.047 \end{bmatrix}$$

$$\mathbf{X'y} = \begin{bmatrix} 194 \\ 100 \\ 206 \end{bmatrix}$$

$$\mathbf{X'X}^{-1}\mathbf{X'y} = \begin{bmatrix} 0.99 \\ 0.26 \\ -0.01 \end{bmatrix} = \mathbf{b}$$

$$\hat{\mathbf{y}} = 0.99_{x1} + 0.26_{x2} - 0.01_{x3}$$

Of the three predictor variables, responsiveness appears to have the strongest effect on overall satisfaction. Note that had we wanted an intercept term ($\mathbf{B}_o$), a vector of ones would have been placed on the far left of the data matrix **X**.

Inverting the matrix **X′X** is a critical step in regression analysis. The determinant of a matrix **X** is denoted $|\mathbf{X}|$. If the determinant of a matrix is zero, no inverse for the matrix exists.

Linear dependencies within a data set are responsible for small or even zero determinants. Collinearity is discussed in chapter 5 of this book. The linear dependencies associated with collinearity are integrally linked to the inversion of **X′X**.

The following matrix **X** is a 2 × 2 matrix characterized by an exact linear dependency. That is, the first column can be used to predict exactly the second column. In this case $x_2 = 2_{x1}$. Calculating a determinant by hand is an easy matter for a 2 × 2 matrix but requires a computer for larger order matrices.

$$\mathbf{X} = \begin{bmatrix} 2 & 4 \\ 4 & 8 \end{bmatrix}$$

To find the determinant of $\mathbf{X}_{2\times 2}$ requires that

$$|\mathbf{X}| = \begin{bmatrix} x_{11} & x_{12} \\ x_{21} & x_{22} \end{bmatrix} = x_{11}x_{22} - x_{12}x_{21}$$

The determinant of **X** is zero

$$\mathbf{X} = \begin{bmatrix} 2 & 4 \\ 4 & 8 \end{bmatrix}$$

$$|\mathbf{X}| = (2 \times 8) - (4 \times$$

$$|\mathbf{X}| = 0$$

which means no inverse for **X** exists. It is a rare instance in applied customer satisfaction research that we encounter an exact linear dependency. More frequently, we encounter a situation similar to that in matrix **A**.

$$\mathbf{A} = \begin{bmatrix} 3 & 3 \\ 4 & 5 \end{bmatrix}$$

$$|\mathbf{A}| = (3 \times 5) - (3 \times 4)$$

$$|\mathbf{A}| = 3$$

An examination of the determinant of a matrix is an excellent shortcut to understanding the level of collinearity present in the data. As the determinant approaches zero, which is indicative of an exact linear dependency, regression models become increasingly unstable.

Matrix algebra remains a very useful tool for researchers. It represents a powerful shorthand for many analyses. Virtually all advanced books on multivariate statistical analysis assume the reader has a fundamental understanding of matrix algebra. This appendix cannot provide a comprehensive treatment of the subject. Hopefully, the examples presented will spark or rekindle an interest in the subject.

Glossary

Alpha-Trimmed Mean — See *Trimmed Mean*

Beta Coefficient — An optimized weight encountered in dependence models, such as regression analysis, that is indicative of the magnitude of effect a given predictor variable has on the outcome variable.

Bivariate Statistics — Any measure used to summarize the relationship between two variables regardless of their measurement level (that is, nominal, ordinal, interval, or ratio).

Boxplot — Frequently used in exploratory data analysis (EDA) to assess the extent to which a variable's univariate distribution is normal. Potentially troublesome distributional characteristics are readily identified using this simple graphical tool. Both SPSS and SAS produce boxplots in their univariate procedures.

Broadened Median (BMED) — A member of the family of L-estimators, the broadened median (BMED) preserves the median's robustness with respect to outliers. Its real benefit is that it is less sensitive to observation grouping. This is because the BMED averages the median and two or three neighboring values, making it less volatile.

Canonical Correlation — The correlation between two sets of variables. One is generally considered the predictor set, and the other is considered to be the outcome set. A single coefficient represents the extent to which the two sets of variables are linearly dependent.

Causal Modeling — A family of analytical techniques (for example, path analysis) that employ cross-sectional data and make inferences concerning the causal relations among variables. Although causality is not proven, researchers can conclude that the relations in the data are consistent with the causal hypotheses.

Collinearity — A mathematical problem especially troublesome in dependence models. It occurs when the relationships among predictor variables are very strong resulting in a very unstable model. Manifestations of this condition include sign reversals associated with beta coefficients and large standard errors around beta estimates.

Communalities In common factor analysis, communalities are estimated for all variables typically based upon the squared multiple correlation (SMC) of each variable with the others. This provides a basic estimate of the unique and common variance associated with each variable. It is also the basis for the most troublesome problem associated with common factor analysis: factor indeterminacy.

Condition Index A means of diagnosing the extent to which collinearity may be degrading a dependence model. Levels greater than 90 indicate substantive problems.

Confirmatory Analysis Any analysis that requires the researcher to specify *a priori* the hypothesized outcome. Factor analysis, for example, can be exploratory or confirmatory. In the latter case, the researcher specifies which variables are expected to load on which factor(s).

Correlation A wide variety of correlations exist for different data situations. All bivariate correlations reflect the extent to which two variables covary. Correlation does not, by any means, imply or demonstrate causality.

Dependence Model Dependence models involve the extent to which a single variable or set of variables is dependent upon a set of one or more predictor variables.

Dependent Variable In dependence models, the dependent variable is the outcome variable. It is considered to be dependent upon one or more predictor variables. See also *Endogenous Variable.*

Derived Importance Derived importance is based upon leveraging the covariation between a critical outcome variable like overall satisfaction and specific, actionable predictor variables. Typically, derived importance implies the use of multiple regression analysis, but this need not be the case. Derived importance should be differentiated from stated importance measures in which respondents are asked to indicate how important various product and service issues are to them.

Discriminant Analysis A dependency model characterized by a series of predictor variables of various types (for example, nominal, ordinal, interval, and ratio) and a single nominal-level dependent variable.

Dominance Analysis A dependence model technique for deriving the importance of a series of predictor variables. Dominance analysis is unique in that it focuses on the average marginal contribution each predictor has on the squared multiple correlation.

Eigenvalve Eigenanalysis is at the heart of many multivariate dimension reducing procedures. The technique reduces a data set into a series of eigenvectors and corresponding eigenvalues. In factor and principal components analysis (PCA), the eigenvectors are orthogonal linear combinations of the original variables, and the eigenvalues represent variance accounted for in the original data matrix. In principal components analysis, a simple transformation of the eigenvectors yields the variable loadings on each component. As many eigenvectors and eigenvalues as there are variables can be extracted from a data matrix. The first extraction accounts for the greatest proportion of variance, and subsequent eigenvector/eigenvalue pairs represent diminishing proportions of variance.

Endogenous Variable Endogenous variables are outcome or dependent variables. Overall customer satisfaction is frequently an endogenous variable; it is dependent upon a variety of service and product quality variables.

EQS A computer program for developing structural equations models.

Exogenous Variable Exogenous variables are predictor or independent variables. Service and product quality are typically used as exogenous variables in dependence models characterized by some measure of overall satisfaction as the outcome variable.

Exploratory Data Analysis (EDA) Exploratory data analysis is recommended before complex multivariate analyses are undertaken. EDA permits researchers to unearth univariate pathologies that may be more difficult to detect in a multivariate context.

Exploratory Analysis Unlike confirmatory analysis, exploratory analysis involves no *a priori* specification of a hypothesized structure. Typically, multiple regression analysis is used in an exploratory fashion; no effort is made to test hypotheses regarding which predictor variable will have the greatest (or most trivial) affect on the outcome variable.

Factor Analysis

An interdependence technique geared toward data reduction. The objective is to reduce the dimensionality of a data set and reveal a smaller set of underlying factors that account for as much of the original data matrix variance as possible.

Communality Indeterminacy

One of the most problematic aspects of factor analysis, factor indeterminacy refers to the mathematical and conceptual difficulties associated with generating common factors. Because factor analysis assumes all variables have common and unique variance, this must be initially estimated. Typically, the squared multiple correlation (SMC) is employed for the initial estimate and this coefficient is used along the diagonal of the correlation matrix that is decomposed. The trouble, of course, is that the communalities cannot be known until the factors are known, and the factors cannot be known until the communalities are known (hence, the use of the SMC as a communality estimate). This is not a problem in principal components analysis (PCA) because there are no underlying assumptions concerning each variable's common and unique variance; ones are used in the correlation matrix diagonal for PCA.

Factor Loading

A number ranging from +1.00 to -1.00 indicating the extent to which a given variable is related to a factor. When squared, the factor loading indicates the proportion of variance the variable and factor have in common. The sum of all squared factor loadings for a given variable will sum to one.

Factor Rotation

A mathematical approach to interpreting the results of factor or principal components analysis (PCA). Factor rotation may be orthogonal or oblique. In the former case, the zero correlations among the factors are maintained. In the case of oblique rotation, factors are allowed to correlate. Some have argued that imposing orthogonality on latent structures in customer satisfaction research is unrealistic because the constructs are theoretically related.

Factor Score

Factor scores may be generated for any observation included in a factor analysis and are standardized over all observations; the mean of all observations on any factor will be zero, and the standard deviation will be one. Unless oblique rotation has been performed, a correlation analysis using factor scores as input will reveal zero correlations among all the factors. Factor scores may be generated and output to other procedures such as regression analysis.

Goodness-of-Fit Statistic Used in confirmatory analyses such as confirmatory factor analysis or path analysis to assess the extent to which the data are consistent with the hypothesized structural or measurement models.

Heteroscedasticity In regression analysis, this condition reflects an undesirable distribution of the residuals. For example, as values of one or more of the predictor variables increase, the residual value (that is, error in prediction) increases. This violates one of the fundamental assumptions of regression analysis.

Homoscedasticity In regression analysis, this desirable property indicates that the residuals are uniform across values of the predictor variables. In short, heteroscedasticity indicates that the regression analysis performs equally across all ranges of the predictor variables. Homoscedasticity is a basic assumption of regression analysis.

Identification A term frequently used in structural equation modeling, identification refers to the relation between the number of available observations and parameters to be estimated. A just-identified (saturated) model has as many observations as parameters. More problematic is the underidentified model in which there are more parameters than observations, making estimation impossible.

Identity Matrix The identity matrix **I** in matrix algebra is equivalent to 1 in scalar mathematics. Any matrix multiplied by the appropriate-sized identity matrix will equal itself, **AI = A.** The identity matrix is composed of ones on the diagonal. All off-diagonal elements are equal to zero.

Ill-conditioning A mathematical problem especially troublesome in dependence models. It occurs when the relationships among predictor variables are very strong, resulting in an unstable model. Manifestations of this condition include sign reversals associated with beta coefficients and large standard errors around beta estimates.

Imputation A process conducted to rectify problems associated with missing values in multivariate data. A variety of approaches to imputing missing values are available. These range from rather simplistic mean substitution techniques to more sophisticated regression-based procedures.

Independent Variable Typically in dependence models, the independent variable(s) are presumed to affect one (or more) outcome variables.

Interdependence Model Interdependence models do not differentiate between dependent and independent variables. Instead, interdependence models reveal how we naturally group variables into conceptually distinct sets. In the case of interdependence models such as principal components (PCA) and factor analysis, the objective is to establish which variables are naturally grouped together based upon their covariation.

Influential Observation With respect to multiple regression analysis, an influential observation is one that exerts excessive influence on the beta coefficients. Removal of such influential observations can sometimes substantively change the regression equation.

Interval Data Endpoint-anchored Likert scale data that employ five or more points are typically treated as interval-level data. The characteristics that distinguish interval level data include valid inferences concerning the distance between each scale point. With interval data, one can reasonably conclude that a score of 4 represents twice the level of a given attribute than does a score of 2. Interval (or ratio)-level data are assumed on the dependent side of a multiple regression equation.

Inverse In matrix algebra, the inverse of a matrix is equivalent to the reciprocal of a scalar. Inasmuch as 10 times its reciprocal (1/10) equals one, a matrix times its inverse equals the identity matrix. Note that calculation of the inverse plays an important role in many multivariate dependence models and that a perfect linear relationship between two variables (or rows) will preclude calculating an inverse.

Key Driver Analysis Generally any dependence model designed to assess the effect of various predictor variables on a single outcome variable. Examples include regression analysis, logistic regression analysis, and discriminant analysis.

Kruskal's Relative Importance A dependence model technique known to be robust with respect to collinearity. The technique produces a metric that represents the average, squared partial correlation over all permutations of independent variables.

Kurtosis Kurtosis reflects the peakedness (or lack thereof) of a univariate distribution. Either extreme is a departure from the normal distribution. A distribution that is very flat is called platykurtic, whereas an excessively peaked distribution is said to be leptokurtic.

Latent Variable A latent variable is inherently unobservable. Factor analysis and other similar procedures are frequently used to facilitate the understanding of latent variable structure. Examples of latent variables include intelligence and motivation. These are typically measured using test instruments in the form of questionnaires with predetermined scales, which ostensibly reflect the underlying latent constructs.

Leptokurtic Distribution A very peaked, univariate distribution.

L-Estimators A set of univariate statistics that are robust to deviations from the normal distribution. Among these are the broadened median, trimmed mean, and trimean.

LISREL A software application developed by Jöreskog and Sörbom specifically for latent variable path model applications.

Logistic Regression Analysis Logistic regression analysis is a dependence model appropriate for binary dependent variables. Such cases violate a fundamental assumption of Ordinary Least Squares regression—that the dependent variable is normally distributed. Logistic regression employs a nonlinear link that permits more robust model development using binary outcome variables.

Loyalty A latent construct that is frequently and erroneously confused with its behavioral manifestations. Loyalty is an attitudinal state focused on an organization, service, or product that results in desirable behaviors such as repurchase or tenure as a customer. Measuring the behaviors is not the same as measuring the attitude.

Manifest Variable Whereas a latent variable is unobservable (for example, intelligence), a manifest variable is more tangible. The actual questions in survey instruments represent manifest variables. Techniques such as factor analysis permit us to understand the latent dimensions underlying sets of manifest variables.

Matrix A "block" of numbers characterized by *n* rows and *r* columns. In customer satisfaction research, a matrix is typified by *n* rows (where *n* = number of observations) and *k* columns each of which relates to a specific variable. Using matrix algebra, complex analyses can be conducted and communicated in an especially parsimonious fashion. Ordinary Least Squares regression, for example, is represented as $\mathbf{b} = (\mathbf{X}'\mathbf{X})^{-1}\mathbf{X}'\mathbf{Y}$, which produces a vector of beta weights.

Matrix Algebra
Matrix algebra is used extensively in modern statistical analysis and applied customer satisfaction research. It is a very convenient way to express complex statistical formulae.

Measurement Model
In structural equation model (SEM) with latent variables, the measurement model represents the confirmatory factor analytic portion of the architecture. The measurement model specifies the relationships between the manifest and latent variables.

Missing Values
Missing data are especially problematic in multivariate analyses because most statistical packages exclude any observation that does not have valid data for every variable in a given multivariate procedure. Missing values occur when respondents fail to answer a question, skip patterns force a respondent to not answer certain questions, key punching errors occur, and a variety of other reasons.

Monotonic Transformation
A means of transforming the values of a variable in an effort to change the overall distribution. A monotonic transformation preserves the *ordering* of the observations.

Multicollinearity
See *Collinearity*.

Multiple Correlation Coefficient
Represented with an uppercase R to differentiate it from the simple bivariate correlation coefficient, the squared multiple correlation coefficient plays a pivotal role in assessing the efficacy of multiple regression analyses. The multiple correlation coefficient is analogous to the simple bivariate correlation, but it reflects the extent to which a series of variables covaries with a single "outcome" measure.

Multivariate Data Analysis
A data set is considered multivariate if each observation (row) has more than two variables. Multivariate data analysis subsumes all statistical techniques, which operate on more than two variables per observations simultaneously. Thus, factor analysis, multiple regression analysis, and path analysis all represent multivariate statistical techniques despite their rather divergent objectives.

Nominal Scale
Nominal data are categorical in nature. There is no inherent ordering associated with values of a nominal-level variable. Examples of nominal variables include eye color or body type.

Nonrecursive Causal Model
In structural equation modeling (SEM), causality is typically assumed to have a unidirectional flow. This is known as a recursive model. Reciprocal causation is permitted in the case of nonrecursive causal models. In this case, we may permit two variables to cause one another. This assumes that product and service quality affect overall satisfaction (y_1), which in turn cause customer loyalty (y_2), which would represent a simple recursive causal model. To make this a nonrecursive model, we would estimate an additional path from loyalty to satisfaction. The implication of this is that satisfaction causes loyalty, and loyalty also causes satisfaction. Such reciprocal causal relationships are not uncommon when modeling psychological phenomena. Nonrecursive SEMs are somewhat problematic from an identification perspective. See *Identification*.

Normal Probability Plot
Also known as the quantile-quantile plot, this tool is used in exploratory data analysis (EDA) to facilitate an understanding of a variable's distribution. If normally distributed, the data points will fall roughly along a diagonal across the plot. Distributions that are heavily left- or right-skewed or have very heavy/light tails will produce normal probability plots with very recognizable characteristics.

Oblique Rotation
In factor analysis and principal components analysis (PCA), rotation is used to maximize simple structure in the factor loading pattern. The objective is to have each variable load very highly on one factor with near zero loadings on the remaining factors. Oblique rotation strives for simple structure but relaxes the orthogonality constraint. In effect, the factors (or components) are permitted to correlate, which, according to some researchers, yields a more realistic solution.

Ordinal Data
Ordinal data are ordered. Inferences may be made concerning the order of ordinal data values but not their relative position. For example, if all students in a class were assigned a rank with respect to their height, this would be ordinal data. We could conclude that one student was taller than another but not how much taller.

Orthogonal Rotation
When principal components (PCA) or factor analysis is conducted, the initial solution is typically rotated in an effort to achieve simple structure and facilitate an understanding of the underlying dimensionality of the

data. Orthogonal rotation maintains the zero correlation among the factors.

Overidentified Model In confirmatory analyses where goodness-of-fit must be assessed, model identification plays a pivotal role. An overidentified model permits parameter estimation and is desirable, as is the just-identified model.

Partial Least Squares (PLS) An approach similar to regression analysis that is also employed in latent variable structural equation modeling. PLS, and more specifically the NIPALS algorithm, constructs a new set of regressor variables that are a linear combination of the original independent variable set. These new linear combinations are created in a way that maximizes their covariance with the dependent variable and maintains orthogonality among successive linear combinations. The technique is very popular in chemometrics and has only recently been adopted by marketing researchers.

Path Analysis This technique was developed in the early 1900s by Sewall Wright and represents the structural foundation for latent variable path modeling. It is included in the broad class of techniques known generally as causal modeling.

Path Coefficient A path coefficient in path analysis is equivalent to a standardized beta coefficient and reflects the extent to which one variable "influences" another.

Platykurtic Distribution A very flat univariate data distribution.

Principal Components Regression (PCR) Involves the use of principal components analysis (PCA) to reduce a set of predictor variables into a more manageable, smaller group of orthogonal component scores. With orthogonal components on the predictor side of the regression equation, there is no concern that collinearity will degrade the model. This approach is frequently used to circumvent the degrading effects of ill-conditioned data and, less commonly, to reduce a predictor variable set to more manageable numbers. The latter usually implies the former problem, of course.

Principal Components Analysis (PCA) A dimension reducing technique used frequently in customer satisfaction research to reduce collinearity attributable to too many variables or variables that are too highly intercorrelated. The technique is conceptually and mathematically similar to factor analysis but does not assume that variables can be decomposed into their unique and common variance. As a result,

PCA does not suffer from the factor indeterminacy problem associated with the estimation of communalities in common factor analysis. Component scores are frequently used subsequently in regression analysis due to their orthogonality. See *Principal Components Regression*.

Quadrant Chart

Used extensively in customer satisfaction research, the quadrant chart typically has a y-axis (vertical) that indicates importance (derived or stated) and an x-axis (horizontal) that reflects performance level in terms of respondent satisfaction. Thus, four quadrants based upon the integrated importance-performance data are possible. Each represents a different combination of importance and performance (for example, high importance and low importance). The strategic implications with respect to the product or service quality issues that fall into each quadrant can help organizations to maximize their customer satisfaction.

Quantile-Quantile Plot

See *Normal Probability Plot*.

Q-Factor Analysis

A special form of factor analysis in which the data matrix is transposed. The columns (variables) become the rows (observations), and vice versa. The net effect is a clustering of respondents. The technique is sometimes used in segmentation studies.

Ratio Data

Ratio data represent the richest data from an analytical standpoint. They are ordered; inferences can be made about the relative magnitude of different values, and, perhaps most importantly, there is a natural zero. Income represents a ratio-level variable.

Recursive Causal Model

In a recursive structural equation model (SEM), causal flow is assumed to be unidirectional. For example, consider a simple path model with two independent and two dependent variables. The independent variables, product and service quality, are assumed to affect the first dependent variable (overall satisfaction), which, in turn, affects the second dependent variable (loyalty). In the recursive model environment, we cannot permit the second dependent variable to "loop back" and affect the first. To do so would be to posit a nonrecursive causal model.

Regression Analysis

A dependency model that is used to assess the extent to which a set of predictor variables affect a single, interval- or ratio-level outcome variable.

Relative Importance In the realm of key driver (multiple regression), relative importance implies a metric that will permit interval- or ratio-level inferences concerning the relative effects of two predictor variables. Note that when evaluating beta weights, it is only possible to make ordinal (rank order)-level judgments about how two competing variables affect an outcome variable.

Ridge Regression A special form of multiple regression analysis employed when collinear data are especially problematic. Ridge regression involves using a *ridge estimator* value (usually between zero and one), which is added to the data matrix. The resulting regression equation generally is more stable.

***R*-Square Statistic** In regression analysis, the squared multiple correlation coefficient represents the proportion of dependent variable variance accounted for by the set of predictor variables. In applied customer satisfaction research, it is not uncommon to encounter *R*-square statistics greater than 0.80. R^2 is the multivariate equivalent of the bivariate correlation coefficient squared (rij^2).

SAS Statistical Analysis System. A comprehensive programming and statistical package used extensively in marketing research generally and customer satisfaction research specifically.

Saturated Model In causal modeling, a saturated model is one in which all possible paths are estimated. No exogenous variables are constrained to zero with respect to any of the dependent variables. A saturated model is able to exactly replicate the original data covariance of matrix and therefore has perfect goodness-of-fit.

Scalar In matrix algebra, a scalar is a single number. A scalar may be added to or used to multiply a vector or matrix if its dimension is equivalent.

Simple Linear Regression A regression equation characterized by a numeric outcome variable and a single predictor variable. This is differentiated from multiple regression analysis, which includes more than one predictor variable.

Simple Structure In factor analysis and principal components analysis (PCA), rotation is typically conducted in an effort to achieve simple structure. This term was first coined by Thurstone (1947) and involves a factor loading pattern in which each variable loads very highly on only one factor.

Skewness Skewness refers to a distribution's tails. Negative skewness is associated with distributions that have a long thin tail to the left, and positive skewness suggests the similar phenomenon on the right-hand side of the distribution. See also *Kurtosis*.

SPSS Statistical Package for the Social Sciences. An advanced statistical analysis program used extensively in marketing research and customer satisfaction research.

Stated Importance Stated importance relies upon the respondent's introspective capacity to communicate which product and service quality issues are important. This is typically achieved through the use of survey instruments that ask respondents to indicate how important various issues are to them. Stated importance has been criticized on several grounds. Among these are respondents tendency to indicate all issues are important, thus minimizing the variance of responses across items.

Stem-and-Leaf Plot A graphic tool frequently used in exploratory data analysis (EDA) that depicts the extent to which a distribution deviates from normality.

Stepwise Selection Used extensively in multiple regression analysis when collinearity is problematic. This is a purely mechanical procedure that checks the residual sum of squares as each variable is entered into the equation. Variables that fail to meet the entry criterion (frequently referred to as the "F-to-enter") are dropped from the model because their unique contribution to accounting for variance in the dependent variable is trivial. Stepwise selection can be forward or backward. The latter refers to a reversal of the procedure in which an "F-to-remove" is calculated for each variable, and those that do not exceed the criterion are dropped. It is possible for a variable to be initially included in the model selection process and subsequently dropped as other variables are added.

Structural Equation Model In structural equation modeling (SEM) with latent variables, the structural model depicts the causal relationships among latent variables. The structural model is rooted in path analysis, which was developed in the early 1900s by Sewall Wright.

Top-Two Box Score The top-box and top-two box scores are metrics frequently employed when presenting univariate customer satisfaction data. Many organizations track the proportion of respondents who rate their product or service on a Likert scale's top one or two numeric categories. The top-box score when using a five-point Likert scale is the proportion of respondents who indicated their satisfaction level was a 5.

Transpose A matrix operation that involves interchanging a matrix's rows and columns. In survey research applications, this typically means the rows (observations) become the columns (variables), and vice versa. The transpose operation plays an integral role in matrix algebra.

Trimean The trimean is one of several L-estimators that comprise a set of robust univariate statistics. The trimean includes an averaging of the mean and the values of the distribution's upper and lower fourths.

Trimmed Mean Involves dropping a proportion of the distribution equally from both tails prior to calculating the mean. This approach tends to be robust to extreme outliers. It is also known as the alpha-trimmed mean where alpha is the proportion of the distribution removed prior to the mean calculation.

Underidentified Model In confirmatory analyses where goodness-of-fit must be assessed, model identification plays a pivotal role. An underidentified model has an infinite number of solution. There is no unique solution to the problem.

Univariate Statistics Focuses on individual variables and their distributions. Univariate profiles derived through the systematic examination prescribed in exploratory data analysis (EDA) approaches represents an excellent idea prior to undertaking more complex multivariate analyses. Univariate examination will reveal any pathological conditions at this level and can lead to correction through various transformations.

Variance-Covariance Matrix In matrix algebra, the variance-covariance matrix is a square matrix with variances along the diagonal and covariances on the off-diagonal. This matrix plays an integral role in statistical analysis.

Variance Inflation Factor (VIF) An indicator of the extent to which collinearity in a regression model is degrading. Variance inflation factors help statisticians diagnose the collinearity problem and assess the extent to which different variables contribute to the condition. See also *Condition Index.*

Varimax Rotation In factor analysis and principal components analysis, varimax is the most commonly used means of orthogonal factor rotation. Numerous other factor rotation approaches are available, but they all strive for the same objective: simple structure. Simple structure is a desirable factor pattern characterized by each variable having a single high loading on one factor and very low loadings on the remaining factors.

Vector In matrix algebra, a vector may be further identified as a row vector or column vector. With respect to a matrix, a vector has only one column or one row. The row vector **b** = [2 3 4 6] has four elements.

Bibliography

Asher, H. B. 1983. *Causal modeling.* Newbury Park, CA: Sage Publications Quantitative Applications in the Social Sciences Series.

Basilevsky, A. 1994. *Statistical factor analysis and related methods.* New York: John Wiley and Sons.

Bearden, W., and J. Teel. 1983. Selected determinants of consumer satisfaction and complaint reports. *Journal of Marketing Research* 20:21–28.

Becker, S. 1954. Why an order effect. *Public Opinion Quarterly,* 18:271–78.

Belsley, D. A. 1991. *Conditioning diagnostics: Collinearity and weak data in regression.* New York: John Wiley and Sons.

Belsley, D., E. Kuh, and R. Welsch. 1980. *Regression diagnostics: Identifying influential data and sources of collinearity.* New York: John Wiley and Sons.

Birkes, D., and Y. Dodge. 1993. *Alternative methods of regression.* New York: John Wiley and Sons.

Blakeslee, J. 1999. Implementing the six sigma solution. *Quality Progress* July: 77–85.

Blalock, H.M., Jr. 1964. *Causal inferences in non-experimental research.* Chapel Hill: University of North Carolina Press.

Blunch, N. 1984. Position bias in multiple-choice questions. *Journal of Marketing Research* 21:216–20.

Bollen, K. A. 1989. *Structural equations with latent variables.* New York: John Wiley and Sons.

Boomsma, A. 1982. The robustness of LISREL against small sample sizes in factor analysis models. In *Systems under indirect observation: Causality, structure, prediction* (Part 1), ed. K.G. Jöreskog and H. Wold. Amsterdam: North Holland.

———1983. *On the robustness of LISREL against small sample size and non-normality.* Amsterdam: Sociometric Research Foundation.

Breyfogle, F. W. 1999. *Implementing six sigma: smarter solutions using statistical models.* New York: John Wiley and Sons.

Budescu, D. 1993. Dominance analysis: A new approach to the problem of relative importance of predictors in multiple regression. *Psychological Bulletin* 114:542–51.

Bullock, H. E., L. L. Harlow, and S.A. Mulaik. 1994. Causation issues in structural equation modeling. *Structural Equation Modeling: A Multidisciplinary Journal* 3:253-67.

Buzzell, R., and B. Gale. 1987. *The PIMS principles.* New York: The Free Press.

Byrne, B. M. 1989. *A primer of LISREL: Basic applications and programming for confirmatory factor analytic models.* New York: Springer-Verlag.

Carp, F. 1974. Position effect on interview responses. *Journal of Gerontology* 29:581–87.

Chin, W.W. 1998. The partial least squares approach to structural equation modeling. In *Modern methods for business research,* ed. G.A. Marcoulides. Mahwah, NJ: Lawrence Erlbaum Associates.

Chou, C., and P. Bentler, 1995. Estimates and tests in structural equation modeling. In *Structural Equation Modeling*. R.H. Hoyle ed. Thousand Oaks, CA. 37–55.

Churchill, G., and C. Surprenant. 1982. An investigation into the determinants of customer satsifaction. *Journal of Marketing Research* 19:491–504.

Clancy, K., and R. Wachsler. 1971. Positional effects in shared-cost surveys. *Public Opinion Quarterly* 35:258–65.

Council on Financial Competition. 1989. *Service quality.* Council on Financial Competion.

Danaher, P., and R. Rust. 1996. Indirect financial benefits from service quality. *Quality Management Journal* 3:63–75.

Devlin, S., H. Dong, and M. Brown. 1993. Selecting a scale for measuring quality. *Marketing Research* 5:12–18.

Dick, A., and K. Basu. 1994. Customer loyalty: Toward an integrated conceptual framework. *Journal of the Academy of Marketing Science* 22:99–114.

Dillon, W.R., John B. White, V.R. Rao, and D. Filak. 1997. Good science: Use structural equation models to decipher complex customer relationships. *Marketing Research* Winter:23–31.

Dillon, W. R., and M. Goldstein. 1984. *Multivariate analysis: Methods and applications.* New York: John Wiley and Sons.

Ding, L., W. Velicer, and L. Harlow. 1995. Effects of estimation methods, number of indicators per factor, and improper solutions on structural equation model fit indices. *Structural Equation Modeling,* 2, 119–143.

Draper, N. R., and H. Smith. 1981. *Applied regression analysis.* New York: John Wiley and Sons.

Everitt, B. S. 1998. *The Cambridge dictionary of statistics.* Cambridge: Cambridge University Press.

Eves, H. 1966. *Elementary matrix theory.* Toronto: General Publishing Co.

Fornell, C., and F. Bookstein. 1982. Two structural equation models: LISREL and PLS applied to consumer exit-voice theory. *Journal of Marketing Research* 19:440–52.

Geladi, P, and B. Kowalski. 1986. Partial least-squares regression: A tutorial. *Analytica Chimica Acta* 185:1–17.

Goodall, C. 1983. Examining residuals. In *Understanding robust and exploratory data analysis,* ed. D. C. Hoaglin, F. Mosteller, and J. W. Tukey. New York: John Wiley and Sons.

Grapentine, T. 1994. Problematic scales. *Marketing Research* Fall:8–13.

———1997. Managing multicollinearity. *Marketing Research* Fall:11–20.

Harman, H. H. 1976. *Modern factor analysis.* Chicago: The University of Chicago Press.

Hatcher, L. 1994. *A step-by-step approach to using the SAS system for factor analysis and structural equation modeling.* Cary, NC: SAS Institute Inc.

Hayes, B. E. 1998. *Measuring customer satisfaction.* Milwaukee, WI: ASQ Quality Press.

Heck, R. H. 1998. Factor analysis: exploratory and confirmatory approaches. In *Modern methods for business research,* ed. G. Marcoulides. Mahwah, NJ: Lawrence Erlbaum Associates.

Helland, I. 1988. On the structure of partial least squares regression. *Communications in Statistics, Simulations and Computation* 17:581–607.

Hoaglin, D. C., F. Mosteller, and J. W. Tukey. 1983. *Understanding robust and exploratory data analysis.* New York: John Wiley & Sons.

Hosmer, D. W., and S. Lemeshow. 1989. *Applied logistic regression.* New York: John Wiley and Sons.

Hoyle, R. H. 1995. *Structural equation modeling.* Thousand Oaks, CA: Sage Publications.

Hu, L., and P.M. Bentler. 1995. Evaluating model fit. In *Structural equation modeling,* ed. R. Hoyle. Thousand Oaks, CA: Sage Publications.

Hu, L., P. M. Bentler, and Y. Kano. 1992. Can test statistics in covariance structure analysis be trusted? *Psychological Bulletin* 112:351–62.

Jackson, J. E. 1991. *A user's guide to principal components.* New York: John Wiley and Sons.

Jolliffe, I. T. 1986. *Principle component analysis.* New York: Springer-Verlag.

Jöreskog, K. G. 1963. *Statistical estimation in factor analysis.* Stockholm: Almqvist and Wiksell.

Jöreskog, K. G., and D. Sörbom, 1993. *LISREL® 8: User's reference guide.* Chicago Scientific Software International, Inc.

Kahn, R., and D. Cannell. 1957. *The dynamics of interviewing.* New York: John Wiley and Sons.

Kerlinger, F. N. 1986. *Foundations of behavioral research.* 3d ed. New York: Holt, Rinehart and Winston.

Kraut, A., A. Wolfson, and A. Rothenberg. 1975. Some effects of position on opinion survey items. *Journal of Applied Psychology* 60:774–76.

Kruskal, W. 1987. Relative importance by averaging over orderings. *The American Statistician* 41:6–10.

Little, R. J. A., and D. B. Rubin. 1987. *Statistical analysis with missing data.* New York: John Wiley and Sons.

Lohmoller, J. 1989. *Latent variable path modeling with partial least squares.* Heidelberg, Germany: Physica-Verlag.

Marcoulides, G. A., ed. 1998. *Modern methods for business research.* Mahwah, NJ: Lawrence Erlbaum Associates.

Marcoulides, G. A., and R. E. Schumacker, eds. 1996. *Advanced structural equation modeling: Issues and techniques.* Mahwah, NJ: Lawrence Erlbaum Associates.

Marcus, M., and H. K. Minc. 1964. *A survey of matrix theory and matrix inequalities.* Toronto: General Publishing Co.

Marsh, H. W., J. R. Balla, and K. Hau. 1996. An evaluation of incremental fit indices: A clarification of mathematical and empirical properties. In *Advanced structural equation modeling,* eds. G. A. Marcoulides and R. E. Schumacker. Mahwah, NJ: Lawrence Erlbaum Associates.

McCullagh, P., and J. Nelder. 1983. *Generalized linear models.* London: Chapman-Hall.

McDonald, R. P. 1996. Path analysis with composite variables. *Multivariate Behavioral Research* 31:239–70.

McLachlan, G. J., and T. Krishnan. 1996. *The EM algorithm.* New York: John Wiley and Sons.

Naes, T., and H. Martens. 1985. Comparison of prediction methods for multicollinear data. *Communications in Statistics, Simulations and Computation* 14:545–75.

Nunnally, J. C. 1978. *Psychometric theory.* 2d ed. New York: McGraw-Hill Book Company.

Oliver, R. 1980. A cognitive model of the antecedents and consequences of satisfaction decisions. *Journal of Marketing Research* 42:460–69.

Oppenheim, A. 1966. *Questionnaire design and attitude measurement.* New York: Basic Books.

Overall, J. E., and C. Klett. 1983. *Applied multivariate analysis.* Malabar, FL: Robert E. Krieger Publishing Company.

Parasuraman, A., L. Berry, and V. Zeithaml. 1985. A conceptual model of service quality and its implications for future research. *Journal of Marketing* 14:41–50.

———1988. SERVQUAUL: A multiple-item scale for measuring customer perceptions of service quality. *Journal of Retailing* 16:12–40.

Perlis, S. 1991. *Theory of matrices.* New York: Dover Publications.

Perreault, W. 1975. Controlling order-effect bias. *Public Opinion Quarterly* 39:545–51.

Reichheld, F. and W. Sasser. 1990. Zero defections: quality comes to services. *Harvard Business Review* 68:105–11.

Rigdon, E. E. 1998. Structural equation modeling. In *Modern methods for business research,* ed. G. A. Marcoulides. Mahwah, NJ: Lawrence Erlbaum Associates.

Rosenberger, J. and M. Gasko. 1983. Comparing location estimators: Trimmed means, medians, and trimean. In *Understanding robust and exploratory data analysis,* ed. D. C. Hoaglin, F. Mosteller, and J. W. Tukey. New York: John Wiley and Sons.

Rummel, R.J. 1970. *Applied factor analysis.* Evanston, IL: Northwestern University Press.

Rust, R. and A. Zahorik. 1993. Customer satisfaction, customer retention, and market share. *Journal of Retailing* 69:193–215.

Rust, R., A. Zahorik, and T. Keiningham. 1994. *Return on quality (ROQ): Making service quality financially accountable.* Cambridge, MA: Marketing Science Institute.

SAS Institute. 1990. *SAS/STAT users guide.* Version 6. 4th ed. Cary, NC: SAS Institute Inc.

Schott, J. R. 1997. *Matrix analysis for statistics.* New York: John Wiley and Sons.

Schumacker, R. E., and R. G. Lomax. 1996. *A beginner's guide to structural equation modeling.* Mahwah, NJ: Lawrence Erlbaum Associates.

Searle, S. R. 1982. *Matrix algebra useful for statistics.* New York: John Wiley and Sons.

Steiger, J. H. 1990. Structural model evaluation and modification: An interval estimation approach. *Multivariate Behavioral Research* 25:173–80.

Steinberg, D. I. 1974. *Computational matrix algebra.* New York: McGraw-Hill.

Teas, K. 1993. Expectations, performance evaluation and consumers' perceptions of quality. *Journal of Marketing* 57:18–34.

Thurstone, L. L. 1935. *The vectors of mind.* Chicago: University of Chicago Press.

———1947. *Multiple factor analysis.* Chicago: University of Chicago Press.

Tukey, J.W. 1977. *Exploratory data analysis.* Reading, MA: Addison-Wesley.

Tunali, I. 1990. *Econometrics.* J. Eatwell, M. Milgate, P. Newman (Eds.). London: McMillan

Wittink, D., and L. Bayer. 1994. *Statistical analysis of customer satisfaction data: Results from a natural experiment with measurement scales.* Working paper 94–04, Cornell University Johnson Graduate School of Management.

Wright, S. 1918. On the nature of size factors. *Genetics* 3:367–74.

———1921. Correlation and causation. *Journal of Agricultural Research* 20:557-585.

———1960. Path coefficients and path regressions: Alternative or complementary concepts. *Biometrics* 16:189–202.

Zeithaml, V., L. Berry. and A. Parasuraman. 1996. The behavioral consequences of service quality. *Journal of Marketing* 60:31–46.

INDEX

A

Action PC case study (principal components analysis (PCA) and action analysis), 163–169
Advertising, word-of-mouth, 6
AGFI, 190
American Express, 18
Analytical approaches to satisfaction data, 55–68
 bivariate, 57–58
 framework for, 60
 key driver, 61–65
 levels of, 56
 multivariate, 58–61
 multivariate hybrid models, 66–68
 multivariate interdependence models, 65–66
 univariate, 56–57
Anchored scale, 19
Anchors. *See* Endpoint anchors
Answer choice ordering, 34
Aquarian Electric Utility case study (structural equations with latent variables), 192–198
Assurance scale, 3
Atheoretic approach, 158
Attitude scales, 8
Attitudinal item, 9
Attitudinal survey research applications, 51
Attrition, 6–7, 10–18
 risk model, 13
Automobile repurchase reasons, 7

B

Behavior, 7
Behavioral psychology, 162
Bentler's Comparative Fit Index, 190
Beta coefficients, 62
Bias, 31, 34
Big Auto Co. case studies
 diagnostics of collinearity, 116–120
 variable profiles, 102–116
Binary, 12, 58, 63
Binary dependent variables, 89
Binary predictor variables, 21–22
Binary scales, 21, 25
Biserial correlation, 58
Bivariate data analysis, 57–58, 156
Bivariate statistics, 44
Bollen's Indices, 190
Bonus plans, 25
Boxplots, 100
Brand image, 8
Broadened medians (BMED), 99

C

Canonical correlation analysis, 59, 64, 69, 86
Case studies
 diagnostics of collinearity (Big Auto Co.), 116–120
 missing values (Globe Bank), 41–51
 modeling customer retention (SuperBank), 10–17
 path analysis (discount auto parts), 139–142
 path analysis (OilTech), 142–148
 principal components analysis (PCA) and factor analysis (Action PC), 163–169
 scale equivalencies (Omnikote Manufacturing), 29–34
 structural equations with latent variables (Aquarian Electric Utility), 192–198
 variable profiles (Big Auto Co.), 102–116

Causal chain, 8–10
Causal modeling, 66, 129–148
 criteria for, 130–131
 criticism of, 130
 multiple predictors, 132
 nature of, 130–133
 See also LISREL; Path analysis
Cause-and-effect relationships, 59
Channel preference, 10–11
Chi-square statistic, 138, 189–190
Closed-end items, 34
Collinearity, 97–98
 diagnosis of, 116–120
 See also Exploratory data analysis and problems in regression analysis
Column and row diagnostics, 97–127
 See also Exploratory data analysis and problems in regression analysis
Common and unique variable variance, 158
Common factor model, 159
Communalities, 158
Communality indeterminacy, 158
Compensation, 25
Competitive advantage, 6
Condition index, 118–119
Confirmatory factor analysis, 171–175, 178
 See also Principal components analysis (PCA) and factor analysis; Structural equations with latent variables
Confirmatory factor analytic representation of measurement model, 187
Confirmatory versus exploratory models, 136–137, 150–152
 See also Causal modeling; Path analysis; Principal components analysis (PCA) and factor analysis
Control groups, 16
Corporate altruism, 5
Correlation coefficients, 73–75
 Pearson, 57–58
 Spearman rank-order, 22, 44, 58
Correlation matrix, 44–45, 50, 153–156
 as data, 52–54
 and path analysis, 137, 139–140
 and principal components analysis (PCA) and factor analysis, 165–171
 and rotation, 166–168
Cost-benefit analysis and interventions, 16–18
Council on Financial Competition, 5
Covariance matrix, 137, 139, 153–154
Covariation, 26, 28, 32, 46, 57–58, 135
 and derived importance models, 71
COVRATIO, 121–124
 See also Influential observations in regression analysis
Cramer coefficient C, 58
Cross-sectional data, 129–131
CSM. *See* Customer Satisfaction Measurement
Customer attrition, 10–12
 See also Attrition
Customer loyalty versus satisfaction, 7–10
Customer retention, 6, 9–10, 17
 case study for modeling (SuperBank), 10–17
 See also Attrition
Customer Satisfaction Measurement (CSM), 25
Customer satisfaction, psychometric aspects of, 20–25
Customer satisfaction research, future of, 17–18
Customer satisfaction research historical roots, 1–18
 background, 1–3
 case study: modeling customer retention, 10–17
 customer loyalty versus customer satisfaction, 7–10
 linking satisfaction to the bottom line, 5–6
 six sigma approach, 3–5

D

Data
historical, 29, 32
interval-level, 21–22
ratio-level, 21
Data cleaning, 41
Data matrix, 154–155
transposing, 170–171
Data reduction, 66
Data transformations, 28, 41
common, 52–53
Data warehouse, 10–11, 17
Date entry errors, 51
Defectors, 12
Demographics, 10, 12
Dependence models, 3, 21, 48, 59–65, 69–95
See also Dependence models and relative importance
Dependence models and relative importance, 69–95
canonical correlation analysis, 86
correlation coefficient, 73–75
dominance analysis, 83–85
integrating performance and importance data, 92–95
Kruskal's approach, 81–83
marginal resource allocation models (derived importance models), 70–72
multiple linear regression, 78–80
multiple linear regression with stepwise selection, 80–81
multiple logistic regression, 87–91
multivariate correlation analysis, 76–78
nature and derivation of importance, 69–70
presentation of derived importance data, 91–92
simple linear regression, 75–76
Dependent variable placement, 35–37
Derived importance, 62, 69–70
presentation of data, 91–93
See also Dependence models and relative importance
DFBETAS, 121–124
See also Influential observations in regression analysis
DFFITS, 121–124
See also Influential observations in regression analysis
Dimension reducing techniques, 59, 152
See also Principal components analysis (PCA) and factor analysis
Dimensionality, 149–175
See also Principal components analysis (PCA) and factor analysis
Discount auto parts case study (path analysis), 139–142
Discriminant analysis, 59
Disparities affecting service quality, 2
Distributional abnormalities, 51–52
Dominance analysis, 83–85
"Don't know" category, 42–43

E

EDA. *See* Exploratory data analysis and problems in regression analysis
Eigenvalues, 119–120, 160–161, 166
EM algorithm, 47–48
Empathy scale, 3
Empirical relationships, 17
Endogenous variables, 182–189, 194–195, 201
See also Exogenous variables; Matrix algebra; Structural equations with latent variables
Endpoint anchors, 20, 23–25
EP. *See* Evaluated performance model
EQS, 177
Error variance, 135
Evaluated performance (EP) model, 20
Exogenous variables, 182–189, 194–198, 201
See also Endogenous variables; Matrix algebra; Structural equations with latent variables

Experimental designs, 16
Experimental treatment groups, 16
Exploratory data analysis and problems in regression analysis, 97–104
  background of exploratory data analysis, 97–104
  diagnosis of collinearity, 116–120
  influential observations in regression analysis, 121–127
  variable profiles, 104–116
Exploratory versus confirmatory models, 136–137, 150–152
  See also Causal modeling; Path analysis; Principal components analysis (PCA) and factor analysis

F
Factor analysis, 65
  See also Principal components analysis (PCA) and factor analysis
Factor loading, 195
Factor rotation, 162
Factor scales, 170
Feedback, 25
Fit statistics, 137–138
Five-point scales. *See* Scale selection
Forecasting, 6
Formative indicators, 200–201
  See also Reflective indicators

G
GIFCO Products Customer Satisfaction Study, 185
Globe Bank case study (missing values), 41–51
Goodness-of-fit, 151, 189–191
GRI, 190

H
H-spread, 100
Hat matrix diagonal elements, 121
Heteroscedasticity, 131
Heuristic approach, 159–161
Histograms, 103–104
Historical data, 29, 32
Homoscedastidity, 131
HugeCo (and regression techniques), 72–85
Hybrid models. *See* Multivariate hybrid models
Hypothesized factor structure, 172

I
Identification (in confirmatory analysis), 190–192
Identity matrix, 181
Ill-conditioned data, 55, 98, 116–117
Importance, 70
  integrating performance and importance data, 92–95
  See also Dependence models and relative importance
Imputation, 41
Inferences, 19
Influence diagnostics. *See* Influential observations in regression analysis
Influential observations in regression analysis, 121–127
  See also Exploratory data analysis and problems in regression analysis
Instrumentation
  structured instrument, 37–40
  survey design, 34–35
Interdependence models, 149–175
  See also Dimensionality; Principal components analysis (PCA) and factor analysis
Interval-level data, 21–22
Interval-level scale, 23–24
Intervention measures, 11–12, 15–17
Item text rotation, 35
Iterative nature of confirmatory factor analysis, 153

K
Key drivers, 71
  analysis of, 61–65
Kruskal's Relative Importance, 59, 81–83
Kurtosis, 101

L
L-estimators, 99
Latent constructs, 156–157
Latent variable extension, 134
Latent variable models, 129
Latent variables, 66–67, 177–202
  See also Structural equations with latent variables
Least squares regression, 210–214
Leptokurtic distributions, 101
Levels of customer satisfaction data analysis, 56
Likert scales, 51, 101, 169
LISREL, 26, 66, 134, 177, 198–199, 201–202
  See also Causal modeling; Path analysis; Structural equations with latent variables
Listwise deletion, 54
Logistic regression analysis, 64, 87, 90
Logistic regression models, 12–13
  See also Regression
Longitudinal changes, 19
Lower predictive capacities, 26
Loyalty
  affective dimension of, 8–10
  cognitive dimension of, 8–10
  definition of, 8
  questionnaire for, 9
  versus satisfaction (of customers), 7–10

M
M-estimators, 99–100
MAD. *See* Median absolute deviation
Malcolm Baldrige National Quality Award, 1, 3
Manifest variable path analysis, 178
Manifest variables, 177–202
  See also Structural equations with latent variables
Marginal resource allocation, 62
  models for, 70–72
Matrix algebra, 178–186, 203–214
  definition of matrix, 179
  identity, 181
  least squares regression, 210–214
  multiplication, 180–181, 205–210
  scalars, 179–181, 203–214
  summary of SEM nomenclature, 184
  transposing, 180
  vectors, 179–181, 203–214
Mean substitution, 46–47
Measurement model, 178, 186–188
Median absolute deviation (MAD), 100
MGV method, 47–48
Missing data. *See* Missing values
Missing values, 41–51, 55, 153
  evaluating data sets for, 51
  regression models for, 48
Model evaluations, 137–138
Model fit, 137–138, 140
  See also Fit statistics
Monotonic transformation, 52
Motorola, 4
Multicollinearity. *See* Collinearity
Multiple correlation coefficient, 74
Multiple linear regression, 78–80
  with stepwise selection, 80–81
Multiple logistic regression, 12–13, 87–91
Multiple predictor causal model, 132
Multiple regression, 47, 61, 136
  logistic, 64
Multiple-choice questionnaire, 34–35
Multipoint scales. *See* Scale selection
Multivariate correlation analysis, 76–78
Multivariate data analysis, 50, 58–61
  dependence models, 59–65
  hybrid models, 66–68
  interdependence models, 65–66
Multivariate dependence models, 21
Multivariate hybrid models, 66–68
Multivariate interdependence models, 65–66
Multivariate statistical models, 28–29, 31
Multivariate techniques, 45

N
Nested structure, 37–39
Nominal scales, 21–22
Normal probability plot, 103–104
Normality, 153–154

O

Oblique rotation, 161–162
OilTech case study (path analysis), 142–148
OLS. *See* Ordinary least squares
Omnibus studies, 34
Omnikote Manufacturing case study (scale equivalencies), 29–34
Ordinal scales, 22–23
Ordinal-level metrics, 62
Ordinary least squares (OLS) regression, 182
Orthogonal rotation, 77, 161–162, 194
Outliers, 51, 99
Overall satisfaction measure, 35–36
Overidentification (in confirmatory analysis), 190–191

P

Pairwise association, 58, 153
Pairwise deletion, 54
Partial correlation, 76
Partial least squares (PLS), 117
  and latent variable path modeling, 198–202
Path analysis, 40, 129–148
  case study: discount auto parts, 139–142
  case study: OilTech, 142–148
  and causal modeling, 129–130
  confirmatory versus exploratory models, 136–137
  direct, indirect, and total effects for, 142
  model, 141
  model input, 137–138
  nature of causality, 130–133
  with two dependent variables, 133
  See also Structural equations with latent variables
Path coefficients, 135
PCA. *See* Principal components analysis (PCA) and factor analysis
Pearson correlation coefficient, 57–58
Performance and importance data integration, 92–95
Platykurtic distributions, 101
PLS. *See* Partial least squares
Predictive models, 11–12
Predictor variables, 13–14, 36–37
Principal components analysis (PCA) and factor analysis, 65, 136
  background, 150
  case study: Action PC, 163–169
  confirmatory factor analysis, 171–175
  data structures for, 152–154
  definition factor analysis, 156
  definition of PCA, 154
  differences between, 150, 156–159
  exploratory versus confirmatory analysis, 150–152
  factor analysis variants, 169–171
  number of, 159–161
  rotating, 161–163
Process variance reduction, 4
Product quality gaps, 5
Product usage, 10–11
Psychometric aspects of customer satisfaction, 20–25
Psychometric data, 134

Q

Q-factor analysis, 170–171
Quasi-confirmatory model-building, 138

R

R-estimators, 99–100
R-factor analysis, 169–170
Random error, 157
Ratio scales, 24–25
Ratio-level data, 21
Reallocation tool, 62
Reciprocal of a scalar, 181
  See also Matrix algebra
Reflective indicators, 200–201
  See also Formative indicators
Regression, 21, 48
  and HugeCo, 72–85
  imputation on variable correlations, 50
  imputation on variable distributions, 49

influential observations in, 121–127
least squares, 210–214
linear, 29
models used for missing value imputation, 48
multiple, 47, 52–53, 61, 136
multiple linear, 78–80
multiple logistic, 12–13, 64, 87–91
ridge, 117
simple linear, 75–76
techniques and importance of, 72–73
See also Exploratory data analysis and problems in regression analysis
Regression analysis, 3, 40
Parallel, 36
Regression models, 12, 36, 40
Relative importance, 62–63, 69–95
See also Dependence models and relative importance
Reliability scale, 3
Research
academic, 1, 6, 26
applied, 1, 55
future of customer satisfaction, 17–18
historical roots of customer satisfaction, 1–18
industry, 6, 26
Residuals, 121–123
Resource allocation, 3
Responsiveness scale, 3
Retention. *See* Customer retention
Return on quality (ROQ), 6
Ridge regression, 117
Risks, 14–15
Robust central tendency measures, 100
Robust data analysis, 98
Robust estimators, 57
Robust inferences, 131
Root cause analysis, 4
Root mean square error of approximation (RMSEA), 190
ROQ. *See* Return on quality
Rotation, 161–163, 166–168, 194
factors with perfect simple structures, 163
See also Principal components analysis (PCA) and factor analysis
Row and column diagnostics, 97–127
See also Exploratory data analysis and problems in regression analysis
Row-deletion statistics, 121–127
See also Influential observations in regression analysis

S

SAS (Statistical Analysis System), 47–48, 165, 177
Saturated model, 139
Scalars. *See* Matrix algebra
Scale conversion, 32–33
Scale selection, 19–34
background, 19–20
case study: scale equivalencies (Omnikote Manufacturing), 29–34
distribution of scores using different points, 27
interval, 23–25
nominal, 21–22
number of scale points, 25–29
ordinal, 22–23
ratio, 24–25
Scale truncation, 20
Scree test, 160–161
SEM. *See* Structural equation modeling
Semipartial correlation, 76
Service quality
disparities affecting, 2
and market-share growth, 5
psychometric aspects of, 2
SERVQUAL, 2–3
scale dimensions of, 3
Seven-point scales. *See* Scale selection
Simple linear regression, 75–76
Simple structure, 162–163
Simulation applications, 18
Six sigma approach, 3–5
Skewness, 28, 31–32, 41, 51–52, 55, 154
and data transformation, 52
positive and negative, 101
SMC. *See* Squared multiple correlation

Spearman rank-order correlation coefficient, 22, 57–58
SPSS (Statistical Package for the Social Sciences), 48, 165, 177
Squared multiple correlation (SMC), 165
SSCP. *See* Sums of squares and cross products
Stated importance, 70
Statistic significance, 12
Statistical Analysis System. See SAS
Statistical Package for the Social Sciences. See SPSS
Statistical packages, 66
Stem-and-leaf plot, 104
Stepwise selection, 80–81
Structural equation modeling (SEM), 18, 66–67, 177–202
  with latent variables, 67
  summary of matrix nomenclature
  See also Structural equations with latent variables
Structural equations with latent variables, 67, 177–202
  assessing the model, 189–190
  background, 177–178
  case study: Aquarian Electric Utility, 192–198
  identification, 190–192
  latent variable path modeling with partial least squares (PLS), 198–202
  matrix algebra, 178–186
  the measurement model, 186–188
  the structural model, 188–189
Structural model, 178, 188–189
Studentized residuals. *See* Residuals
Sums of squares and cross products (SSCP), 207–210
SuperBank case study (modeling customer retention), 10–17
Survey instrument design, 34–35

T

T-statistic, 196
Tangible scale, 3
Ten-point scales, 72–73
  See also Scale selection
Top box scores, 56–57
Top-two box scores, 25–27, 31–33, 51–52, 56–57
Transpose of a matrix, 170–171, 180–181
Trends, 5
Trimean, 57, 99
Trimmed means, 57, 99

U

Unique and common variable variance, 158
Univariate data analysis, 56–57, 101–116
  variable = overall satisfaction, 102–103
  See also Analytical approaches to satisfaction data; Exploratory data analysis and problems in regression analysis
Univariate statistics, 44

V

Validation, 14–15
Variable profiles (Big Auto Co. data set), 104–116
  acceleration univariate, 105, 112–113, 116
  design univariate, 105, 108–109
  overall satisfaction univariate, 104–105
  quality univariate, 105, 107
  safety univariate, 114–116
  See also Exploratory data analysis and problems in regression analysis
Variables, 12
  binary predictor, 21–22
  dependent, 24
  independent, 24
  predictor, 36–37
Variance, 36
  reducing, 4
Variance Inflation Factors (VIF), 118
Variance-covariance matrix, 52–53
Variation, 46
Varimax rotation, 194

Vectors. *See* Matrix algebra
VIF. *See* Variance Inflation Factors

W
Word-of-mouth advertising, 6

Z
Z-test, 56
Zero baseline, 24
Zero defect services, 4
Zero value, 24